WILLIAM FAULKNER'S
AS I LAY DYING
A Critical Casebook

Dianne L. Cox

GARLAND PUBLISHING, INC. • NEW YORK & LONDON
1985

Library of Congress Cataloging in Publication Data
Main entry under title:

William Faulkner's As I lay dying.

  (Garland Faulkner casebooks ; vol. 3)
  1. Faulkner, William, 1897–1962. As I lay dying—
Addresses, essays, lectures. I. Cox, Dianne L.
II. Series: Garland Faulkner casebooks ; v. 3.
PS3511.A86A869 1985   813'.52   84-13793
ISBN 0-8240-9228-7 (alk. paper)

The following have granted permission to reprint
the essays in this book: C. Patten; the essays by S.M.
Ross, W. Branch, and W. Rossky, University of Texas
Press; J.M. Garrison, Jr.; E.P. Dagenfelder and *Style*
(University of Arkansas); C. Bedient and *Modern
Language Quarterly*; C. Palliser and Duke University
Press; C. Rooks and *Arizona Quarterly*; G.M. Mor-
rison; M.J. Dickerson and *Mississippi Quarterly*.

Printed on acid-free, 250-year-life paper
Manufactured in the United States of America

Acknowledgments

My work on William Faulkner and particularly on *As I Lay Dying* began when I was a doctoral student under the guidance of Professor James B. Meriwether. Specific instances of my indebtedness to Professor Meriwether are mentioned in the notes to my Introduction for this volume, but his assistance and encouragement have been far more thoroughgoing than these can indicate. I am deeply grateful for his generous and rigorous attention to my work.

The research collection of the William Faulkner Room at the University of South Carolina, maintained under Professor Meriwether's supervision, has been invaluable to me in compiling the annotated bibliography for this volume. In addition, several of the contributors to the collection, including the editor, have been assisted by the staff of the Alderman Library at the University of Virginia. Thanks are owed to both institutions.

Mrs. Meredith L. Smith shared with me the hours of collation that lie behind the textual history included in the Introduction, and Dr. Gail Morrison has graciously read and critiqued the Introduction on several occasions.

Finally, thanks are due to Mrs. Jill Faulkner Summers for her permission to quote from the manuscript of *As I Lay Dying* in Sister Catherine Patten's "The Narrative Design of *As I Lay Dying*."

Contents

Series Editor's Preface

Work on the writings of William Faulkner shows no sign of slackening. Articles and books reflecting an ever-widening range of interpretations and critical approaches continue to appear with such frequency that the thickets of Faulkner criticism are in some ways becoming even more tangled and bewildering than those of Yoknapatawpha County itself. In spite of several excellent bibliographical guides, the problem, even for veteran Faulknerians, of keeping up with, sifting through, and evaluating the field, are formidable; for the non-specialist—the student, the professor who simply wants to be a better teacher of Faulkner—these problems are frequently overwhelming.

Garland's Faulkner Casebook Series is designed to come to the aid of both specialist and non-specialist; each volume, devoted to a single Faulkner work, is designed to provide, as it were, a place to start, as well as a place to come back to. Each volume in the series is edited by a scholar who has specialized knowledge of, and, in most cases, who has been a principal contributor to, the scholarship on a particular Faulkner novel. Each editor has been asked to select "the best and most useful" of the available scholarship on that novel for inclusion in the volume, as well as to commission new essays to fill gaps in the scholarship. Writers of previously published essays being anthologized in a volume have been invited to re-write, correct, or simply to update their essays, in light of developments in Faulkner scholarship since the essay's publication.

Each volume will contain (1) an editor's introduction, designed to provide an overview of scholarly study of the novel; (2) an essay, new or old, which brings together all of the available information about the novel's genesis—the inception, the writing, revisions, publication—based upon examination of manuscripts and upon other biographical data; (3) the body of essays described above; and (4) an annotated bibliography of criticism of the novel. The bibliography is *highly* selective for the years prior to 1973, the cut-off date of Thomas L. McHaney's *William Faulkner: A Reference Guide*, in order to provide a key to "the best and most useful" material; an effort has been made to be *complete* for the period since 1973.

Noel Polk
Series Editor

INTRODUCTION

Dianne L. Cox

Faulkner's comments about his novel, *As I Lay Dying*,
are remarkable both for their similarities and, paradoxically,
for their contradictions. From 1933[1] on, Faulkner repeatedly
emphasized in interviews and in essays that he considered the
novel a *tour de force*,[2] but the value he placed on the work
varied. Sometimes he claimed it was a favorite,[3] but he was
just as likely to name it as his least favorite for the very
reason that it was a *tour de force*, that it had cost him no
trouble in the writing.[4] Placed in the context of all that
we know through Faulkner's accounts and from other sources
about the circumstances under which *As I Lay Dying* was composed,
these contradictions are readily reconciled. But the complexity
they imply in Faulkner's relationship to his work is not to be
ignored.

As I Lay Dying was written at a crucial point in Faulkner's
personal life and in his professional career as well. His first
publisher, Horace Liveright, had published *Soldiers' Pay* on
the recommendation of Sherwood Anderson. But Liveright did
not especially care for Faulkner; he wrote Anderson in 1926:

> About Faulkner; I don't want to say much just
> yet. He's a peculiar man and my heart didn't warm
> to him when I met him here in New York.... [H]e's
> not the man that I can write to frankly and inti-
> mately and whole-heartedly.[5]

After *Soldiers' Pay* and *Mosquitoes* failed to sell, Liveright's
firm rejected *Flags in the Dust*, and Liveright released
Faulkner from his contract.[6] *Flags* was offered to several
publishing houses before Harrison Smith, then an editor at
Harcourt, Brace, recommended that his firm accept it.[7]
Harcourt, Brace published it only after substantial cutting,
however, and under the new title, *Sartoris*. Then, in early
1929, Faulkner's next novel, *The Sound and the Fury*, was ill-
received by Harcourt, Brace.[8] The first five years of Faulkner's
novel-writing career had been disappointing ones, and it may

well have seemed to the young writer that he would never be
able to find a publisher who could see that he was a serious
writer and who had sustained confidence in his ability.

Hal Smith was still demonstrating faith in his talent,
however, and he was already negotiating carefully for the
transfer of the typescript of *The Sound and the Fury* from
Harcourt, Brace to his newly created firm of Jonathan Cape
and Harrison Smith; a contract for the novel was drawn up
18 February 1929.[9] For the first time in his career, Faulkner
could feel that he had a publisher who was willing to make a
commitment to him. Hal Smith had liked *Soldiers' Pay*;[10] he
had been influential in persuading Harcourt to take *Sartoris*;
and he actively sought to make Faulkner one of his authors
when setting up his own firm.

After his discouraging experience with *Flags in the Dust*,
Faulkner had put aside his hopes of writing marketable, or
even publishable, novels. When he wrote *The Sound and the
Fury*, he said in 1932, "I believed then that I would never be
published again. I had stopped thinking of myself in publishing terms."[11] Years later, in 1946, he said much the same
thing in a letter to Robert Linscott, of Random House, implying his gratitude to Smith:

> I reckon I wrote TSATF for fun. The one before
> that had been turned down by everybody I sent it to
> and so I was disabused of hopes of printing; had never
> had any about making money writing anyway.... Didn't
> think anybody would print it and was correct, until
> Hal Smith who had tried to get Harcourt to take it,
> set up for himself and printed it.[12]

Smith published *The Sound and the Fury* knowing it would
not sell, and Faulkner himself was aware of this. He wrote,
"[Smith] warned me ... it [*The Sound and the Fury*] would not
sell."[13] And he had told an interviewer in 1931, "'We both
believed we wouldn't sell a copy.'"[14] With his next novel,
Sanctuary, Faulkner hoped to make a profit for himself and
his publisher. Though he revised it in galley proof at considerable personal expense to make it a work of which he
would not be ashamed, originally, he admitted, "it was deliberately conceived to make money."[15] In late May, 1929, he sent
the typescript to Smith.[16]

By this time Faulkner had decided to marry Estelle Oldham
Franklin,[17] the woman he had loved before her marriage to
Cornell Franklin in 1918--and whose marriage had been dissolved
earlier in 1929. She had come home to Oxford, Mississippi,
with her two children. She and Faulkner were married on 20
June, about three weeks after the completion of the typescript
of *Sanctuary*.[18] The marriage did not please Estelle's father,

Lemuel Oldham; nor did it seem wise to Faulkner's long-time
friend, Phil Stone, nor to his brother Murry ("Jack") Falkner,
because they felt Faulkner's future as a professional writer
was still too uncertain, and both told Faulkner so.[19] Faulkner
was probably well enough aware of the financial burden he was
undertaking. He had published only three novels by this time,
and none of them had made him very satisfactory returns for his
effort.[20] He was apparently surprised to find that *The Sound
and the Fury* could be published at all, and even as late as
October, 1930, when *As I Lay Dying* was published, he wrote to
Hal Smith, "I dont think it'll sell, either. Dont think I'll
ever crash through with a book."[21]

His doubts about the practicality of writing as a profession
must have been aggravated by his awareness of the lack of confidence friends and family had in him as a provider. With two
small children, there was no question of Estelle's working--even
if she had wanted to or had been trained for work, or if her
parents or Faulkner's pride would have allowed it. The children themselves were not likely to be a direct financial burden
since their father was supporting them.[22] But this very support,
coming from the man whom Estelle had married partly because
her family considered his prospects so much better than Faulkner's, may have constituted a challenge to his pride and to his
confidence in himself as a professional writer such as he had
not yet had to confront.

Thus, some time in the late spring or early summer of
1929, Faulkner asked Hal Smith for an advance of $500 on his
next book, promising delivery by March 1, 1930.[23] This request
surely took place after Smith had received *Sanctuary*, but
probably before he had informed Faulkner that it "'was too
tough. He wouldn't publish it then'"[24]; it is unlikely that
Faulkner would have made such a request had he known that
Smith thought *Sanctuary*, for which he recently received a $200
advance,[25] was inappropriate for publication. Since Faulkner
promised the next book by March 1, it is tempting to speculate
that his request for the advance was made around the first of
June--giving him a round nine months to produce the novel. If
so, the advance must have reached him before his wedding and
been intended to see him through the summer in Pascagoula,
Mississippi, where he and Estelle honeymooned. This chronology
would seem to be partially confirmed in his interview with
Marshall J. Smith as printed in the Memphis *Press-Scimitar*:

> "Spent the $500.
> "Got a job rolling coal in a power plant."[26]

The job was begun on his return to Oxford, in the fall of 1929.
While in Pascagoula, Faulkner had read the proof of *The
Sound and the Fury*,[27] but there is no evidence that he worked

on anything else during the time--unless he was then re-working
"Father Abraham," his Snopes novel that would not be published
until 1940, when it appeared under the title, *The Hamlet*. No
stories were sold to magazines,[28] and the royalties from *Sartoris*
could not have amounted to much after the advance was deducted.
The Sound and the Fury would not be published until October 7.[29]
Owing Smith either a book or $500, having made little or nothing
on his writing since his marriage, and having learned some time
during the summer that *Sanctuary* not only would not make him
money, but that Smith thought it unfit to publish, Faulkner
took on hourly labor for the first time since his days as post-
master at the University of Mississippi in 1924. As he tells
the story in his introduction to the 1932 Modern Library reissue
of *Sanctuary*, Smith wrote to him on receiving *Sanctuary*, "'Good
God, I can't publish this. We'd both be in jail.'" And Faulkner's
reaction to this news was to tell himself, "'You're damned.
You'll have to work now and then for the rest of your life.' That
was in the summer of 1929. I got a job in the power plant, on the
night shift, from 6 p.m. to 6 a.m., as a coal passer."[30]

   As I Lay Dying was begun, then, on 25 October 1929,[31]
under considerable financial and professional pressure. Under
his agreement with Smith, Faulkner had only four months to
produce this novel, and whether it would be saleable or not,
it had to be a responsible job. He could scarcely afford another
counter productive venture such as *Sanctuary* seemed to have
been. Moreover, as the reviews of *The Sound and the Fury*
came in, it became apparent that that novel was a critical
success.[32] Even as he began to write *As I Lay Dying*, Faulkner
was receiving the positive recognition he had hoped for, and
he apparently felt that his professional career could not now
afford being cheapened by the easy production of inferior
works.[33]

   As he worked on the novel, he seemed to be in good spirits.
He was working productively at night in the power house. Some
time around mid-November he wrote Smith that he was about half-
finished with a novel "that is a son bitch sho enough." And
he added in a postscript, "Name of the new novel is 'As I Lay
Dying'. How's that for high?"[34] The manuscript was end-dated
December 11, 1929, and the typescript 12 January 1930, six
weeks before the promised date of delivery. Though the book
was written under pressure and turned out in about twelve weeks,
Faulkner took pride in it from the beginning, as the letter
quoted above indicates. He seems to have been as proud of his
ability to produce such a work in "six weeks," roughly the
time taken for the composition of the manuscript, as in the
merits of the book itself; he wrote in 1932:

> I wrote *As I Lay Dying* in six weeks, without
> changing a word. I sent it to Smith and wrote
> him that by it I would stand or fall.[35]

A year later, in contrasting the mode of composition of *As
I Lay Dying* with that of *The Sound and the Fury*, his tone was
more restrained though he was in essence saying much the same
thing about the novel:

> ...As I Lay Dying... would be a deliberate book.
> I set out deliberately to write a tour-de-force.
> Before I ever put pen to paper and set down the
> first word, I knew what the last word would be and
> almost where the last period would fall. Before I
> began I said, I am going to write a book by which,
> at a pinch, I can stand or fall if I never touch ink
> again.[36]

This was the first time Faulkner called the novel a *tour
de force*. He quoted himself many times later--sometimes in a
tone of dismissal--but initially the term was applied in
pride.[37] *As I Lay Dying* was not the same kind of rite of
passage for him that *The Sound and the Fury* was, but in a personal sense for Faulkner it represented a confirmation of his
mature powers as a professional writer; the writing of it may
well have enabled Faulkner to demonstrate to himself at a
crucial time in his publishing career that he was indeed a
professional in every sense of the word. His statement that
the book was intended as one by which he could stand or fall
if he never wrote another implies that he had considered the
possibility that his writing career was over. *As I Lay Dying*
may then have been a conscious test case by means of which
Faulkner would decide whether or not it made sense for him to
continue as a professional writer. Writing it under pressure
of time and finances, he learned that he could, in fact, write
a "deliberate" book--and this was no disparagement. On demand,
at will, he could turn out a work which represented neither a
cheap idea nor any other compromise with his standards as a
writer, and which, though it might not sell, would be an
intentional repetition of the craftsmanship he achieved in
The Sound and the Fury.

In his introductions to both *Sanctuary* and *The Sound and
the Fury*, Faulkner called *As I Lay Dying* a book by which he
would "stand or fall"; in doing so Faulkner implicitly attested
to what its achievement meant to him. The phrase is adopted
from Joseph Conrad's 1914 introductory remarks to *The Nigger
of the "Narcissus"*[38]--a work comparable to *As I Lay Dying* in
scale, design, and themes, and which is frequently echoed in
Faulkner's novel. There Conrad said of his short novel, "the

book written round him [James Wait] is not the sort of thing
that can be attempted more than once in a life-time. It is
the book by which, not as a novelist perhaps, but as an artist
striving for the utmost sincerity of expression, I am willing
to stand or fall." It has been pointed out that the cynical
tone of Faulkner's introduction to the Modern Library *Sanctuary*
is parodic of a passage in Hemingway's *The Torrents of Spring*,
and was intended to demonstrate Faulkner's divergence from his
contemporary, Hemingway;[39] in echoing also Conrad's frank pride
in his achievement with *The Nigger*, Faulkner simultaneously
placed himself in the company of one of that illustrious group
of "masters" he sought to emulate.[40] If this is what he had
in mind when he wrote the introduction, then he thought of *As
I Lay Dying* as an initiation indeed--as a kind of rededication
to his profession despite personal difficulties and the temporary lapse from the standards of his craft that *Sanctuary* had
initially represented. (*As I Lay Dying* also marked a less
personal turning point in Faulkner's publishing career. It
was the first in an unbroken series of his novels to be accepted
without question by his publishers; never afterward did he need
to wonder whether his novels would be published, or by whom.)

Faulkner's dedication of *As I Lay Dying* to his publisher,
Hal Smith, stands as an acknowledgment of Smith's staunch
support of Faulkner early in his career when other publishers
were luke warm toward this young novelist who was still only
"promising." Evelyn Harter Glick, the book designer for Cape
and Smith, and later for Smith and Haas, and Random House,
feels that Smith's reinforcement was so crucial to Faulkner's
career that he might have ceased to pursue his profession without it. And from what Faulkner has said of his feelings about
himself as a published writer at this time, she may well be
correct in her assessment:

> It's my conviction that Faulkner wouldn't have
> gone on writing during those years that were so
> tough if Hal Smith hadn't given him advance after
> advance which was never earned; if Hal hadn't
> spent his nights roaming around and talking to
> him. I think Hal kept him going. It's true he
> had some magazine sales to the big magazines,
> but whether he would have gone on if his books
> hadn't been published is for me a question.[41]

Faulkner once flippantly acknowledged his debt to Smith as
his publisher and financial backer in a letter to Evelyn Glick.
She had asked him to write something for Elmer Adler's *Colophon*
series, "Breaking into Print." He responded: "Tell him [Adler]
the best way I know to get published is to borrow advances
from the publisher; then they have to print the stuff [...]."[42]

This seemingly hard-boiled approach should be read as Faulkner's joking with a member of the publishing staff who was whole-heartedly behind both Faulkner and Smith, and who would under-stand perfectly well that the butt of the joke was Faulkner himself as much as it was Smith. In the context of his other expressions of gratitude to Smith, there is every reason to read this, too, as yet another oblique one. This and later letters, Faulkner's naming Smith godfather to his daughter Jill,[43] and the dedication of *As I Lay Dying* to him, all rein-force Evelyn Glick's perception that Hal Smith played a vital supporting role as friend and publisher at a critical stage in Faulkner's professional career. Moreover, Faulkner's acknow-ledgment of Smith's support in the dedication for *As I Lay Dying* (rather than *The Sound and the Fury*, or *Sanctuary*) seems to me to reinforce the evidence of his introductions and inter-views that *As I Lay Dying* was for him the novel which stood at the fork in the road for him professionally. Because of Smith's support—and even more because of his own mature powers—he was able to create a novel by which, professionally, he stood rather than fell. Though not a commercial success, it confirmed Faulkner as a professional writer.

Later in his career Faulkner continued to label *As I Lay Dying* a *tour de force*, claiming that the writing of it had been simple since "all the material was already at hand."[44] In a sense this is true; despite the often brilliant individuality of the novel, many of its techniques and themes had been ex-plored earlier in his fiction. Faulkner had been experimenting with interior monologues almost from the beginning of his fic-tion-writing career. Several of the sketches published in 1925 in the New Orleans *Times-Picayune* and the *Double Dealer* employ this technique.[45] It appears again in the passages of Donald Mahon's deathbed stream-of-consciousness and Margaret Powers' memories of her dead husband in *Soldiers' Pay*,[46] and in Gordon's stream-of-consciousness in *Mosquitoes*,[47] where the intelligence and sensitivity of the latter character adumbrate the streams-of-consciousness of Quentin Compson and Darl Bundren. In *The Sound and the Fury* Faulkner had managed most of an entire novel in interior monologues which not only provided convincingly individual voices for the three brothers who, each in his own way, focused obsessively upon a single feminine figure, their sister, but which also effectively exploited the potential and solved the problems of narrating through such circumscribed perspectives, telling the story and yet ordering the material so that the successive monologues reverberate among and amplify one another.

The early novels, too, had taken focus and structure from the common attention of their various characters to a central event, or concern, often involving death or mortality. In *Soldiers' Pay* a remarkably dissimilar group of characters is

clustered around the usually unaware, dying Donald Mahon. Those
who grieve, or ought to (Margaret, Emmy, Cecily), form an inner
circle who are themselves the focus of attention for those who
desire (Gilligan, Januarius Jones, George Farr), and death and
sex are paired at every level. As with Addie in *As I Lay Dying*,
Donald's helplessness in death, his dependence on family and
community to administer the last rites of the wounded and dead,
is stressed--as is the theme of self-interest and the irrepress-
ible demands of the living despite the presence of death. The
fact of death functions in both novels much as the physical
confinement of the characters on the *Nausikaa* does in *Mosquitoes*: it serves to condense and focus the sum of man's
experience into a single period of crisis during which each
man's approach to life and his relationships with other men
stand in special relief, uncluttered by extraneous detail and
experience. Like the ship-of-fools technique, Faulkner's
practice of structuring his novels around a single intensely
desired or intensely mourned individual allows him, in effect,
to place his characters in a controlled environment, to circum-
scribe their action so as to make more clear its motivations
and significance.

    Mosquitoes, though not a tragic novel like his others, uses
the microcosm/ship-of-fools technique to explore the relationships among a diverse group of artists and non-artists, again
stressing themes of mortality and sexuality (or its analogue,
creativity). This convention provides a relatively plausible
narrative framework in which varying points of view may be
brought to bear on a common experience. To the detriment of
the novel, the shipboard experience often proved too trivial
to provide sustained dramatic focus, and the characters' concerns
are so widely divergent that there are few illuminating over-
lappings. But with this experiment under his belt, Faulkner
was able to draw on it as well as on *Soldiers' Pay* for the
narrative framework and focus of *As I Lay Dying*, where the tensions among his characters are revealed and heightened through
their common concern with the death--and the sexuality--of the
mother, Addie Bundren, and through their forced interaction on
their "ship," the wagon that takes them to Jefferson. It is
this latter kind of structural unity--a kind not employed in
The Sound and the Fury--that helps to anchor and make cohere the
more numerous perspectives that comprise *As I Lay Dying*.

    In fact this central structuring device accounts for the
major technical shift from *The Sound and the Fury* to *As I Lay
Dying*. When Faulkner decided to provide focus not only in the
dead Addie, but also in the journey to her burial ground, he
created for this stream-of-consciousness novel a narrative
present which existed in *Soldiers' Pay* and *Mosquitoes*, but
not in *The Sound and the Fury*, except for the fourth section,

which is objectively narrated, and for one level of Benjy's monologue. This made for more monologues of immediate perception than in *The Sound and the Fury*, and for a smaller proportion of memory. (*As I Lay Dying* is primarily a treatment of present loss, whereas *The Sound and the Fury* is a treatment of the memory or persistence of loss.) Faulkner's choice of a present-tense narration to coincide with the present of events created technical difficulties not encountered in *The Sound and the Fury*, where most of the events of the monologues are events of the past. But for Faulkner the technical shift was a minor, and logical, extension of what he had been doing very effectively with *The Sound and the Fury*.

Faulkner's earlier use of the themes of death, sex, and human isolation or self-interest have been touched on; other themes explored in *As I Lay Dying* which had been treated in earlier work include the effect of words in frustrating the desire to communicate (*Mosquitoes*); the failure of familial love (*The Sound and the Fury*, *Flags in the Dust*); the potency (and rarity) of natural sexual love (*Soldiers' Pay*, *The Sound and the Fury*). Many of the characters of *As I Lay Dying* are adumbrated in prior creations as well: Anse in the father of Elmer Hodge,[48] in the Henry Armstid of "Aria Con Amore," and "As I Lay Dying,"[49] and even in the whining, selfish Caroline Compson of *The Sound and the Fury*; Cash in the MacCallums of *Flags in the Dust*, but also in the injured Henry Armstid; Darl in such psychically wounded war veterans as the narrator of "The Lilacs,"[50] Donald Mahon, and Bayard Sartoris, and in such ineffectual figures as Galwyn (*Mayday*[51]), Horace Benbow of *Flags* and—chiefly—Quentin Compson; Jewel in the reckless John Sartoris and, in his grief and guilt, Bayard Sartoris as well; Dewey Dell in such natural young women as Juliet Bunden in "Adolescence"[52] and Emmy in *Soldiers' Pay*, as well as in the defiantly sexual Caddy Compson and her daughter Quentin. Skeet MacGowan is reminiscent of Jason Compson. Doctor Peabody first appears in *Flags*,[53] and the Bundrens' neighbors are imported from the drafts of "Father Abraham" and related material that would become, by 1940, *The Hamlet*.[54]

It was primarily through his work on *The Hamlet* that Faulkner had so much of the *As I Lay Dying* material ready to hand in 1929. He had been working on his Snopes novel at least as early as 1926 or 1927,[55] and this material itself was adumbrated in the Al Jackson letters that Faulkner and Sherwood Anderson exchanged in 1925 and that he attributed to the Anderson-like Dawson Fairchild in *Mosquitoes*,[56] and in his sketch "The Liar," printed in the New Orleans *Times-Picayune* in 1925.[57] Indeed, when, in May or June of 1929, Faulkner promised a new novel to Hal Smith, it is entirely possible that the novel he had in mind was the Snopes novel rather than

As I Lay Dying. The novel he sent to Smith in the winter of
1930 was clearly an outgrowth of Snopes material, but much
simpler in scope, more focused and less episodic in structure
than *The Hamlet* would prove to be. The surviving drafts of
pre-*Hamlet* material, variously titled "Father Abraham,"
"Abraham's Children," "As I Lay Dying," and "Aria Con Amore,"
reveal the degree to which Faulkner had conceived in detail
his microcosm of Yoknapatawpha hill farmers. In these versions,
early treatments of Flem Snopes and his marriage to Eula
Varner, and of the auction of the wild spotted horses to Flem's
all-too-willing neighbors, the horses' subsequent escape, Henry
Armstid's injury in the stampede and Mrs. Armstid's futile
attempt to recover the purchase price of Henry's horse,
Faulkner's themes of greed, lust and sterility are already
sketched in relief against the fecund natural environment.
Clearly from the beginning Faulkner thought of this world of
hill farmers as a wasteland where men blundered in their blindness and ineffectuality just as they did in post-war Jefferson,
or for that matter in the pre-war world of the Compsons. Though
the action of *The Hamlet* antedates *As I Lay Dying* by twenty
or thirty years, it was a simple thing for Faulkner to adopt
this hill community and advance it into the post-war era for
As I Lay Dying, because he had initally developed it as a
wasteland environment similar to that in *Flags in the Dust*--
in effect imposing through hindsight certain perspectives of
the malaise of the 1920's on a fictional world of the 1890's.
The briefest time references and details making Darl a war
veteran, along with a few details of urban technology (tele-
phones, graphophones and autos), are all that distinguish the
world of *As I Lay Dying* from that of *The Hamlet*.

It is possible, then, that the existence of *As I Lay Dying*
is owed to Faulkner's difficulties in handling his more
ambitious Snopes novel within the constrictions of time he
had accepted. Presumably at some point in the fall of 1929
he recognized that producing the Snopes novel before March
first was not possible, so he devised a new plot using some
of the setting, characters and concerns of the Snopes material,
and drawing, too, on the techniques and themes of earlier work.
It is likely that this is what Faulkner meant when he wrote
that *As I Lay Dying* was a "deliberate" book--this cool-headed
and thrifty borrowing of an existing conception to produce
a new work with its own integrity and that yet would not pre-
empt his later development of the original and more complex
conception in the Snopes trilogy. And this very careful pre-
servation of the material for the Snopes trilogy implies that
even as Faulkner worked on the book by which he would stand
or fall professionally, he was keeping his options open,
planning for his future, as a professional writer. And that,

too, confirms that the writing of *As I Lay Dying* was Faulkner's
personal rededication to his craft and his career.

    As I Lay Dying, Faulkner's "deliberate" book that was
written in twelve weeks after a gestation period of three
years if one reckons from the conception of the Snopes
material (nine months if one reckons from the time of the
promise made to Hal Smith), was published on October 6, 1930,
by Cape and Smith. In the process of its publication, the novel
seems to have received no editorial attention. Though the typescript setting copy now in the Faulkner Collection of the
Humanities Research Center at the University of Texas, in
Austin, shows that the designer of the book, Evelyn Harter,
took care to give the printer instructions about the handling
of problematical passages, such as the spaced setting of
"Chuck.   Chuck.   Chuck." on a line of its own on the second
page of the novel,[58] it reveals no evidence of copy-editing.
Indeed, Evelyn Harter Glick recalls that Cape and Smith really
had no copy-editor.[59]
    This lack of editorial attention was a mixed blessing.
Though the novel was not subjected to wholesale restructuring,
as was *Sartoris*, nor to the editorial tampering and second-
guessing that *Absalom, Absalom!* later suffered at Random House,[60]
neither did it receive the kind of careful copy-editing that
might have led to the correction of more of the errors in
Faulkner's typescript than actually were caught--either by an
alert printer or by Faulkner himself when he read proof. At
the same time, *As I Lay Dying* was subjected to a rather thorough
process of regularization in its spelling and punctuation,
a process which, for example, denied Faulkner his use of archaic
but acceptable spellings and his system of punctuation with
ellipses of varying lengths from three to as many as twelve
points. This regularizing may have been done by a Cape and Smith
proofreader; or it may have been done by the printers at Vail-
Ballou, either as part of their normal handling of a typescript
setting copy with its share of typographical errors and out-
right misspellings, or with instructions from Cape and Smith.
    In addition, there are errors in the text of the first
edition that were not present in Faulkner's typescript. Some
of these are simple printer's mistakes, such as the failure to
provide a paragraph indentation at 25.23. But many are the
results of a misunderstanding of Faulkner's use of dialect and
the consequent substitution of proper grammatical constructions
for the more realistic vernacular of his characters. Further
errors derive from a misunderstanding of Faulkner's unconventional use of italic and roman passages to indicate the various
levels of consciousness flowing together within a character's
thought processes. Thus, periods were sometimes added at the
end of italic passages where none were intended by Faulkner--

to the potential confusion of readers struggling to comprehend
Faulkner's innovative narrative technique. Though Faulkner read
proofs for *As I Lay Dying* carefully enough to decide that a
few substantive changes were in order, the deviations from his
typescript mentioned above are of the sort that might easily
escape his notice. Nevertheless, in the aggregate they substantially misrepresent his intentions and could be corrected,
thanks to the existence and availability of the typescript.

A second printing of *As I Lay Dying* was issued in 1933,
under the imprint of Harrison Smith & Robert Haas. Though this
printing has new preliminaries, the text is virtually unchanged.
Machine collation of the two printings shows that a few lines
were adjusted or reset. Perhaps this reflects a shifting of the
type while it was in storage; Evelyn Harter Glick recalls that
the book was printed from standing type rather than plates.[61]
One additional change—the deletion of the periods spaced
after the word "clopping" at 245.2 and at 245.5—makes the
second printing slightly less accurate than the first.[62]

The first English edition (London: Chatto & Windus, 1935)
is based on the 1930 edition and repeats most of its errors,
though a few are corrected. The English text has been house-
styled in accordance with English spelling and usage; for
example, labored (1930 18.8) becomes laboured (1935 17.8), and
apostrophes are restored to Faulkner's "cant," "dont," "wont,"
etc. Spot collation reveals, too, that a few additional errors
were made in this text.

Though an inquiry apparently was made about the possibility of reissuing *As I Lay Dying* in Random House's Modern
Library series in 1931,[63] the book did not appear under that
imprint until 1946, when it was published in one volume with
The Sound and the Fury. A new typesetting was done for this
edition, using the first printing as setting copy. There is
no evidence that Faulkner saw proofs, made suggestions or corrections, or in any way participated in the preparation of the
edition. Though a few of the more obvious errors in the 1930
edition are corrected in this edition, as in the English edition (for example, the apostrophe in "wasn't" is restored at
1946 362.9 and 362.11, and the misspelling "infinitestimal"
at 1930 155.11 is corrected at 1946 458.11), by far the
majority of the errors in the 1930 edition are carried forward
into the 1946 edition. Moreover, sample collation reveals that
new errors and another layer of regularizing were introduced
in this printing; e.g., apostrophes are imposed on Faulkner's
usual spellings "cant," "wont" and "dont"; hyphenation is
regularized; punctuation is added or dropped.

In 1964, Random House issued a new edition of the novel
which incorporated corrections suggested by Professor James B.
Meriwether after he had compared the 1930 edition with the

typescript setting copy and the manuscript. This edition
restores many of Faulkner's typescript readings, yet not
all that should, ideally, be restored to the text. Moreover,
the text that Meriwether submitted to Random House was copy-
edited there before printing, and also at the proof stage,
without his knowledge or approval. Thus some of his careful
textual work was undone.[64] Finally, a few new printer's errors
were introduced in this edition: or woman (1964 144.4) for
TS or a woman; little black (1964 187.24) for TS little tall
black; go if (1964 217.30) for TS go to if. The 1964 edition,
then, is preferable to the 1930 edition, because it is more
faithful to Faulkner's typescript, and because it contains
fewer printer's errors. Nevertheless, it is still desirable
that a new edition be prepared in accordance with the guidelines of the Center for Scholarly Editions. Until this is
done, readers can have little confidence that the difficulties
they encounter in this often problematical novel are not of a
printer's or a copy-editor's making.[65]

NOTES

1. Faulkner first made the statement in his 1933 introduction for *The Sound and the Fury*, which was not published in
his lifetime, but which was edited by James B. Meriwether, in
Southern Review, n. s. 8 (October 1972), 705-710.

2. Faulkner made similar statements in his introduction
to *Sanctuary* (New York: Modern Library, 1932), p. vii; to
Malcolm Cowley in 1945 (*The Faulkner-Cowley File: Letters
and Memories, 1944-1962*, [New York: Viking Press, 1966], p. 25);
in Japan in 1955 (*Lion in the Garden: Interviews with William
Faulkner, 1926-1962*, James B. Meriwether and Michael Millgate,
eds. [New York: Random House, 1968], p. 180); in Paris in
the same year (*Lion in the Garden*, pp. 222, 244); and in
1957 to students at the University of Virginia (*Faulkner
in the University: Class Conferences at the University of
Virginia, 1957-1958*, Frederick L. Gwynn and Joseph L. Blotner,
eds. [New York: Vintage, 1965], pp. 87, 113, 115, 207).

3. In a 1932 interview with Henry Nash Smith, Faulkner
apparently indicated that *As I Lay Dying* was the novel he
liked best (*Lion in the Garden*, p. 32); in 1945 he wrote
to Malcolm Cowley, "*As I Lay Dying* is simple *tour de force*,
though I like it" (*Faulkner-Cowley File*, p. 25).

4. See *Lion in the Garden*, p. 180.

5. Walker Gilmer, *Horace Liveright, Publisher of the
Twenties* (New York: David Lewis, 1970), p. 126.

6. See Joseph Blotner, *Faulkner: A Biography*, 2 vols.
(New York: Random House, 1974), I, pp. 559-560, 586.

7. Blotner, I, p. 580.

8. See *Selected Letters of William Faulkner*, Joseph Blotner, ed. (New York: Random House, 1977), pp. 42–43; Faulkner wrote to Alfred Harcourt on 18 February 1929 (the date on which he signed a contract for *The Sound and the Fury* with Cape and Smith):

> About the Sound & Fury ms.... I am sorry it did not go over with you all, but I will not say I did not expect that result. Thank you for delivering it to him [Hal Smith].

9. See Blotner, I, p. 603; James B. Meriwether, "Notes on the Textual History of *The Sound and the Fury*," *Papers of the Bibliographical Society of America*, 56 (1962), 292, n. 33.

10. Blotner, I, p. 580.

11. "Introduction" to the Modern Library issue of *Sanctuary*, in *Essays, Speeches & Public Letters*, James B. Meriwether, ed. (New York: Random House, 1966), p. 177.

12. *Selected Letters*, p. 236.

13. "Introduction" to *Sanctuary*, *Essays, Speeches & Public Letters*, p. 177.

14. Interview with Marshall J. Smith in *Lion in the Garden*, p. 7.

15. See the "Introduction" to *Sanctuary*, *Essays, Speeches & Public Letters*, pp. 176–177. However, one should not take too literally Faulkner's implication here of a cause-and-effect relationship between the acceptance of *The Sound and the Fury* and his renewed hope that he could write a profitable novel. The beginning of *Sanctuary*'s composition dates from January 1929; the transfer of the typescript of *The Sound and the Fury* from the Harcourt, Brace files to those of Cape & Smith was accomplished in mid-February. See Blotner, I, pp. 614, 603; *Selected Letters*, pp. 42–43.

16. The typescript is end-dated 25 May 1929; presumably Faulkner mailed it to Smith soon after finishing the typescript. See James B. Meriwether, *The Literary Career of William Faulkner: A Bibliographical Study* (1961; authorized reissue, Columbia: University of South Carolina Press, 1971), p. 66.

17. Murry C. Falkner, *The Falkners of Mississippi: A Memoir* (Baton Rouge: Louisiana State University Press, 1967), p. 125; Blotner, I, p. 618.

18. Blotner, I, pp. 193–205, 613, 619.

19. Blotner, I, pp. 619-620; Falkner, p. 125.

20. According to Gilmer, pp. 126-127, neither *Soldiers'
Pay* nor *Mosquitoes* sold well enough for Liveright to recover
the advances he had paid to Faulkner. *Sartoris* had only one
Harcourt, Brace printing, was not reviewed especially well,
and it, too, seems to have made little for author or publisher.
See James B. Meriwether, "The Text of Faulkner's Books: An
Introduction and Some Notes," *Modern Fiction Studies*, 9 (1963),
167; O.B. Emerson, "William Faulkner's Literary Reputation in
America," unpublished dissertation, Vanderbilt University,
1962, pp. 13-15, and Blotner, I, pp. 610-612.

21. *The Making of William Faulkner's Books, 1929-1937:
An Interview with Evelyn Harter Glick*, James B. Meriwether, ed.
(Columbia, S.C.: University of South Carolina Southern Studies
Program, 1979), p. 15.

22. Blotner, I, p. 620.

23. *Lion in the Garden*, p. 8; *Selected Letters*, p. 236.

24. *Lion in the Garden*, p. 8.

25. James B. Meriwether, "Some Notes on the Text of Faulkner's *Sanctuary*," *Papers of the Bibliographical Society of
America*, 55 (1961), 192, n. 2; Blotner, I, p. 613.

26. *Lion in the Garden*, p. 8.

27. *Selected Letters*, p. 44.

28. Faulkner's first sale of a full-length story to a
national magazine was in January of 1930, when *Forum* bought
"A Rose for Emily"; see Hans H. Skei, "*bold and tragical and
austere*: William Faulkner's *These 13*. A Study," (Oslo, Norway:
University of Oslo Department of Literature, 1977), p. 6.

29. Meriwether, "Textual History of *The Sound and the
Fury*," 287.

30. *Essays, Speeches & Public Letters*, p. 177.

31. This date appears on the first page of the manuscript,
now in the William Faulkner Foundation Collection in the Manuscripts Department at the University of Virginia Library.

32. For a summary of the reviews, see O.B. Emerson, pp.
15-27.

33. Faulkner's statement in his introduction to *Sanctuary*
suggests that he considered *The Sound and the Fury* and *As I
Lay Dying* mature, professional works against which he was at
that time measuring all his other novels; when he rewrote
Sanctuary in galley proofs he was "trying to make out of it

something which would not shame *The Sound and the Fury* and *As I Lay Dying* too much... " (*Essays, Speeches & Public Letters*, p. 178).

34. *The Making of William Faulkner's Books*, p. 5.

35. "Introduction" to *Sanctuary*, *Essays, Speeches & Public Letters*, pp. 177-178.

36. Introduction for *The Sound and the Fury*, *So Rev*, 709.

37. Later, when he persisted in applying the term *tour de force* to the novel, its connotation became less positive. Gradually, as he achieved more and even better novels, Faulkner naturally took relatively less pride in *As I Lay Dying*. Then the term *tour de force* became a kind of pat response when he was put on the spot by an interviewer. It was usually coupled with a mention of the simple idea around which the plot was constructed, and these comments functioned to deflect Faulkner's interrogators from the more complex matters of narrative technique his memory no longer retained in clear detail. His tone of dismissal would seem to have arisen more from his desire to dismiss such topics of discussion than from any genuine disparagement of his work.

38. "To My Readers in America," *The Nigger of the "Narcissus"* (Garden City and New York: Doubleday, Page & Co., 1926), pp. ix-x.

39. See Thomas L. McHaney, "Anderson, Hemingway, and Faulkner's *The Wild Palms*," *PMLA*, 87 (May 1972), 471 and n. 42.

40. See Michael Millgate's discussion of Faulkner's division of those writers who influenced him into "contemporaries" and "masters" in "Faulkner's Masters," *Tulane Studies in English*, 23 (1978), 145-155.

41. *The Making of William Faulkner's Books*, p. 6.

42. *The Making of William Faulkner's Books*, pp. 6-7. Evelyn Glick thinks that some of the money Harrison Smith "advanced" Faulkner was out of his own pocket rather than from Cape and Smith coffers (interview 12 July 1978); if so, when Cape and Smith went into receivership in 1931, Faulkner remained in debt to Smith while forfeiting substantial earnings; see his letter to Smith in *Selected Letters*, p. 72.

43. See *Selected Letters*, p. 346.

44. *Lion in the Garden*, p. 244.

45. See the separate monologues of "New Orleans" and also "Home" and "The Cobbler" in William Faulkner, *New Orleans Sketches*, Carvel Collins, ed. (New York: Random House, 1968).

46. (New York: Boni and Liveright, 1926).

47. (New York: Boni and Liveright, 1927).

48. See "A Portrait of Elmer," in *Uncollected Stories of William Faulkner*, Joseph Blotner, ed. (New York: Random House, 1979), pp. 610-641. This story was written before December 1931, but the conception of it, and a draft of the unfinished novel from which it was drawn, date from 1925 when Faulkner was in Paris. See William Faulkner, "Elmer," edited by Dianne L. Cox, with a foreword by James B. Meriwether, *Mississippi Quarterly*, 36 (Summer 1983), 337-460, and *Selected Letters*, p. 94.

49. Carbon typescripts in the Faulkner papers at the University of Virginia Library, Manuscripts Department. These are early drafts of the auction of the spotted horses in *The Hamlet*.

50. First published in the *Double Dealer*, June 1925, and collected in *A Green Bough* (New York: Smith and Haas, 1933).

51. This allegorical piece was not published in Faulkner's lifetime, but it was composed by 27 January 1926, the date on the hand-lettered copy Faulkner made for Helen Baird. A facsimile of this booklet was issued, with an afterword by Carvel Collins, by the University of Notre Dame Press in 1977.

52. "Adolescence" was written, according to Faulkner, in the early 1920's (see Meriwether, *Literary Career*, p. 86). It was published only recently in *Uncollected Stories of William Faulkner*, pp. 459-473.

53. The character in *Flags*, however, is older, heavier, and less energetic than in *As I Lay Dying*. Though the time of both novels is post-World War I, Peabody is only seventy years old and 225 pounds in *As I Lay Dying* ([New York: Random House, 1964], pp. 41-42), whereas he is eighty-seven years and 310 pounds in *Flags* ([New York: Random House, 1973], p. 87; originally published in shorter form under the title *Sartoris* [New York: Harcourt, Brace, 1929]). This suggests that Faulkner may at one time have postulated a pre-war date for *As I Lay Dying*. If the action of *Flags* occurs in 1919 and 1920, then *As I Lay Dying* would be set in 1902 or 1903. But this date is contradicted by the scene in which Uncle Billy recalls that the bridge was built in 1888 and that no one has "touched hammer to it" in twenty-five years (*AILD*, p. 83). The evidence of this passage places the action of the novel no earlier than 1913. But even this requires an inference that Uncle Billy means no one has worked on the bridge since it was built. As the passage stands, in the post-war time frame of the novel, one must assume that he means the bridge was built in 1888 and it was last repaired twenty-five years ago. On the other

hand, Samson's reference (p. 106) to Jewel's Snopes horse might be construed to imply a date in the early 1900's, if one assumes that he means the horse is actually one of those sold at the horse auction and not the descendant of one, as is specified on p. 127. But the evidence is not strong for any particular or consistent pre-war setting at any stage of the novel's composition, and all the other time references in manuscript, typescript, and published book point to a time in the 1920's for its action--indeed, to a time later than the action of *Flags* (Peabody's relative ages notwithstanding), since the war has been over and Darl has been home for some time.

54. Typescript and manuscript drafts survive in the Faulkner papers in the University of Virginia Library, Manuscripts Department, and in the Arents Collection of the New York Public Library.

55. See James B. Meriwether, "Sartoris and Snopes: An Early Notice," *The Library Chronicle of the University of Texas*, 7 (Summer 1962), 36-39.

56. This point is made by James B. Meriwether in an unpublished paper, "The Beginnings of the Snopeses," presented in April, 1976, at the Georgia Technological Institute conference, "William Faulkner: Fifty Years After *Soldiers' Pay*."

57. See *New Orleans Sketches*, pp. 92-103.

58. William Faulkner, *As I Lay Dying* (New York: Jonathan Cape: Harrison Smith, 1930).

59. *The Making of William Faulkner's Books*, p. 27.

60. See Michael Millgate, *The Achievement of William Faulkner* (New York: Random House, 1966), pp. 150-151, for a brief account of the editorial treatment of *Absalom, Absalom!*.

61. *The Making of Faulkner's Books*, p. 7.

62. I am grateful to Professor James B. Meriwether for sharing with me the results of his machine collation of the two printings.

63. *The Making of Faulkner's Books*, p. 7.

64. Interview with Professor James B. Meriwether, May, 1974.

65. In recent years, several other editions of *As I Lay Dying* have been published, none of which has any authority. These include the 1963 Penguin paperback; the text printed in the English collection, *Faulkner's County* (London 1955);

a book club edition issued by the Literary Guild and also by the International Collectors Library in 1970 (based on the 1964 text); a printing in *Nobel Prize Library* (New York and Del Mar, California, 1971); and a large print English edition published in Bath by the Lythway Press, 1977.

As I Lay Dying

THE NARRATIVE DESIGN
OF *AS I LAY DYING*

Catherine Patten, R.S.H.M.

When the reader encounters *As I Lay Dying* for the first
time, the experimental form of the novel strikes him most
forcefully. Told in fifty-nine sections and from fifteen
different points of view, *As I Lay Dying* significantly
modifies a technique Faulkner first used in *The Sound and
the Fury*. In that book three of the four sections are
ascribed to a character who tells the story from his point
of view; the fourth has an omniscient narrator. However, the
increase in the number of narrators in *As I Lay Dying* and
the fact that they alternate in telling the story greatly
complicate the question of narrative management.

Faulkner indicates the time of the narration in his
earlier novel by placing a date at the beginning of each section
and then telling the story in the past tense, the usual mode
of story-telling in English. In past-tense narration the point
in time when the narrator tells the story and the point in
time when the action narrated takes place do not coincide.
This narrative form gives an author certain obvious advantages.
He can create an illusion of present time while remaining
free to telescope events by skipping over unimportant time
periods in a phrase (i.e., "three days later"). He can also
anticipate the future without breaking his illusion (i.e.,
"John did not yet know that ... "). Moreover, the separation
of narrator from event allows the narrator to comment on
events, even in first person narration, from the vantage of
later time.

Although Faulkner often uses past-tense narration in *As I
Lay Dying*, he departs daringly from the traditional procedure
by mixing his narrative modes. The book begins, in fact, with
present-tense narration which continues for a significant
portion of the novel.

An author limits himself severely by using present-tense
narration. The point in time when the narrator tells the
story and the point in time when the action takes place coincide. Moreover, the point at which the reader experiences the

action also coincides with both the action itself and the
narrator's telling of it. If, as in *As I Lay Dying*, the
narrators are also participating in the actions they are
describing, the reader plunges into a world of pure subjectivity; external chronological reality is revealed only through
its impingement on the consciousness of the speaker. When only
one narrator exists, such a story becomes a study of his mind;
when many such narrators exist, the whole question of perception assumes paramount importance.

An example from *As I Lay Dying* illustrates the problem.
Cora says that Darl wanted to stay home until Addie died and
that Jewel forced him to go--"for three dollars, denying his
dying mother the goodbye kiss."[1]

But in Darl's description of the same event he subtly con-
trols the situation by playing on Anse's greed and Jewel's
impatience. In the manuscript of this section Faulkner originally had Darl say "Come on" and lead the way to the wagon. Then
he changed it so that Jewel takes the initiative:

> "~~Come on, Jewel," I say, going down the steps~~
> "Come on," Jewel says, going down the steps. Pa
> is still talking.[2]

The final version characterizes Jewel as the brother frustrated
by inaction and waiting, while it shows Darl's ability to get
what he wants from other members of the family because he
knows their weaknesses. As the story continues and Darl's perception is consistently verified, the Tulls' misunderstanding
of what happened also marks them as unreliable interpreters
of events.

Since the reader participates in the action of the novel
through the subjectivity of the characters, any examination
of *As I Lay Dying* must begin by studying the question of
narrative management. I believe that the neglect of just such
a study accounts in large measure for the numerous conflict-
ing interpretations which scholars have given the novel.

R.W. Franklin argues in his "Narrative Management in *As
I Lay Dying*" that Faulkner establishes present-tense narration as the pattern in the first quarter of the novel but that
"Past narration becomes so prevalent in the latter part of
the book that it constitutes a shift in the narrative
arrangement."[3] After discussing the difficulties inherent
in present-tense narration, Franklin concludes:

> Instead of attempting forced explanations, we are
> more accurate simply to judge the anachronisms in-
> consistent, the narrative management faulty, and
> to recognize that *As I Lay Dying* shows the great
> haste in which it was written.[4]

Franklin's analysis is perceptive and his reasoning cogent, but he begins by assuming that:

> This novel utilizes present-tense narration, which makes the points of narration and action simultaneous. Or to be more accurate, only a point of action exists since there is no narrator *per se*. Each of the minds is its own persona telling its part of the story through unconscious, involuntary narration.[5]

Two of these statements need questioning: first, that the novel does indeed use present-tense narration *as the controlling form*; and second, that each mind tells its story through unconscious, involuntary narration.

Since, by his own analysis, Franklin shows that present-tense narration in its pure form exists only in the first part of *As I Lay Dying*, is it not possible to look for some other narrative pattern around which Faulkner organized his novel? If the book is so admittedly experimental in structure, might it not also be experimental in this regard? Franklin judges *As I Lay Dying* against a known narrative pattern and finds it wanting. Suspending both assumption and judgment for the moment, let us look more closely at the narrative management of the novel.

Any discussion of narrative management in *As I Lay Dying* must distinguish at least three interwoven structural patterns. The first of these, chronological linear time in which external events occur, is clearly established in the book. A comparison of the manuscript and text shows how carefully Faulkner revised the novel to clarify any ambiguity in the temporal sequence of events. The second structural pattern creates suspense and then resolves it. Closely related to "plot," this pattern governs the giving of information to the reader and the organization of the book as a whole. While the first structure is linear, temporal, and spatial, the second is geometrical and centrifugal with the atemporal *Cora/Addie/Whitfield* triptych at its center.

The third structural pattern, perhaps the most important one, evolves out of the consciousness of the characters and their gradual growth of perception. Here we move from external to internal time, from objectively reported events to subjectively perceived experience. Because only characters who participate in the narrative present are revealed so fully, the third pattern concerns Darl, Jewel, Dewey Dell and Vardaman almost exclusively. The pages that follow examine each pattern in turn in an attempt to illuminate the intricate, and radically experimental, narrative management of *As I Lay Dying*.

The first and most basic pattern concerns the time when events occur. Even a cursory comparison of the manuscript and text shows that Faulkner not only had the linear chronology of *As I Lay Dying* firmly in mind, but that he revised with great care to eliminate any confusion or inconsistency in the time scheme. One reason for this concern is that the precise external chronology forms the framework around which Faulkner built his more experimental arrangements.

Faulkner achieves such clarity by two means. First, he keeps before the reader a linear movement in space which parallels the movement in time; where the Bundrens are at any given point helps the reader to determine the time of events. Second, because the perceptions of the various narrators agree in their recording of external time, the reader has a clear chronology to follow. Numerous references to the time of day or day of the journey make it possible to state clearly that the novel covers ten days: Addie dies on the evening of the first and is buried on the ninth; Anse introduces the new Mrs. Bundren to his family on the morning of the tenth day as they are about to leave Jefferson.[6]

The manuscript of the novel shows that when Faulkner thought the time references inconsistent or confusing, he revised accordingly. For example, when Tull describes the funeral and then lapses into italicized thought, both manuscript and text begin: *"She laid there three days in that box ..."* (p. 86). Then the manuscript makes explicit the meaning of such a delay:

> Three days in July, with rain-spells just making the air hotter for the sun to shine in, curdling milk in the spring house, even. (MS. p. 36)

Faulkner inserted the next time reference in the margin of the manuscript:

> [m][On the 4th day Darl and Jewel got back and they loaded it onto the wagon and started and it already too late.
>
> ~~Take my team, Anse, I said.~~
> ~~We'll wait for ourn. She'll want hit so.~~
> ~~"You cant get a team across that ford. The water's~~
> ~~rising every day, and there aint a team forded hit in~~
> ~~10 years.~~ You'll have to go all the way down to Samson's bridge. It'll take you a day for that. Then you'll be 50 miles from Jefferson. Take my team, Anse.
> We'll wait for ourn. She'll want hit so.] (MS. p. 36)

In the text the first sentence quoted does not appear; the second passage begins *"On the third day"* and ends *"forty miles"* from Jefferson, not fifty.

The change of day may depend on how Faulkner was counting. If the day on the evening of which Addie dies is counted as the first, the brothers return on the fourth day. If, however, the first full day on which Addie is dead, the day of the funeral, is counted as the first, the brothers return on the third day. Samson's statement after the Bundrens' first day of travel that "Quick had been to the funeral three days ago" (p. 107) supports this reasoning. The change in the mileage from Samson's bridge to Jefferson makes more plausible the fact that although Samson's is out of the way, it is not farther from Jefferson than the Bundrens'. Early in the novel Tull speaks of Jefferson as "a day's hard ride away" and New Hope as "not three miles away" (p. 28). The journey, then, takes Anse past New Hope to Samson's, a day's ride, and then back past New Hope, close to home, to Tull's bridge where he finally crosses the river.

Such an understanding helps explain the next time change from manuscript to text. Samson says:

> So I left them there, squatting around the wagon.
> I reckon after 2 days they was used to it. (MS. p. 46)

However, earlier on the same manuscript page he had referred to Addie as "a woman that's been dead in a box 4 days" and soon after the changed sentence he thinks about his wife's anger:

> And I imagined a lot of things coming between us,
> but I be durn if I ever thot it would be a body
> 4 days dead and that a woman. (MS. p. 47)

It seems clear that Faulkner had his time scheme firmly in mind and that the "2 days" was not a slip. In context the "2 days" could refer to the length of time the Bundrens have been watching the corpse since the funeral rather than to the length of time that Addie has been dead. If this is so, "2 days" is correct. Probably Faulkner decided that the distinction would confuse his readers without providing any greater understanding; therefore he changed the text to read "four days."

Another time reference in the manuscript, changed in the text, seems to be an error. In the manuscript Tull says: "I had not thot water in August could be so cold" (MS. p. 65); in the text the month is July (p. 151). Since the previously quoted passage from manuscript page 36 also refers to July, Faulkner apparently wrote "August" to make his cold water seem more unusual, and then realized his inconsistency.

Faulkner was equally meticulous in establishing the ages of the Bundren children. In the manuscript of Darl's flashback section recalling the summer when Jewel was fifteen,

Vardaman comes to the field with the lunches and Anse sends him back to find Jewel (MS. p. 51). In the text, Dewey Dell performs this chore. At the end of the same section Vardaman, oblivious to the family emotion which Jewel's arrival with his horse has caused, repeats "Let me ride, Jewel," sounding "like a cricket in the grass, kind of" (MS. p. 53). Probably Faulkner has Dewey Dell bring the lunches in the text because Vardaman would have been too young to carry the pails. He probably replaced "kind of" in the last quotation with "a little one" in the text (p. 129) for the same reason.

In Dewey Dell's last section Anse rages: "My own ~~daugh~~ born daughter that has et my food for 16 years, begrudges me the loan of $10.00" (MS. p. 106). In the final version he says "seventeen years" (p. 246) which agrees with Dewey Dell's answer to Moseley when he asks her age (p. 190). Again, as Cash ponders why he feels closer to Darl than to the others, he thinks:

> It's because me and Darl was born close together, and it was nigh 8 years before Jewel and Dewey Dell and Vardaman begun to come along. (MS. p. 95)

In the text, Faulkner changed this to "ten years" (p. 224).

The reader can, therefore, ascertain the ages of the Bundren children with some accuracy. Given the fact that Dewey Dell is seventeen at the time of the action and that she was born soon after Jewel to "negative" him, he is probably eighteen or nineteen years old. If so, his fifteenth summer when he earned his horse would have been three or four years earlier. Since Vardaman at that time could speak but was too young to perceive what was happening, and since Vardaman during the novel's action is still a "little tyke" (p. 32) overwhelmed by death, he is probably seven or eight years old. This conclusion agrees substantially with the findings of Floyd C. Watkins and William B. Dillingham who have suggested that Vardaman is a normal child of six to eight years old confused by his confrontation with death.[7] Moreover, since ten years elapsed between Darl's birth and Jewel's, and Jewel is now eighteen or nineteen, Darl must be twenty-eight or twenty-nine and Cash a year or two older.

Manuscript evidence indicates, then, that Faulkner not only had his chronology firmly in mind, but that he also considered the accuracy of his time-scheme to be of importance to the novel as a whole. Indeed, the linear chronology of external events provides a structural framework essential to the more experimental narrative arrangements in *As I Lay Dying*. In fact, the chronological clarity of the novel may be one reason its intricate narrative design has generally escaped notice.

The second structural pattern of *As I Lay Dying* exists
as a counterpoint to the linear chronology of the first. By
this pattern Faulkner creates suspense for the reader, keeping
from him crucial pieces of information until the appropriate
time. Organized around Addie as central figure and her section
as center of the book, the pattern keeps us asking on first
reading what happens to Addie--or, her body--and why. On
subsequent readings we perceive the design created by careful
placement of sections.

Even small changes in the manuscript indicate that Faulkner
had such an ordering in mind. For instance, in the opening
section Darl thinks that Cash:

> holds the two boards on the trestle, fitted
> along the edges in ~~the-shape-of-half-a-box~~
> ~~the-coffin~~ a quarter of the coffin . . . .
> Maw could not want a better one, a better
> box to lie in. (MS. p. 1)

The text reads:

> He holds the two planks on the trestle, fitted
> along the edges in a quarter of the finished
> box . . . . Addie Bundren could not want a better
> one, a better box to lie in. (pp. 4-5)

The change from "Maw" to "Addie Bundren" and from "coffin"
to "box" in the text delays information which the reader needs
to understand even this first section.[8]

In a larger sense, Darl's opening description of Jewel and
himself walking across the cottonfield prepares for the revelation of their relationship to each other. Darl's second section
furthers this revelation when he describes, clairvoyantly,
Jewel and his horse. But the reader has to wait until section
32 to learn how Jewel purchased the horse and what its acquisition meant to the family; not until *Addie* section 40, which
completes the explanation, does the reader understand Darl's
preoccupation with Jewel.

A revision of *Cora* 6 further supports the idea that
Faulkner deliberately withheld information to create suspense.
In both the manuscript and text, Cora knows that Addie "was
not cold in the coffin before they were carting her 40 miles
away to bury her. Refusing to let her lie in the same earth
with those Bundrens" (MS. p. 9). Although Cora seems to know
that the Bundrens have set out on their journey, in the text
she does not know that they have had problems crossing the
river. In the manuscript Cora does know and judge this:

> It was a judgment, the drowning of that team. It
> was the hand God trying to wipe forever from the
> face of man the ingratitude of those people, taking

> her unto him beneath the waters, coffin and team
> and all. But even that would not content them.
> They must haul her back into the world like it was
> a ~~bag of~~ bale of hay. ~~Ref~~ They would let the team
> drown, but not her. They must haul her back out of
> the very hand of the Lord that would have hid her
> outrage and her shame beneath His own waters that
> He sent for that purpose, to drag her on in the
> sight of man in outrage and in shame. (MS. p. 10)

As it stands, the passage concerns a future event in chronological time, told in the past tense by a character who is standing
beyond both the chronological present of the novel and the
present of the event. Faulkner may have deleted the passage
because it places Cora too far into the future or because
it short-cuts his gradually unfolding revelation. Since he
allows the complexity of the narrative management to remain,
it seems probable that Faulkner changed it because he did not
want to give away the coming dramatic action too soon.

   Another example of the same kind of revision occurs when
Darl thinks about Addie's partiality for Jewel. The manuscript
illustrates the skill with which Faulkner revised to give Darl
knowledge of Jewel's parentage and yet keep the secret from
the reader:

> ^{m}[I ~~tell~~ told them that's why ma] ~~Maybe-that's-why-ma~~
> always whipped him and petted him more. ~~Or-maybe~~
> Because he was peakling and around the house more.
> ~~Or-maybe-his-name~~ [That's why she named him] Jewel.
> I told them. (MS. p. 7)

   After he is familiar with *As I Lay Dying*, the reader
realizes that the second structural pattern, which creates
aesthetic effect, also determines the ordering of sections.
R.W. Franklin, after pointing out that the *Cora/Addie/Whitfield*
sections are largely atemporal, concludes that "the Cora-Addie-
Whitfield grouping was indeed made in defiance of his original
narrative intention."[9] However, further analysis shows that
Faulkner placed his triptych carefully. The Bundrens cross
the river almost at the exact center of the book. The major
revelations in the novel frame the event. Darl recalls the
story of Jewel and his horse just before they cross the
river; the *Cora/Addie/Whitfield* sections immediately follow
the daring of the river. Both the information contained in
these sections and their placement in the novel make clear
their importance. After the triptych, the reader can evaluate
more accurately the characters' perceptions and understand
more clearly the pattern of relationships that is being worked
out during the journey.

Addie is at the center of the novel because Addie is in
a real sense at the center of her family's lives. The best of
the traditional criticism of *As I Lay Dying* emphasizes this
point.[10] Yet Addie's centrality is not without irony and
ambiguity. In the triptych her plea for experience, not empty
words, is surrounded by the thoughts of people pre-eminent
for the disparity between word and deed. Again, the motives
of her family revealed during the journey belie their stated
purpose—to keep their word to bury Addie with her kin. Indeed,
by the time the Bundrens reach Jefferson, Cash merely alludes
to his mother's burial in a subordinate clause: "But when we
got it filled and covered and drove out the gate ..." (p. 227).
Anse's final words: "Meet Mrs Bundren" (p. 250) bring the cycle
to a close. We may think of the second narrative pattern either
as a tent-like one hovering over the chronological line or
as a circle of which Addie is the center. With Addie at the
apex or core, this structure, while neither the primary focus
nor the central fact about the novel, influences all else in
As I Lay Dying.

The geometrical precision of the second pattern leads in
turn to the third and most complex pattern. Here present-tense
narration assumes prime importance as Faulkner uses it to
explore the developing perceptions of his characters. When
the book opens, Darl is speaking in the present tense:

> Jewel and I come up from the field, following the
> path in single file. Although I am fifteen feet ahead
> of him, anyone watching us from the cottonhouse can
> see Jewel's frayed and broken straw hat a full head
> above my own. (p. 3)

Here the point in time of Darl's perception and narration
(narrative present) and the point in time of the events
narrated (chronological present) coincide. In the first
sections of *As I Lay Dying* Faulkner carefully establishes
the reality of the external chronological present by having
different speakers record the same events. Darl, Jewel and
Cora all record Cash's sawing, the Tulls' waiting, and Dewey
Dell's fanning. Nevertheless, the first five sections of the
novel, all in the narrative present, differ significantly
in the levels of consciousness they reveal.

Darl in section 1 describes Jewel and himself in minute,
almost scrupulously exact detail. The intensity of his gaze
as it records Jewel's movements tells much about Darl:

> Jewel, fifteen feet behind me, looking straight
> ahead, steps in a single stride through the window.
> Still staring straight ahead, his pale eyes like

> wood set into his wooden face, he crosses the
> floor in four strides with the rigid gravity of a
> cigar store Indian dressed in patched overalls and
> endued with life from the hips down, and steps in
> a single stride through the opposite window and
> into the path again just as I come around the corner.
> In single file and five feet apart and Jewel now in
> front, we go on up the path toward the foot of the
> bluff. (p. 4)

His visual acuity--"Between the shadow spaces they are yellow
as gold, like soft gold, bearing on their flanks in smooth
undulations the marks of the adze blade ..." (p. 4)--and
auditory sensitivity--"I go on to the house, followed by the

> Chuck.   Chuck.   Chuck.

of the adze" (p. 5)--forecast the qualities of Darl's mind
which intensify as his breakdown progresses.

In the next section, Cora's remembering--"So I saved out
the eggs and baked yesterday" (p. 6)--and her description
of Addie--"The quilt is drawn up to her chin, hot as it is,
with only her two hands and her face outside" (p. 8)--place
her clearly in the same time continuum with Darl. But most of
Cora's section seems a conscious conversation with an imagined
audience to whom she communicates her self-justification. Cora
worries about monetary loss and gain every bit as much as she
worries about spiritual accounting, and she is as preoccupied
with her own concerns as Darl is with Jewel.

Still another kind of subjectivity emerges in *Darl* 3
which begins with objective description reminiscent of
section 1:

> Pa and Vernon are sitting on the back porch. Pa
> is tilting snuff from the lid of his snuff-box into
> his lower lip, holding the lip outdrawn between
> thumb and finger. They look around as I cross the
> porch and dip the gourd into the water bucket and
> drink. (p. 10)

Anse's question "Where's Jewel?" awaits an answer while Darl
recalls, mostly in images, boyhood pleasures: drinking water
from a cedar bucket, especially at night, and lying naked in
the dark "feeling the cool silence blowing upon my parts"
(p. 11). He notices the details of Pa's and Vernon's appearance:
"Pa's feet are badly splayed.... Vernon has been to town. I
have never seen him go to town in overalls"; then he attends
to his own motion--"I fling the dipper dregs to the ground"
(p. 11)--and answers Pa's question. The framing action of
drinking from the gourd establishes the relatively short time
lapse in which Darl's reflections take place.

Interior time, while verbally extensive because words form
the medium of the book, still clearly differs from the external
chronological time of actions and dialogue. In other words,
there are levels of consciousness in *As I Lay Dying* which
external chronological time cannot measure. Notice Darl's
"thoughts" after he answers Pa's question--"Where's Jewel?"
Here Darl moves to clairvoyant imaginative projection totally
concerned with Jewel and his horse. Because Darl's preoccupation with Jewel is so complete, the reader's awareness that
this is Darl's subjectivity fades. In one short section, then,
Darl moves through various levels of consciousness prodded by
external associations. The drink of water reminds him of his
first realization that cedar water tastes better. Then he
remembers drinking water alone at night, which in turn makes
him think of lying awake in darkness in adolescence. Answering
Anse's question reminds Darl of Jewel and the level of consciousness from here on seems to be neither objective description nor flash of memory but some deep, almost wordless,
submerged awareness of his brother.

If this analysis is correct, Faulkner deviates early from
strict present-tense narration. Even while the external chronological present remains, the variations in consciousness create
passages which defy an exact congruity of event, narration,
and reader awareness. Jewel's section underscores the point.
While the external chronological present remains clear and in-
tact--Jewel resents Cash's sawing, Dewey Dell's fanning, and
the Tulls' waiting--the import of the section is its revelation
of Jewel's unspoken rage. Although Darl focuses on him, Jewel
focuses on Addie and those surrounding her, claiming her attention. Just as Darl's "thoughts" about Jewel are non-verbal
images somewhere below the level of consciousness, Jewel's
rage seems to move from conscious fury--"I told him to go
somewhere else. I said Good God do you want to see her in it"
(p. 14)--to a deep unconscious desire:

> It would just be me and her on a high hill and me
> rolling the rocks down the hill at their faces,
> picking them up and throwing them down the hill
> faces and teeth and all by God until she was quiet
> and not that goddamn adze going One lick less. One
> lick less and we could be quiet. (p. 15)

In addition, a change in the manuscript supports the view
that the simultaneity of the external chronological present
and the narrative present breaks down early in the novel.
After what is now the last line of section 3, a crossed-out
sentence in the manuscript--"We watch him come around the
house" (MS. p. 5)--parallels the opening of section 5: "We
watch him come around the house. [sic] and mount the steps"

(MS. p. 7). If he had left the first sentence in, Faulkner
would have clearly established the contemporaneity of the
end of section 3 and the beginning of section 5. Such a repetition would support the thesis that *Jewel* 4 occurs apart from
external chronological time. While it may be argued that
Faulkner crossed out the sentence for just that reason, his
use of overlapping phrases and events elsewhere in the novel
suggests that the change was made for aesthetic reasons. Darl's
personal intrusion at the end of section 3--"We watch him come
around the house"--would have weakened the powerful climactic
ending:

> "Eat," he says. "Get the goddamn stuff out of
> sight while you got a chance, you pussel-gutted
> bastard. You sweet son of a bitch," he says. (p. 13)

But not only the immeasurable interior time of a character's
mind breaks the simultaneity of the external chronological
present and the narrative present. Early in *As I Lay Dying*
Faulkner has characters speak in the past tense about events
which have not yet happened. For example, in section 6 Cora
speaks in the past tense from the vantage of future time.
Therefore the narrative present (and Cora's perceptual present)
is in the future on the external chronological continuum.
Nevertheless, the events she describes are partly present,
partly future. Faulkner limits the future by having Cora say:
"Why, for the last three weeks I have been coming over every
time I could" (p. 21). Obviously she is speaking sometime soon
after the funeral. Perhaps the narrative problem accounts for
Faulkner's elimination of a passage in the manuscript which
experiments with different tenses:

> ~~But maybe bereavement will change them. Maybe they~~
> ~~will realise what they have lost. And then even~~
> ~~bereavement has not changed them. Alive, they suffered~~
> ~~her maybe because with a woman's great heart she~~
> (MS. p. 9)

The manuscript of *As I Lay Dying* shows clearly that
Faulkner was aware of the narrative complexities he was
creating and that he revised carefully to be sure his use of
tenses was consistent.[11] But as the examination of the first
six sections shows, much more than tense must be considered.
Rather, in this novel of subjectivity, we must ask where the
character's perceptual present (point of narration) is in
relation to the chronological present. Moreover, we must ask
whether that subjectivity represents conscious or unconscious
"thought" and determine the relationship of that "thought"
to temporal progression. Because Faulkner establishes a clear
chronological sequence of events early in the novel, he can

move the point of narration forward or backward on the time
continuum and shift levels of consciousness without causing
confusion. But the reader who understands this understands
also that in *As I Lay Dying* the chronological present must
always be subservient to the perceptual present, the subjective development of the characters.

Such a frame of reference for the novel helps explain
why Faulkner consciously created, not just tolerated, overlapping passages. Several times in the novel two different
characters report a fragment of dialogue or an event in
subsequent sections. Faulkner uses the device to keep the
reader aware of the external chronology and also to verify
a character's perception. For example, at the end of section 6
Cora reports:

> "What you want, Darl?" Dewey Dell said, not
> stopping the fan, speaking up quick, keeping even
> him from her. He didn't answer. He just stood and
> looked at his dying mother, his heart too full
> for words. (pp. 23-24)

In the next section Dewey Dell reveals her inner preoccupations. Beginning with the memory of Lafe--"The first time
me and Lafe picked on down the row" (p. 25)--she then skips
briefly from one member of the family to the next. Associational
rather than logical progression, unfinished sentences, and the
use of pronouns rather than nouns--"And so it was because I
could not help it" (p. 26)--all contribute to the impression
that section 7 represents a working of Dewey Dell's mind
below the level of consciousness. She "thinks" about her
communication with Darl "without the words" and then comes
to conscious thought:

> He stands in the door, looking at her.
> "What you want, Darl?" I say.
> "She is going to die," he says. And old turkey-
> buzzard Tull coming to watch her die but I can fool
> them.
> "When is she going to die?" I say.
> "Before we get back," he says.
> "Then why are you taking Jewel?" I say.
> "I want him to help me load," he says. (pp. 26-27)

Several important things happen in this passage. First,
Darl's coming to the door and Dewey Dell's question verify
Cora's report, but in the previous section Cora says "He
didn't answer." The placement of Darl's exchange with Dewey
Dell immediately after her "thoughts" about communicating with
him without words makes the silence of these questions and

answers clear. Second, Dewey Dell, unlike Cora, knows that
Darl is taking Jewel, not *vice versa*, and that he is deliberately depriving Jewel of being at his mother's side when she
dies. Third, the repeated conversation establishes the simultaneity of the passage with the previous section. Therefore
it is not strict present-tense narration: a passage intervenes
which is somehow beyond time in the depths of a character's
consciousness.

A similar repetition of Addie's last cry: "'Cash,' she
says; 'you, Cash!'" (p. 45) occurs at the end of Peabody's
section 11 and the beginning of section 12. While Peabody
notices Addie's repudiation of him, Darl records her desire
to see Jewel (p. 46); but the primary purpose of the overlapping is to verify Darl's clairvoyant narration of Addie's
death. Here Darl again assumes, except in the italicized
passages, the objective descriptive voice of the opening
of the novel.

Faulkner uses the same technique in sections 13 and 14
to place a subjective experience on the external chronological
continuum. Vardaman hears Dewey Dell call him: "Vardaman....
You, Vardaman" (p. 55) and she repeats the call on page 60.
Sometimes Faulkner uses a variation of the technique when two
narrators describe, in the present tense, the same action.
For example, Vardaman in section 24 says Dewey Dell gets into
the wagon (p. 95) and then Darl describes the same event in
section 25:

> She sets the basket into the wagon and climbs in,
> her leg coming long from beneath her tightening
> dress.... (p. 97)

Another, more complex type of overlapping can be seen in
MacGowan 55 and *Vardaman* 56. MacGowan tells in the past tense
about his seduction of Dewey Dell. In the manuscript his
section ends:

> "Aint you going to pay me first?" I said.
> She didn't look at me. She held the box,
> looking at the capsules. "Are you sure it'll
> work?" she says.
> "Sure it'll work," I says.
> So we went down cellar and I give her what she
> asked for. She said she wanted something more in her
> belly than what she had. And we dont never let a
> customer complain. We replace the article, if
> necessary. At least, I will. (MS. p. 102)

But Faulkner changed the ending in the text:

> I gave her the box of capsules. She held the
> box in her hand, looking at the capsules.

>   "Are you sure it'll work?" she says.
>   "Sure," I says. "When you take the rest of
> the treatment."
>   "Where do I take it?" she says.
>   "Down in the cellar," I says. (p. 238)

Besides being more dramatic, the revision ends with dialogue
and an illusion of present time which moves easily into the
actual present of Vardaman's narrative of the same event.
Nevertheless, MacGowan tells his story from some future point
in chronological time whereas Vardaman stands squarely in the
present of the novel.

The overlapping, then, verifies the perceptions of a character or places him in relationship to external chronological
time. If the important development in *As I Lay Dying* has to
do with a character's subjectivity, rather than with the
development of events, Faulkner's technique becomes an aid
to the reader, a clever narrative device rather than a weak-
ness. The reader who begins by assuming that present chronological time is absolute in this narrative has missed the
point entirely. Much of *As I Lay Dying* works to demonstrate
that time is relative to perception.

However, the problem of past-tense narration remains.
Even assuming, as I do, that the point of narration can move
at will along the external continuum, the relationship between
present and past-tense narration must be established. Why would
Faulkner begin in the present tense, so carefully establish
his chronology of action, and then switch to past-tense
narration? Did he lose control of his narrative? If a character speaks in the past tense in a book such as this, how
important is his point of view?

A close look at the temporal structure of the novel sheds
light on some of these complexities. If we compare the chronological present of the events described in each section with the
point of narration, several illuminating explanations emerge.
First, some points of narration are simultaneous with the points
of action, they describe, as we have seen in *Darl* 1. However,
Faulkner needed to develop some way to cover a period of time
quickly. How, in present-tense narration, can the author move
from the night of the first day to the afternoon of the second
without describing all the hours in between? One solution can
be seen in *Tull* 20. Here Faulkner moved the point of narration
to the second afternoon but had Tull recall the pertinent
events of the morning:

>   It was ten oclock when I got back, with Peabody's
> team hitched on to the back of the wagon. They had
> already dragged the buckboard back from where Quick

> found it upside down straddle of the ditch about a
> mile from the spring. It was pulled out of the road
> at the spring, and about a dozen wagons was already
> there. It was Quick found it. He said the river was
> up and still rising. He said it had already covered
> the highest water-mark on the bridge-piling he had
> ever seen. "That bridge wont stand a whole lot of
> water," I said. "Has somebody told Anse about it?"
> (p. 80)

The recollected conversation with Quick and Armstid at the
end of the passage creates an illusion of present time which
makes the transition to the actual present almost unnoticeable:

> "Then he better get at it soon as he can,"
> Armstid said.
> Anse meets us at the door. (p. 81)

This may be precisely the reason Faulkner rewrote the opening
paragraph to include dialogue. Faulkner's struggle with verb
tenses in the manuscript supports such an idea:

> I slept late and so it's ten oclock when I get
> back, with Peabody's team hitched on behind. They
> had ~~done all rea~~ already dragged the buckboard back.
> It was pulled out of the road at the spring, and
> about a dozen wagons were already there, and so I
> decided they had persuaded Anse to bury her at New
> Hope even before I heard how high the river was and
> still rising. And when I got there and found they
> was going to have the funeral at the house, I knew
> so. Until I found out that Anse was wishing[12] that
> Darl and Jewel would hear about it and put the load
> off and come on back, so they could get across the
> river before it rained again.
> Anse meets us at the door. (MS. p. 34)

Faulkner employs the same device to telescope time in
Anse 28, an interior monologue. Here Faulkner moves the chronological present and the point of narration to the evening of
the fourth day. As Anse thinks about the land he saw on the
way to Samson's--"Eight miles of the sweat of his body washed
up outen the Lord's earth, where the Lord Himself told him
to put it" (p. 104)--he recalls: "We drove all the rest of
the day and got to Samson's at dust-dark and then that bridge
was gone, too" (p. 105). Anse's final thought--"But now I
can get them teeth. That will be a comfort. It will" (p. 105)--
supports the placing of his monologue in the chronological
present of the evening of the fourth day. Clearly, he has not
yet faced the fifth day's trauma of the river crossing and
he still expresses optimism about the journey.

The next section, Samson's, moves the point of narration
to the morning of the fifth day, shortly after the Bundrens
have left his house. Samson's reference to MacCallum, who was
on the porch with him the night before, places him in time:

> If they was bent on going to Jefferson, I reckon
> they could have gone around up by Mount Vernon, like
> MacCallum did. He'll get home about day after to-
> morrow, horseback. (p. 112)

However, the events he tells presumably anticipate Anse's
monologue in section 28 when they go back to the previous
evening at sunset when the Bundrens arrived. Thus Faulkner
effectively moves the point of narration to the fifth day
and gives an outsider's comment on the Bundrens' journey.
When the next section begins with Dewey Dell's seeing the
New Hope sign, the reader recognizes the continuity of the
narrative present.

Faulkner also uses this technique in two *Darl* sections,
42 and 57. In the first, Darl speaks in the past tense while
narrating how they got from the river to Armstid's. However,
interspersed italicized sentences indicate his obsessive
concern with Jewel, and the last italicized passage shifts
to the narrative present:

> *When I looked back he was leading the horse into
> the barn* he was already talking about getting
> another team, and by supper time he had good as
> bought it. *He is down there in the barn, sliding
> fluidly past the gaudy lunging swirl, into the
> stall with it.* (p. 174)

This extremely important section, Darl's first after the
crossing of the river, reveals his dissociation from himself.
Darl's real presence is to Jewel and the horse, not to the
journey itself. But in terms of narrative management it serves
the same foreshortening purpose as the others we have examined;
it moves the point of narration to a future which becomes the
new narrative present by the end of the section.

The same technique appears again in Darl's last section,
57. His dissociation from himself reaches a climax here when
he speaks of himself in the third person, but the point of
narration is, once again, clear. Darl speaks from his cell in
Jackson as he clairvoyantly sees his family in Jefferson sitting
in the wagon eating bananas.

> The wagon stands on the square, hitched, the
> mules motionless.... Darl is our brother, our brother
> Darl. Our brother Darl in a cage in Jackson where,
> his grimed hands lying light in the quiet interstices,
> looking out he foams. (p. 244)

His description of the train ride is memory: "Darl has gone
to Jackson. They put him on the train, laughing, down the
long car laughing ..." (p. 243). Thus, Faulkner establishes
the point of narration as the tenth day. Unlike some of the
other narrators, Darl always speaks from an immersion in the
present time of the novel. If the reader establishes where in
time Darl is, he will know where in time the Bundrens are.
The fullness of Darl's presence at any moment in *As I Lay
Dying* combines with his great number of sections to give him
a special claim on the reader's attention.

Nevertheless, Faulkner frequently uses characters whose
point of narration lies somewhere in the indefinite future
in *As I Lay Dying*. In almost every instance these characters
assume importance as tellers of and commentators on the story,
rather than as participants in the action. At least once, in
Tull 16, Faulkner seems to have adopted such a stance to avoid
confusion, because Vardaman in section 15 and Darl in section
17 narrate events of the same night in present time. Faulkner
also employs this technique to foreshorten time in *Tull* 20,
Armstid 43, *Moseley* 45, and *MacGowan* 55.

Faulkner developed, then, two techniques to foreshorten
time. The first was to place a narrator slightly ahead on the
time continuum in a new present. From this point the narrator
can recall intervening events and then become immersed in the
new present. The second foreshortening technique is that of
placing a narrator in an indefinite future time and having
him narrate events in the past tense, from memory.

Tull 20 illustrates both these techniques. We have already
seen how he placed Tull's point of narration ahead of the
events narrated to foreshorten time at the outset. After the
funeral, however, Faulkner had to bridge the gap between the
afternoon of the second day and the morning of the fourth
when Jewel and Darl return. He solved the problem by using
italics to indicate the displacement in time: "*On the third
day they got back and they loaded her into the wagon and
started*" (p. 87). Then the narrative of the Tulls' trip home
after the funeral on the second day resumes, but now narrated
from an indefinite future point in time. Faulkner thereby
manages to leap the third day completely; when the next
section opens in the present time of the morning of the fourth
day, the reader follows easily.

Placing the point of narration in the indefinite future
also has the effect of distancing these characters in the
reader's perception. Such distancing seems to be the primary
reason for narration from a point in the indefinite future in
Anse 26--the events follow the narrative present exactly--
and in *Tull* 33 and 36. These *Tull* sections which describe
the crossing of the river provide an objective, outside point

of view to complement Darl's and Vardaman's perceptions. As Tull's sections further the action, they also leave the reader with a dual perspective on a most important event. Even as they verify the factual accuracy of what Darl sees, they point up the special characteristics of his mind.

After the crossing of the river the narrative present is associated exclusively with Darl and Vardaman who have ten of the remaining seventeen sections in the novel. But since both brothers are submerged in subjectivity, Faulkner needs some outside narrators to comment on the journey and to carry the external action. These outsiders also provide humor which demands a detachment Darl does not have and a maturity Vardaman does not possess. Although he is a Bundren, Cash fulfills such a narrative role. At the same time, his position in the indefinite future helps explain his lifeless, flat quality; he, too, lives at a distance from the present.

Three sections in *As I Lay Dying* are, as we noted in our discussion of the second narrative mode, completely atemporal: *Cora* 39, *Addie* 40, and *Whitfield* 41. Looking at them in terms of our present discussion of the relationship between a character's perception and external chronology, we discover that the first two could occur any time after the conversation to which they allude; Whitfield's any time after the funeral. Clearly Faulkner placed them together intentionally, as a triptych, at the chronological center (fifth day) and high point (river crossing) of the novel. Cora and Whitfield frame Addie literally and figuratively. They express in words as they formed in life the limits of her action. Against this limit--theological, social, sexual, verbal--Addie rebels. Her rebellion lies behind the psychological complexities of the Bundren family relationships, especially that between Darl and Jewel.

As Faulkner attempted to convey shifts of consciousness and clairvoyant "seeing" in the third narrative mode, he had available a technical resource which he had already used to great effect in *The Sound and the Fury*: italics. A study of the manuscript and text of *As I Lay Dying* shows that Faulkner used italics carefully in developing his experimental narrative form.

Italics first appear in *Darl* 12. Although Faulkner has already described clairvoyant communication (Darl sees Jewel and the horse in section 3 and Dewey Dell reveals her conversation with Darl in section 7) and various levels of consciousness (in *Jewel* 4, *Darl* 3 and *Dewey Dell* 7) here, for the first time, such a transition threatens to be confusing. The manuscript shows Faulkner's struggle with the problem. He wrote in the present tense until he finished the first italicized section (in the text, page 48 lines 20-31). Then he apparently reconsidered the complexity of the narrative arrangement he had created.

Darl begins speaking in the narrative present (point of narration and events coincide) about Addie's last moments. However, Darl is on the road with Jewel, not at home with Addie. When Faulkner shows Darl's deeper preoccupation with Jewel, to whom he is physically present, Faulkner shifts to italics. The technical device signals the reader that two changes are occurring--one physical, one psychological. Darl's deepest "thoughts" begin and end with *"'Jewel,' I say"* (MS. p. 19), a phrase which recalls his taunting of Jewel in section 10 (pp. 38-39).

> "Jewel," I say. Overhead the day drives level and gray, hiding the sun by a flight of gray spears. In the rain the mules smoke a little, splashed yellow with mud, the off one clinging in sliding lunges to the side of the road. The tilted lumber gleams dull yellow, water-soaked and heavy as lead, tilted at a steep angle into the ditch, above the broken wheel; about the shattered spokes [m][and about Jewel's ~~ankles~~ straining ankles] a runnel of ~~yellow water swirls~~ yellow neither of water nor earth, swirls, curving with the yellow road neither of water nor earth, down the hill. [m][dissolving into ~~a dark mass of~~ a streaming mass of dark green neither of earth nor sky.] ~~Jewel's hat droops about his neck, channeling water onto the towsack wrapped about his shoulders as, ankle-deep in the running ditch, he pries with a slipping 2-x-4 at the axel~~. "Jewel," I say. (MS. p. 19)

The passage describes, in mobile images, Jewel's struggle in the rain with the broken wagon wheel. Obviously Faulkner is trying to overcome the temporal linear quality of his medium as he simulates nonverbal perceptions. The images which here appear conjoined in Darl's mind gather meaning as the novel progresses: driving rain, and mud, the yellow, water-soaked boards, the broken wheel and the shattered spokes, the runnel *"neither of water nor of earth."*

After writing the paragraph Faulkner apparently considered recasting the conscious narrative portion in the past tense, while leaving the below-conscious portion as present-tense narration. Accordingly he wrote the past verb form over all the verbs up to that point and finished the section in the past tense. However, his indecision obviously remained because he also left the present-tense verbs intact. Thus the first manuscript paragraph reads:

~~They-can-feel-the-floor-shake-under-Dr.-Peabody's~~
                              stood
~~tread.-Pa-stands-beside-the-bed~~. Pa is standing
                                                    peered
beside the bed. From behind his leg Vardaman peers,

with his round yellow head, his eyes round and his
                                                looked
mouth beginning to open, round too. She looks at Pa.
              was
The repudiation is gone from her eyes; ~~yet~~ as they
                                    appeared
cling to his face all her failing life appears to drain

into them, urgent, irremediable. "It's Jewel she wants,"
              said
Dewey Dell says. (MS. p. 19)

A bit further on in the same section Faulkner faced a
slightly different narrative problem. When Darl breaks his
narrative of Addie's death and foresees Dewey Dell's reaction,
he knows that she will go to the porch and silently implore
Peabody's help in getting an abortion. The shift here is not
only psychological and physical, but also temporal. Dewey
Dell's section 14 attests to the accuracy of Darl's knowledge.
Again, Faulkner uses italics to indicate the shift in time,
place and consciousness.

When he got to the end of the section Faulkner obviously
decided to conclude with the last part of Darl's paragraph
about Jewel quoted above. Consequently he crossed out these
lines where they appear earlier in the manuscript. By the time
he had finished the first draft of *As I Lay Dying*, Faulkner
apparently thought he had solved the narrative problems that
the section illustrates, and he cast the whole of *Darl* 12 in
the typescript and the text in the present tense.

A comparison of the manuscript and text of Dewey Dell's
section 30 further supports the thesis that Faulkner used
italics only as a device for clarity and communication with
the reader. The manuscript begins with two almost completely
italicized paragraphs:

> I dont know whether I can see it or not. But I
> know that I am I and I know that it is it and that
> it is there because I saw it there, curving red away
> in to the pines. And if I see it and it is there, I
> see it. But if I dont see it, it is not there. And
> if it is not there, I am not I. And if I am I, then
> yesterday is not because I dont see it. But I dont

> know if I see it or not. So I dont know if yesterday
> was or not or whether I am or not. But yesterday
> was; that's why I must see it.
>   The signboard comes in sight. And so it is yes-
> terday. And beyond yesterday is the day before
> yesterday. And the day before that. And the day
> before that. That's why I must pass it. I heard that
> my mother died. I wish I had time to let her die. I
> wish I had time to wish I had. And the day before that
> is beyond the wild green-of-the in the wild earth and
> outraged earth too soon too soon   too soon. It's
> not that I would not it's too soon   too soon   too soon.
> (MS. p. 48)

In the text Faulkner has eliminated the italics and rewritten
the opening so that Dewey Dell's attention focuses on the ironic
signboard--"New Hope. 3 mi." The change calls attention to the
sentence which remains italicized:

> That's what they mean by the womb of time: the agony
> and the despair of spreading bones, the hard girdle in
> which lie the outraged entrails of events (pp. 114-115)

Both italics and images suggest that Dewey Dell's words well
up from places below consciousness, that her perception here
is, unlike the first two paragraphs, essentially nonverbal
and unconscious.

Originally Faulkner also italicized the paragraph in section 30 which reveals Dewey Dell's clairvoyant conversation
with Darl. But this in turn created problems. First, the paragraph itself is very confusing in its original version; only
the most discerning reader would realize that it is a conversation. Second, it forces Faulkner to return to regular
type for the next paragraph in which Dewey Dell recalls her
nightmare. In the manuscript, then, the recollected dream
appears to be continuous with the return to the present:
"It blows cool out of the pines, a sad, steady sound" (MS.
p. 48). Faulkner remedied the problem in two stages. On the
manuscript he inserted double vertical lines to indicate
changes from italics to regular type:

> The land runs out of Darl's eyes; they swirl to
> pin-points. They begin at my feet and rise along my
> body, to my face, and then my dress is gone: I sit
> naked on the seat above the mules, above the travail.
> Suppose // "Suppose I tell him to turn, // he says //
> He will do what I say. // Once I waked with a black
> void rushing under me. I could not see. I saw Vardaman
> rise and go to the window and strike the knife into
> the fish, the blood gushing, hissing like steam but

> I could not see. // He'll do as I say. He always
> does. I can persuade him to anything. You know
> I can // Was I dead once? // Suppose I do. We'll
> go to New Hope. We wont have to go to town. //
> I rose taking the knife from the streaming fish the
> knife still hissing I killed Darl. (MS. p. 48)

Later, in the typescript and text, he italicized the dream
paragraph. The final version distinguishes clearly between
Dewey Dell's conscious mind and her other perceptions. It
also clarifies her clairvoyant conversation with Darl by
making clear that it is a conversation. Here, as throughout
the novel, Faulkner used italics deliberately and discrimin-
atingly to convey to the reader shifts in time, place or consciousness which could not be communicated easily using only
regular type.

A study of the third narrative mode in *As I Lay Dying*
leads to several conclusions. First, the fullness of present
time in the novel is always associated with Darl. All his
sections maintain the present-tense narration with which the
novel begins. Immediately, such an insight signifies the
importance of Darl's perception. The fact that Darl narrates
all the major events of the novel reinforces this view. After
opening it, he describes Addie's death and Anse's reaction,
Cash's building of the coffin, Jewel's acquisition of the
horse, the actual river crossing and the loss of the team,
Jewel's diving for Cash's tools, the barn fire, the entrance
into Jefferson, his going to Jackson. The fact that the "object"
of the journey, Addie's burial, is merely alluded to, not
described, supports the idea that *As I Lay Dying* is really
about perception and mental states as much as about events.
As Darl disintegrates mentally, Vardaman's role increases
proportionately. Between them Darl and Vardaman have twenty-
nine, or just half, of the sections in the novel. Like Darl,
Vardaman's point of narration always coincides with the point
of action and like Darl, Vardaman cannot comprehend what is
happening. But Vardaman's lack of comprehension grows out of
his being a child whereas Darl's problem is an acuity of perception which enables him to see things with which he cannot
cope emotionally. Vardaman and Darl draw together because
they share a radical and unspeakable sense of loss. As he
disintegrates under the impact of the journey and lives more
and more on an unconscious level, Darl approaches the child's
concerns and confusion. Vardaman, in his loneliness, responds
to an adult's attention. Only Darl bothers about him. The
growth of the relationship between Darl and Vardaman is especially marked in the part of the book between the river crossing

and the entrance into Jefferson. Of these eleven sections
(42–52), the two brothers have nine.

Dewey Dell also participates in present-tense narration
in three of her four sections. However, she seldom narrates;
rather, she "speaks" interior monologues which throw up images
that suggest her unworded depths. Although Dewey Dell can
converse clairvoyantly with Darl, essentially she is taken up
with her own concerns, mainly getting an abortion. Her last
section, 58, departs from the pattern in that it consists
wholly of dialogue with two framing sentences spoken from the
indefinite future. However, the section actually characterizes
Anse more than Dewey Dell as it describes his taking of her
ten dollars.

Jewel also speaks in the present tense in his one section,
but like Dewey Dell's it is essentially an interior monologue.
Both Jewel and Dewey Dell receive definition in the novel much
more through Darl's perception of them than through their
own words.

Cash presents special narrative problems. The first three
of his five sections (18, 22, 38) are so out of touch with the
external action as to seem obsessive. Jewel's and Dewey Dell's
interior monologues reveal something of their motivations
and preoccupations which in turn are personal. Cash's preoccupation, his workmanship, isolates him from the human reality
around him. At the end of the book, in sections 53 and 59,
Cash suddenly assumes a narrative role which some critics
have said marks a new insight and maturity gained through
suffering.[13] The narrative framework of the novel, however,
argues against such an interpretation. Cash speaks both times
from the indefinite future, he never becomes present to present
action, and he seems to assume his narrative role simply because
no one else is available to do so. More importantly, Faulkner
uses narrative technique to set Cash apart from the other
children.

If all that we have said about narrative management in
As I Lay Dying is true, Faulkner experimented with a totally
new narrative form which allowed him to explore questions of
perception and consciousness without sacrificing completely
the advantages of past-tense narration. He did it by establishing an exact chronology of action and by using various points
of narration on his time continuum. Some characters assume
importance only through what they tell about others. Their
sections usually remain on a conscious descriptive level and
they speak from a point in time beyond the narrative present.
The author thus creates a distance between them and the
reader as well as between them and the Bundrens, for they are
mostly outside the family circle. In contrast, the Bundren
children and Darl in particular, usually speak in a narrative

present which coincides with the point of action. Moreover, their subjectivity becomes important in itself as it reveals patterns of perception, various levels of consciousness, and a complex interaction with each other. An exploration of their subjectivity provides the key to characterization.

Before trusting any statement or perception in *As I Lay Dying*, the reader must ask who makes it and under what circumstances. In addition, he must ask whether it represents conscious thought or some deeper level of the self. As in *Darl* 3 and in the italicized passages mentioned above, Faulkner moves easily in *As I Lay Dying* through the mazes of the mind, even attempting to convey through images the nonverbal self below consciousness. Only characters whose point of narration coincides with the chronological present reveal those levels of consciousness. These are the characters most deeply involved in the psychological journey which parallels the literal one.

By now it should be abundantly clear that the narrative management of *As I Lay Dying* involves the creation of a new narrative pattern. Faulkner wove together skillfully three structural patterns: a linear chronology of events; a symmetrical plot design; a developing subjectivity revealed through the characters' perceptions of events. The first places the book in time and prevents the reader from becoming confused. The second provides the suspense necessary to the plot and sustains an artistic form. The third becomes the key to the characters and thus to the ultimate meaning of the novel. Here Faulkner differentiates the people who merely serve to narrate and comment upon events from those who experience, perceive, and participate psychologically in the Bundren odyssey.

Faulkner once commented on his attitude toward time in an interview with Loïc Bouvard:

> . . . I agree pretty much with Bergson's theory of the fluidity of time. There is only the present moment, in which I include both the past and the future, and that is eternity. In my opinion time can be shaped quite a bit by the artist; after all, man is never time's slave.[14]

His remarks corroborate the findings suggested by an analysis of narrative management. They support the idea that time is relative to man's perception of it, and that life resides in the fullness of the present moment which in turn contains both past and future. Moreover, Faulkner asserts that the artist can shape time, as he does in *As I Lay Dying*.

A close analysis of narrative techniques in *As I Lay Dying*
leads, therefore, to an understanding of the novel as a whole.
Such analysis suggests that Faulkner knowingly experimented
with a hybrid type of narration for a specific purpose, that
he wanted to explore the relationships among various sub-
jectivities, and that he created a form which demands that
the reader attend to the narrative patterns if he wishes to
understand the novel. Further, the narrative patterns suggest
that a psychological journey parallels the physical one and
that those characters who are most present to events are also
the characters whose perceptions are most significant.

NOTES

1. William Faulkner, *As I Lay Dying*, edition revised under
the direction of James B. Meriwether (New York: Random House,
1964), p. 21. Subsequently "the text" refers to this edition
and all citations will be given in the body of the paper.

2. Manuscript of William Faulkner, *As I Lay Dying*, p. 8.
Subsequently all references to the manuscript will be cited
in the body of the paper. Passages underlined or crossed out
are underlined or crossed out **in** the manuscript; ^{m}[ ] indicates
marginal inserts; [ ] indicates inserts within the body of
the manuscript.

3. *Modern Fiction Studies*, 13 (Spring 1967), 64.

4. Franklin, p. 65.

5. Franklin, p. 58.

6. See the appended chronology of the novel, pp. 30-32.

7. "The Mind of Vardaman Bundren," *Philological Quarterly*,
39 (April 1960), 247-251.

8. André Bleikasten notes this in *Faulkner's As I Lay
Dying*, trans. Roger Little (Bloomington: Indiana University
Press, 1973), p. 13.

9. "Narrative Management," p. 62.

10. For example, see Olga Vickery, "The Dimensions of
Consciousness: As I Lay Dying," *The Novels of William Faulkner*,
rev. ed. (1964); rpt. in *William Faulkner: Three Decades of
Criticism*, ed. Frederick J. Hoffman and Olga W. Vickery (1960;
rpt. New York, 1963), pp. 232-247. Hereafter cited as *Three
Decades*.

11. For example, in section 5 Faulkner made several revisions
to keep his tenses consistent.

12. This word is illegible in the manuscript, though I am quite certain it begins with a "w."

13. See, for example, Joseph L. Blotner, "*As I Lay Dying*: Christian Lore and Irony," *Twentieth Century Literature*, 3 (April 1957), 16; Jack Gordon Goellner, "A Closer Look at 'As I Lay Dying,'" *Perspective*, 7 (Spring 1954), 54; Olga Vickery, "The Dimensions of Consciousness: *As I Lay Dying*," in *Three Decades*, p. 233; Frederick J. Hoffman, *William Faulkner* (New York: Twayne Publishers, 1966), p. 62.

14. *Lion in the Garden: Interviews with William Faulkner, 1926-1962*, James B. Meriwether and Michael Millgate, eds. (New York: Random House, 1968), p. 70.

THE CHRONOLOGY OF *AS I LAY DYING*

Catherine Patten, R.S.H.M.

A careful reading of *As I Lay Dying* enables one to determine with some certainty the chronology of the novel. Faulkner's concern with the details of his time scheme points to its importance to him and, consequently, to the reader.

First Day

After Darl and Jewel have left to get wood and Anse has told Vardaman to clean his fish, Anse sees the shadow touch the porch steps and says it's five o'clock (p. 31). Darl notices, when he and Jewel are on the road, that the sun is "an hour above the horizon" (p. 39) but by the time Peabody arrives "the sun has gone down behind a bank of black cloud like a topheavy mountain range" (p. 41). Addie dies in the twilight (p. 48) and it is "nigh to midnight" (p. 65) when Vardaman's knocking wakes the Tulls. Vernon says it was "nigh toward daybreak when we drove the last nail" (p. 69). Darl notices that "toward dawn the rain ceases" and Cash, after packing up his tools, mounts the steps "into faint silhouette against the paling east" (p. 75). It is "almost dust-dawn" when Vernon gets home (p. 69).

Second Day

Tull says it was "ten oclock when I got back" the next morning to view the body and attend the funeral (p. 80).

Third Day

After the funeral Tull thinks: "*She laid there three days in that box, waiting for Darl and Jewel*" (p. 86) and that "*On the third day they got back and they loaded her into the wagon and started*" (p. 87). From the context it seems clear that the three days here mentioned are the day of the funeral and the two days subsequent to it. This third day of the novel, then, is spent waiting for Darl and Jewel to return with the wagon and the team.

Fourth Day

   Darl and Jewel return and the journey begins. Anse says,
"We drove all the rest of the day and got to Samson's at dust-
dark" (p. 105) and Samson says the Bundrens arrived "just before
sundown" (p. 106).

Fifth Day

   After staying overnight at Samson's, the Bundrens leave
the next morning (p. 112) and retrace their steps past New
Hope (p. 114) and Tull's (p. 116). At Tull's bridge they cross
the river and finally arrive, wet and bedraggled, at Armstid's
in time for supper (p. 174).

Sixth Day

   In the morning Anse rides Jewel's horse to Snopes'. He
returns near supper time and Jewel rides off on the horse
(p. 182).

Seventh Day

   Eustace Grimm arrives at Armstid's "about a hour after
breakfast next morning" (p. 183) with Snopes' team, and the
Bundrens again set out. Vardaman asks Darl when they will get
to Mottson and he answers "tomorrow" (p. 187).

Eighth Day

   In Mottson Moseley rebuffs Dewey Dell, Darl buys ten cents
worth of cement, and Moseley says Albert told him "It had been
dead eight days" (p. 193). After they leave Mottson, Cash
protests "Wont we get to Jefferson tomorrow? ... It aint but
one more day" (p. 197) when they pour the cement over his
leg. Jewel returns (p. 198), and they stay at Gillespie's
overnight. During the night Darl sets fire to the barn.

Ninth Day

   Darl says Jewel "got burned in a fire last night" (p. 220)
as the family arrives in Jefferson (p. 221). In the morning
Addie is buried after having "waited nine days" (p. 224),
and Darl is sent to Jackson. Dewey Dell first meets MacGowan
at noon: "It was just a quarter past twelve" (p. 232); and Cash
goes to Peabody's sometime during the day. The only time
reference in the novel which seems inaccurate occurs when Peabody says to Cash: "you rode six days on a wagon without
springs, with a broken leg" (p. 229). Since Cash broke his
leg when crossing the river on the fifth day, and this is
only the ninth day, Cash has not been suffering for six days.

Possibly this is a typical exaggeration of Peabody's or perhaps Peabody just does not know exactly how long ago Cash
broke his leg. At any rate, the statement does not fit the
chronology of the novel. At ten that night, after Anse has
gone to find a new wife, Dewey Dell returns to meet MacGowan
while Vardaman watches in the square (p. 237; 248).

Tenth Day

The "next morning" (p. 248) as they are leaving Jefferson,
Anse introduces the new Mrs. Bundren to his family. Darl,
from his cell in Jackson, sees them eating bananas in the
wagon.

SHAPES OF TIME AND CONSCIOUSNESS
IN *AS I LAY DYING*

Stephen M. Ross

Among Faulkner's many experiments with narrative technique,
As I Lay Dying seems in certain respects the most puzzling.
The novel seems to alternate between stream-of-consciousness
and colloquial storytelling; the use of italics follows no
easily discernible pattern; the author attributes his own
ornate rhetoric to the thoughts of ignorant children; and,
most notably, the book's temporal structure appears to break
down badly, as Faulkner mixes past-tense and present-tense
narration, even switching from one to the other within certain
monologues.

Citing these apparent inconsistencies in the novel, readers
have charged Faulkner with mishandling his own technique. R.W.
Franklin marshals the most complete case against the novel by
arguing that Faulkner, when he began the story with present-
tense stream-of-consciousness, failed to provide his reader
with a "stable present" (which "traditionally ... resides
at the point of narration and is the present of the narrator"),
and so wrote himself into a corner that he could escape only
by jumping out the window, by virtually abandoning the restric-
tive present tense. The results, evident in the book's anachronisms and broken sequence of sections, led Franklin to conclude
that Faulkner blundered, that we must "judge the anachronisms
inconsistent, the narrative management faulty, and ... recognize that *As I Lay Dying* shows the great haste in which it
was written."[1]

But *As I Lay Dying* seems, to me at least, a far better and
more artfully contrived novel than Franklin allows. That
Faulkner wrote the book quickly (he was writing all his books
in this 1929 to 1932 period rather "quickly") does not mean
he wrote it carelessly. He revised the novel while it was still
in manuscript, and again when he made the typescript, so that
we must be cautious before concluding that he was swept away
by his own ingenuity.[2] Franklin's analysis, which does make
the novel seem highly inconsistent and clumsy in its temporal
structure, employs a traditional, sequential time scheme as

the standard for evaluating the story's coherence; but Faulkner, as various critics have suggested, explores in *As I Lay Dying* (and in other works as well) highly unconventional notions about the nature of time, ideas growing primarily out of Bergson's theory of duration.[3] In technique, too, I would argue, Faulkner experiments with time, with ways of representing time through grammar and through the conventions of narration: events that appear inconsistent by standard definitions of fictive time become on closer inspection carefully and intriguingly ordered. If we study Faulkner's alternations in past and present narration--the crux of the book's complex temporal structure--we can discover not only a principle of order but also another of Faulkner's technical innovations.

I

Sorting out the narrative tense of *As I Lay Dying* can be a complicated process, not only because some sections are in past tense and others in present, but also because some monologues mix tenses; there are so many variations to account for that any general statement about the novel's time scheme can become tangled. We can, however, get a clear picture of Faulkner's method by looking first at the monologues of a single speaker, a character allotted enough sections to reflect the book's overall complexity but not so many that we cannot discern pattern in Faulkner's choice of tense. Vernon Tull, as the Bundrens' nearest neighbor, occupies a middle position in the story between the outside observers who relate only one incident in the funeral journey, and the members of the family who are directly affected by Addie's death. Tull narrates six sections: 8/28 (on the porch with Anse) in present tense; 16/65 (night Addie dies) in past tense; 20/80 (the funeral) in past, then present, then past tense; 31/117 (at river) in past, then present tense; 33/130 (crossing river) in past tense; 36/145 (conversation with Cora about events at the river) in past tense.[4]

If we apply to these six sections the normal basis for choosing verb tense--the establishment of an event's position in a temporal sequence--then inconsistencies are glaringly apparent. In section 20, to mention only the most obvious example, past tense is allowed to represent past, future, and present time: the second italicized portion of section 20 describes in past tense events that take place *after* the narrative's "time-present" (the funeral day), and the final incident (finding Vardaman fishing) occurs back once again on the funeral day--but it too is rendered in past tense whereas most of the funeral day has been described in present tense.

Yet Faulkner appears to have selected his tenses deliberately
throughout all of Tull's sections. In section 31, for example,
he has revised verbs to make them consistently past tense up
to the point where the switch to present-tense narration occurs,
after which he has revised verbs again to keep them consistently present tense.[5]

We cannot unravel the complex fictive time created in these
monologues by trying to squeeze them into a consecutive linear
pattern--Franklin shows the difficulties in this. But perhaps
we can come closer to an explanation by regarding these sections in the terms they are given to us, as *interior* monologues.
Instead of asking how the verb tense orders events, we should
ask what the tense has to do with portraying inner experience:
what psychological implications does tense carry that Faulkner
might be trying to capitalize on, or to create, as he records
the thoughts and emotions of his characters? A tentative
answer is inherent in the words "present" and "past" themselves: present-tense narration suggests that events are experienced and felt by the narrator at the same instant they
are told to the reader, while past tense places a buffer of
time between events and the narrator's description of them.
Present implies--and helps create--immediacy of experience,
an intensity of the moment; past implies greater detachment,
a looking back on events, a separation from them.[6] Such a
distinction is, of course, *prima facie*, and stated in abstract
terms seems too inelastic to account for the wide variations
in Faulkner's manipulation of tense throughout *As I Lay Dying*.
"Immediacy" and "detachment" are not absolutes that can be
set up as poles on a scale of psychic intensity, from which
readings can be taken to determine when past tense should
be used and when present--Faulkner does not choose his tense
in any such simplistic fashion. Rather, he alters verb tense
for the same reasons he employs italics, or gives sophisticated
diction to a child's thoughts--that is, to suggest the infinite
variability of human awareness. Tense as Faulkner uses it
helps throw into relief nuances of consciousness in its
temporal dimension. That present tense suggests greater
immediacy than does past allows Faulkner, merely by choosing
one tense over another, to submerge a character more deeply
in his experience, letting the reader then sense the character's
heightened psychic involvement. With past tense, Faulkner can
move a character, in a way that is simultaneously psychological
and temporal, back from an event, permitting speculation on
its meaning.

I would emphasize that in *As I Lay Dying* the significance
of either past or present time, the quality of consciousness
each evokes at any given moment in the story, varies from
speaker to speaker and from monologue to monologue. Faulkner

seeks, through technical means, greater flexibility in the
representation of human experience, not just another rigid
formula that no matter how inventive would only restrict
his ability to portray inner reality. Thus in some monologues
past tense does represent "present" events, in the manner
of the conventional "historical present." In others, however,
past tense contrasts sharply with the immediacy of the present.
We can say that the *relatively* greater immediacy of the present
tense holds throughout the novel, but we cannot find for all
the sections a single scale by which to measure the "intensity
of involvement" or the "degree of detachment" enforced by
tense. Most importantly for our efforts to understand what
appear to be anachronistic passages, we must note that the
use of tense to portray consciousness occasionally supersedes
its function as an indicator of temporal order: a passage may
be narrated in a tense inappropriate to its position in the
sequence of action for the sake of that sense of felt experience
Faulkner wished to create for that character at that point in
the story.

We can see more concretely how and why Faulkner violates
conventional narrative time if we look at Tull's six monologues--
which turn out, in this new light, to be quite consistent.
Both Tull's proximity to the Bundrens and his position as an
outsider are reflected and enforced by the tense in which he
thinks at a given moment: when he is actually with the Bundrens,
both physically and psychically, he uses present tense; when
he is, or feels, separated from them, when he thinks about the
family as from a distance, as an observer instead of a participant, he uses past tense. In section 8 Tull sits on the
Bundrens' porch waiting with Anse--he is present and involved,
though like Anse he merely sits. In section 16, however, when
Tull's attention is focused on Vardaman, he tries to comprehend
the boy's incredible actions more than he participates in
them. He looks back on what happened the night Addie died,
remembering and puzzling over the elemental injustice of
Vardaman's grief. In this section Faulkner carefully keeps
Tull physically as well as temporally separated from events
at the Bundren farm, by bringing him back home ("It was long
a-past midnight when we drove the last nail, and almost dust-
dawn when I got back home and taken the team out and got back
in bed" [p. 69]) before letting him tell us that Vardaman
drilled holes in the coffin to let his mother breathe. None
of the narration in this section occurs while Tull is at the
Bundrens'. His thoughts, more than Vardaman's actions, are
the real subject of his monologue: "Now and then a fellow
gets to thinking. About all the sorrow and afflictions in
this world" (p. 67). Faulkner emphasizes the content of Tull's
speculations rather than the immediate experience of that night,

so the section is in past tense, as a recapitulation, and the
final three paragraphs are devoted entirely to Tull's wander-
ing meditation on God's justice, on his own lack of a young
son, and on Cora's useless piety.

In section 20, the funeral, Faulkner even more carefully
focuses Tull's attention and concern, letting the character's
consciousness create time in its own terms. After the brief
exchange (rendered in past tense) with Armstid and Quick about
Peabody's team, Tull's immediate attention switches to Anse,
and the tense changes to present ("Anse meets us at the door").
The talk among the men proceeds in normal fashion until Tull's
attention turns to Cash; he tries to console Cash about the
way the women have ruined his work on the coffin by putting
Addie in backwards. The talk among the men continues, but
it is now in the background of Tull's awareness, so Faulkner
puts the voices in italics and removes speaker identification,
for Tull is not listening closely enough to note who speaks
which lines. Tull then reports the funeral itself, but only
as it affects him, that is, as disembodied voices:

> In the house *the women begin to sing....*
> *The song ends*; the voices quaver away with a rich
> and dying fall. *Whitfield begins.* His voice is bigger
> than him. It's like they are not the same. It's like
> he is one, and his voice is one.... *Somebody in the
> house begins to cry.* It sounds like her eyes and her
> voice were turned back inside her....
> *Whitfield stops at last. The women sing again.*
> In the thick air it's like their voices come out of
> the air, flowing together and on in the sad, comforting
> tunes. When they cease it's like they hadn't gone
> away.... *Then they finish....*
> *On the way home Cora is still singing.* (pp. 85-86;
> italics mine)

This passage records movement through time, but time marked
by the voices Tull hears instead of by minutes and hours.
His psychological impression of the funeral becomes the time
"span" here, with each change in voice (the sentences I have
italicized) serving as a temporal unit or "moment." Franklin
blames Faulkner for jumping too abruptly from the funeral to
the trip home, but the voices carry over into the trip ("Cora
is still singing") so this belongs to the felt time period
of the funeral itself. An external sequential time pattern
gives way to the portrayal of consciousness.

The italicized portion that follows the funeral has a
detached quality similar to that of the italicized dialogue
going on in the background when Tull is talking to Cash. The
attempt to persuade Anse to get started for Jefferson seems

more half-remembered than immediately experienced by Tull,
as if these fragments were all that remained in his consciousness about the three days following the funeral. The past
tense helps create this impression, as does the jumbled sequence within the passage (Tull refers to Anse as still waiting
after he tells us the boys have returned home and the family
has started for Jefferson). Only bits and pieces have stuck
in Tull's memory, so that is all we get, because these can
suffice to indicate the incident's importance to Tull. The
past tense in the final portion of section 20, when the Tulls
find Vardaman fishing at the slough, not only creates a slight
mental distancing from the farm and the funeral (the Tulls are
now a mile away), but it also is consistent with section 16,
in which Tull puzzles over Vardaman's behavior. Tull certainly
"experiences" Vardaman, of course, but the boy's significance
in the processes of Tull's consciousness is that of someone
pondered rather than someone faced in the immediate instant
without time for wonder and speculation.

Although the movement from past to present in section 31
is simpler and more straightforward than the alternations in
section 20, Faulkner takes no less care in modulating the flow
of Tull's awareness. By beginning with past and changing to
present tense, Faulkner causes the past to continue into the
present; what was and what is blend into a single progression
of experience without a sudden, abrupt jump from past to
present.[7] The movement in time reflects Tull's gradual emergence from the moment that has just passed into the action now
occurring. The sentence stating that he rode from his field to
the river is in simple, definite past tense: "After they passed
I taken the mule out and looped up the trace chains and
followed" (p. 117). When he arrives and first describes the
Bundrens looking at the swollen river, Tull uses more indefinite
verb forms that depict a continuing past time: "was setting,"
"was watching," "was looking" (pp. 117-18). And before talk
commences, in the present tense, Tull describes the river,
using frequentative past which refers to repeated action going
on in the past and carrying into the future: "Sometimes a log
would get shoved over the jam and float on, rolling and turning,
and we *could* watch it go on to where the ford used to be. It
would slow up ..." (p. 118, my italics). Only then does true
present-tense narration begin: "'But that dont show nothing,'
I say.... We watch the log. Then the gal is looking at me
again" (pp. 118-19).[8] This is no arbitrary or careless shifting
of narrative time, but a controlled rendering of Tull's steadily
increasing physical and psychic proximity to the Bundrens at
the river; he is moving into a sharing of their experience,
and Faulkner modulates the temporal dimension of Tull's awareness through the progression of verb tenses--past, continuous
past, frequentative past, present.

Section 33 also demonstrates Faulkner's adherence to consistent psychological criteria for his selection of narrative tense. Here Tull is still with the Bundrens at the river, and he crosses the submerged bridge with Anse, Vardaman, and Dewey Dell. Because of his direct involvement, we might expect present-tense narration; but Tull experiences this moment more as an observer than as a participant: he *feels* detached, apart from what is happening--apart even from himself:

> Like it couldn't be me here, because I'd have had
> better sense than to done what I just done. And
> when I looked back and saw the other bank and saw
> my mule standing there where I used to be and knew
> that I'd have to get back there someway, I knew it
> couldn't be....
>   When I looked back at my mule and it was like
> he was one of these here spy-glasses and I could
> look at him standing there and see all the broad
> land and my house sweated outen it.... (pp. 131-32)

Section 36, Tull's last, brings Cora's judgment of Anse, plus Tull's own rejection of her judgment, to bear on the events at the river. The Tulls are looking back on what Vernon has just been through, so past tense is used. The final portion of the section, after the brief dialogue with Cora, describes action in a vivid historical present, since this experience in Tull's memory demonstrates the irrelevance of Cora's contradictory explanation for the incredible scene Tull has witnessed--Jewel holding the wagon alone against the current, saving his mother (as she predicts) from the flood waters.

II

That conventional notions of fictive time are inadequate for evaluating the coherence of *As I Lay Dying* is evident from the varied shapes that time and consciousness assume in just the six sections allotted Vernon Tull. Faulkner felt free to step out of the regular progression of past-present-future, not believing it necessary to represent time as linear sequence; nor did he find it essential to create for the novel a stable present of narration which mirrors any "correct" ordering of chronology such as Franklin insists upon. We know that Faulkner's conception of time was closely akin to Henri Bergson's: "I agree pretty much," he told Loic Bouvard, "with Bergson's theory of the fluidity of time. There is only the present moment, in which I include both the past and the future, and that is eternity."[9] It is Bergson's conception of "pure duration," not linear, mechanical time (what Mr. Compson in *The Sound and the Fury* sardonically calls "the minute clicking of

little wheels"), that guides Faulkner's choices and experiments
in *As I Lay Dying*. Duration is the temporal dimension all experience has, but this dimension cannot always be represented
as linear progression, for time is not always felt as sequence;
time, like other dimensions of our awareness, varies infinitely,
and intertwines itself with all other qualities of experience--
with gradations in emotional intensity, with our sense of
proximity or detachment, with our sense of stasis or change.[10]

Faulkner's manipulation of verb tense reflects, symbolically,
the constant modulations that the temporal dimension of human
awareness undergoes. Using grammar as a tool for pushing and
pulling at the novel's "time-line," Faulkner tries to warp
time into the shapes of thought and emotion; he creates "duration" by reworking fictive time into a flexible, shifting process that ebbs and flows with the intensity of his characters'
inner lives. This does not mean that he abandons sequential
time altogether. The overall movement of action from before
Addie's death to after her burial is fairly easy to follow;
but in any given monologue Faulkner refracts time through the
narrating consciousness, so that rigid temporal ordering may be
momentarily disrupted. Faulkner alters literary and grammatical
time as we commonly know it in order to achieve psychologicl
verisimilitude. Tull, as we have seen, alternatingly feels
intensely caught up in what he narrates, or more detached
and distant--he has helped Anse so much he can't quit, but he
can pause to ponder the meaning of the events he describes.
Time has, in fact, almost a spatial correlative, since he
narrates in present tense only when he is literally close to
the Bundrens. Faulkner establishes the relationships of other
speakers to the events of the novel in similar, though not
identical, ways: he fuses time with other dimensions of experience to render the organic, fluid nature of human consciousness. All the narrators figuratively (and sometimes literally)
cluster around Addie's death and burial, and each is established
in his or her place in terms of this central event. Such placing occurs in space, in time, and in emotional and moral terms;
such placing is created by the form each monologue assumes
as well as by the content of a character's thought or the circumstances of his participation in the action. While time
may not have such a clear spatial equivalent as it does for
Tull, time does merge with other qualities of psychic life to
help define each character's existential stance in the world
around him.

For someone like Cash, or Cora Tull, "place" in this existential sense is as definite and secure as feet and inches,
or as the number of eggs saved out for baking; for Jewel it
is the equally definite vision of himself on a hill with
Addie, above the others, throwing rocks down upon them. Anse

sees himself stoically absorbing the bad luck that travels a
road--he reasons that if men were meant to travel, God would
have made them horizontal like snakes instead of vertical
like trees. Addie distinguishes the deeds that run powerfully
along the ground from the words that vanish upwards into the
air, and her frustration in life came from the ever-increasing
distance she felt between the two, a distance she ironically
tried to bridge by taking Whitfield as a lover "in order to
shape and coerce the terrible blood to the forlorn echo of
the dead word high in the air" (p. 167). The novel is filled
with this kind of imagery, images of space, of shape and
direction, and of time. The pregnant Dewey Dell feels trapped
in time, which she perceives in the concrete physical terms
of her body: *"That's what they mean by the womb of time: the
agony and the despair of spreading bones, the hard girdle in
which lie the outraged entrails of events"* (pp. 114-15).
Vardaman seeks the impossible security of an eternal present,
since he is unable to accept change and the passage of time.
And to Darl, acutely sensitive to the uncertainty of human
existence, time and space become inextricably one--"the space
between us [is] time: an irrevocable quality" (p. 139).

Perhaps because time is the dimension of experience that
is "irrevocable," its representation constitutes the most
intriguing and thematically important experiment in *As I Lay
Dying*. We are by no means required to share Faulkner's (or
Bergson's) theory about the nature of time, but we should
judge the consistency of *As I Lay Dying* in its terms rather
than from our own *a priori* notions about fictive time. What
seem to be inconsistencies or shifts in method during the
course of the novel are more properly regarded as part of
Faulkner's creation of time appropriate to the narrating mind
in a given monologue. For example, in the sections belonging
to the outside witnesses Samson, Moseley, Armstid, and MacGowan,
the speakers use past tense so conventionally that their sections
do not sound like stream-of-consciousness.[11] Yet the oral,
storytelling tone of these sections augments the speakers'
experience of the funeral journey: not only are they outside
the family, but none of these men is deeply committed to the
Bundrens, in circumstance or in spirit. Samson and Armstid
shelter the family, and marvel at what the Bundrens are doing;
but theirs are the thoughts of incredulous observers whose
particular personalities are not crucial to the story. They
express what amount to communal thoughts. We can readily
imagine their tales being told and retold, being passed along
from farmhouse to store to village throughout Yoknapatawpha
County; their monologues manifest the community's consciousness as well as their own. The witnesses tell their anecdotes
in the colloquial manner, and in ordinary narrative past tense,

because the content of their minds is closer to the surface of
public awareness and memory than are the feelings of someone
like Darl.[12]

Faulkner's portrayal of Cora Tull demonstrates his willingness to sacrifice conventional technical consistency for
psychological realism. Cora's section 6 seems out of place
because it is in past tense whereas the other fourteen of the
novel's first fifteen sections are in present. Cora, in fact,
is given present-tense narration only very briefly, in section
2, when she describes the scene at Addie's deathbed; most of
section 2, however, records Cora's thoughts about yesterday's
baking and her need to justify the expense to Mr. Tull. Cora
always thinks back on events, retelling them in order to
judge others' behavior and justify her own, blanketing everything with her sanctimonious platitudes. Faulkner is consistent
to Cora's character in rendering section 6 not as direct experience, but as grossly inaccurate gossip, "told" after the
fact in Cora's complacently pious fashion. The same can be
said of section 39, when Cora describes her conversation with
Addie and concludes that Addie was too proud to find salvation.
Throughout the novel Cora is detached and protected against
the world by her moralizing; she is always looking back at
others, as Tull beautifully puts it, "with that singing look
in her face like she had done give up folks and all their
foolishness and had done went on ahead of them, marching up
the sky, singing" (p. 146).

Other "anachronisms" noted by Franklin are less trouble-
some once we abandon the supremacy of sequential time and
allow Faulkner to alter chronology in order to shape the
dimensions of psychic experience. The triad of sections (39-
40-41; Cora-Addie-Whitfield) is difficult to fit into a linear
time scheme because we don't know when Cora is recalling her
conversation with Addie, because Addie is already dead when
we hear her thoughts, and because Whitfield has already
arrived at the farm back in section 20. So obviously out
of sequence are these sections that even Franklin thinks
Faulkner has "based the grouping on some other organizing
principle" than simple chronological arrangement.[13] These
sections portray Addie's personality as it was during her
entire life, so that the information contained in all three
monologues could be given at any point in the book. Faulkner
seems to have chosen the triad's position for dramatic reasons:
it comes just after the crossing of the river, during a pause
in the action, and at a turning point in thematic emphasis--
after the crossing, human interference with the journey
becomes more important than the natural catastrophes that
have plagued it so far. The triad forms a cohesive unit
defining the personality against which the rest of the Bundrens

have had, in some way or another, to define themselves.
Cora's judgment of Addie is ridiculed by Addie's angry pride
and strength, while in turn Whitfield's comic monologue mocks
Addie's version of meaningful action--taking this hypocrite
to be the embodiment of powerful, active sin, the "deed" so
far better than Anse's "word." From this point on we can
comprehend the damage worked on human personality, especially
Darl's, by Addie's fierce hatred of life.

    Section 12, which depicts (in present tense) the same
scene described previously in section 11 (also in present
tense), is anachronistic by a standard of sequential time,
but, again, not by the criterion of duration. Both Peabody
and Darl are close enough to Addie's death to face it directly
and intensely, Peabody by being literally present, Darl by
being "present" in his heightened, clairvoyant imagination;
both are present in any sense that matters in *As I Lay Dying*.[14]
Franklin refers to the manuscript as proof that in section 12
Faulkner lost control of his present-tense technique.[15] The
first part of the manuscript, up to and including the first
italics, was originally written in present tense. Faulkner
then went through and wrote past forms above all the verbs
in the first portion in roman type (e.g., $\frac{was}{is}$) without crossing
out the present forms (Faulkner was usually careful to cross
out whatever he changed in a manuscript). The roman portion
after the first italics was written originally in past tense,
as if Faulkner had decided on past. But in the final published
version all verbs in section 12 are in present tense. That
this demonstrates Faulkner's *confusion*, as Franklin claims,
is a highly speculative deduction. It is just as plausible
that Faulkner did not cross out the present verb forms because
he was testing the tense, putting both down to see which would
sound more appropriate for Darl's consciousness at the moment.
All of Darl's clairvoyant narrations are in present tense, so
Faulkner's final decision seems consistent on psychological
grounds. Franklin fails to mention that the italicized portions
in section 12 were never changed, as if Faulkner were considering putting roman type in one tense and italics in another--
something he does in sections 34, 35, 48, and 49. We can of
course never know what Faulkner had in his mind when he wrote
this section, but his revisions suggest deliberate and artful
experimentation, consistent with the rest of the novel, far
more than they prove confused ineptitude.

    Understandably, the members of the family, the most intense-
ly affected by Addie's death, narrate most often in the present
tense; yet their monologues do vary a great deal. Anse (in
three sections) and Jewel (in one) narrate very little action,
expressing their thoughts and feelings directly, and in present
tense. Dewey Dell is committed to going to Jefferson so she

can buy something that will abort her child; the urgency of
her immediate predicament is reflected in her harsh, present-
tense monologues.

In Vardaman's sections Faulkner modulates tense to
emphasize the boy's confused obsession with his mother's
death. He can comprehend the way things are in the present,
but he cannot understand or accept emotionally the passage
of time. Addie continues to live for Vardaman, either in her
coffin or (emotionally at least) as a fish he has caught.
When Darl is taken away to Jackson, Vardaman (in his last
monologue) can recognize the action of going away as past,
but he asserts what is still "present" to him: *"My brother
is Darl.... Darl is my brother. Darl. Darl"* (pp. 241-42).

Three of Vardaman's sections contain past-tense narration
that does not indicate remembered event so much as it signals
the boy's psychological disengagement, compared to events
rendered in present tense. In section 35, for example, he
describes his brothers' struggle in the river in unpunctuated,
run-on narrative, as if the description of action rushes
through his mind automatically, involuntarily. What really
engages his attention is the instant when Darl, who Vardaman
hopes has "caught" Addie, comes up out of the water. The run-
on narrative abruptly stops, while the print switches to italics
and the tense to present, focusing Vardaman's consciousness
on this crucial moment: *"Then he comes up out of the water.
He comes a long way up slow before his hands do but he's got
to have her got to so I can bear it"* (p. 144). When Darl
comes out empty-handed, the past-tense narrative resumes.[16]
In section 49, too, tense change and italics signal differences
in the immediacy of Vardaman's experience. The narrative is
in present tense, telling of Darl and Vardaman "listening"
to Addie in her coffin, and of Vardaman waiting to find out
where the buzzards go at night. While these events are in
the foreground of his consciousness, his seeing Darl set
fire to Gillespie's barn remains in the background, being
less important to the boy than is the coffin or the buzzards.
So seeing Darl is recorded as memory, separated from the rest
of the section by italics and past tense: *"And I saw something
Dewey Dell told me not to tell nobody"* (p. 205).[17]

Darl's monologues, like his psychic states, are the most
complex. Most of his narration is in present tense, for he
experiences the world around him with maddening intensity.
The few past-tense passages (other than those which clearly
are remembered incidents, such as the story about Jewel's
"sleeping") suggest a distancing from that being described.
He narrates section 42, for example, in past tense until his
attention turns to Jewel and the horse, in a last italicized
passage rendered in present tense (p. 174). In section 48

the references to Jewel (all in present tense) are scattered
among narrative sentences (in past tense) telling of Cash
and of the coffin. Clearly it is Jewel, Addie's favored child,
who holds Darl's constant obsessive attention; Darl cannot
find his "place" in time because he has been literally
displaced in Addie's affection by Jewel.

Darl's acute mental powers range beautifully but frantical-
ly through time and space, giving him clairvoyance but also a
tenuous hold on any sense of his identity in the real world.
In an effort to define himself, to declare the nature of
existence in the flux of time, Darl plays with words, with
the past and present forms of the verb of existence:

> And since sleep is is-not and rain and wind are *was*,
> it is not. Yet the wagon *is*, because when the wagon
> is *was*, Addie Bundren will not be. And Jewel *is*, so
> Addie Bundren must be. And then I must be, or I could
> not empty myself for sleep in a strange room. And so
> if I am not emptied yet, I am *is*.
>   How often have I lain beneath rain on a strange
> roof, thinking of home.[18] (p. 76)

But words will not suffice, and Darl is left with only the
despair of not knowing the true nature of his existence.
By the last section, he has lost any cohesive identity,
for there is no place in time for Darl; he becomes disengaged
from himself, narrating in the past tense and the third person--
except when his mind pictures (in present tense) his family
waiting by the wagon in Jefferson. This is Darl's place emotionally, but physically and mentally he is foaming in a
cage in Jackson.

We must not mistake Darl's confusion--one of the novel's
subjects--for Faulkner's experimentation in narrative management. Though not a perfectly executed work of fiction (the
book is perhaps open to Faulkner's own complaint that it was
too much a *tour de force*), *As I Lay Dying* is nonetheless one
of Faulkner's most imaginative and structurally innovative
novels. We may decide that verb tense should not, after all,
carry the psychological burden Faulkner loads it with,
we may conclude that the creation of psychological time does
not work equally well at every point in the novel, but once
we understand Faulkner's incredible virtuosity here, we can
hardly claim that he succumbed to carelessness.

NOTES

1. R.W. Franklin, "Narrative Management in *As I Lay Dying*," *Modern Fiction Studies*, 13 (Spring, 1967), 64, 65.

2. The manuscript at the University of Virginia's Alderman Library, besides exhibiting numerous small revisions, is a composite of pages apparently written at different times: entire passages written on one sheet of paper have been pasted on to the final manuscript page, often with changes (especially in verb tense) to make the pasted-on portion fit into the new version.

   All references to the manuscript of *As I Lay Dying* are to that at the University of Virginia.

3. Various critics have discussed time as a theme in *As I Lay Dying*: see especially Robert Hemenway, "Enigmas of Being in *As I Lay Dying*," *Modern Fiction Studies*, 16 (Summer, 1970), 133-46. Hemenway argues that Faulkner "shows that the boundary of existence is time, that tense serves as the only certain functionary of being" (p. 139). See also Peter Swiggart, *The Art of Faulkner's Novels* (Austin: Univ. of Texas Press, 1962), pp. 109, 123; and Margaret Church, *Time and Reality: Studies in Contemporary Fiction* (Chapel Hill: Univ. of North Carolina Press, 1963), pp. 235-37.

4. All references to *As I Lay Dying* are to the 1964 Random House edition collated with the first edition and manuscript by James B. Meriwether. Double numerical references (e.g., 8/28) indicate section number and the page on which the section begins.

5. Compare manuscript pp. 49-50 with final published version, pp. 118-19.

6. Past is, of course, the more common narrative tense and can represent present as well as past time. When an author uses present tense, however, he not only emphasizes its greater immediacy, but also decreases the illusion that past tense can represent present time.

7. Faulkner uses this same device of bringing action from the past into the present at the beginning of section 20, and in Peabody's first section (11/40): Peabody narrates in past tense until he arrives at the Bundren farm and begins talking with Anse.

8. There may be a further modulation in Anse's first line of quoted dialogue: "'If it was just up, we could drive across,' Anse says" (p. 118). "Says" is used variously in the novel to represent either the correct present-tense "says" or a common colloquial form of the past-tense "said"

(see MacGowan's section, for example). Which it is here is unclear, perhaps deliberately so.

9. *Lion in the Garden: Interviews with William Faulkner, 1926-1962*, James B. Meriwether and Michael Millgate, eds. (New York: Random House, 1968), p. 70.

10. See Henri Bergson, *Time and Free Will*, trans. F.L. Pogson (London: Swan Sonnenschein, 1910), pp. 99-106.

11. Franklin argues, incorrectly I think, that Faulkner virtually abandons the technique with which he started the novel when he introduces the outside witnesses (Franklin, p. 64).

12. At the end of the novel, two sections by Cash and one by Dewey Dell are in past tense and sound more like told stories than is usual for members of the family. Addie has been buried, however, and Darl has been put away, so that the pace of thought, action, and feeling has slowed, relaxing into the more methodical movements of Cash's thinking as he speculates on what has happened. Past tense again reinforces detachment from the central event, now completed.

13. Franklin, p. 62.

14. We must, of course, accept Darl's clairvoyance in order for this (and many other passages) to be comprehensible. Interestingly, Faulkner introduces us to Darl's powers rather gingerly. In section 3, when he first describes Jewel's behavior with his horse, Darl begins "He *will* ... the horse *will* ..." (p. 11; italics mine) before moving into straight present-tense narration. The "will" suggests that Darl is describing something he has seen before, making his description not so much clairvoyance as imaginative reconstruction from past experience. Elsewhere, however, Darl's clairvoyance is not mitigated by verb tense.

15. Franklin, p. 61.

16. Faulkner revised this section to make it internally consistent, by changing verbs ("says" and "begin") originally in present tense in the section's final paragraph, so that they would match the past tense of the earlier, nonitalicized narrative, of which the final paragraph is a resumption (Manuscript, p. 61; published version, p. 144). For a discussion of "voice" in Vardaman's and others' narration, see Stephen M. Ross, "'Voice' in Narrative Texts: The Example of *As I Lay Dying*," *PMLA*, 94 (March, 1979), 300-310.

17. Faulkner even uses tense in section 49 to evoke the merging of dream and reality in Vardaman's mind. Before going to sleep, the boy consciously recalls (in present tense) the

toy train he hopes is still in the store in Jefferson: "It goes round and round on the shining track" (p. 206). After Dewey Dell tells him to go to sleep, he dreams of the train (in past tense): "It was behind the window" (p. 206). Then, as he half-awakens to see the men coming to move Addie's coffin, the image of the train blends into the image of the line of men: "Then it [the train] was pa and Jewel and Darl and Mr Gillespie's boy" (p. 206). Finally, completely awake, Vardaman continues his narration again in present tense: "Mr Gillespie's boy's legs come down under his nightshirt" (p. 206).

There is one error in section 49, in the last lines where a past-tense reference to seeing Darl is not in italics. This may be an oversight in transcription, since the manuscript (p. 89) does indicate italics for these lines.

18. See Hemenway, "Enigmas of Being," for an excellent thematic analysis of this and other passages in which characters explore the nature of existence through the verb "to be."

PERCEPTION, LANGUAGE, AND REALITY
IN *AS I LAY DYING*

Joseph M. Garrison, Jr.

Criticism of Faulkner's *As I Lay Dying* seems to be reaching a dead end. Recent interpretations are still asking essentially the same kinds of questions which produced, in the 1950s and 1960s, some very useful readings.[1] These questions center around the final meaning of the journey. Is it a heroic quest heroically fulfilled, as John Ditsky has suggested,[2] or is it "primarily a nonsense story"?[3] Both conclusions have been defended with varying degrees of persuasiveness, but neither of them is satisfying; and we remain uncomfortable with the Bundrens and their story. My purpose is not to challenge the work which has already been done on this novel: much of it has been incisive; much of it has been helpful; and it has provided further occasions for response. Rather, I want to investigate a new focus for Faulkner's art in *As I Lay Dying* and explore some ways in which it supports another reading.

I will begin with Darl and, for purposes of organization and continuity, will concentrate on him throughout most of my discussion. First of all, he is fascinated with other people's eyes--with what he sees, literally, in the eyeballs of other people. Moreover, he is unusually concerned with his own visual experience and with the language which he uses to describe it. Through him, we can "see" Faulkner's interest in perceptual biases and related cognitive considerations. Here are Darl's first words:

> Jewel and I come up from the field, following
> the path in single file. Although I am fifteen
> feet ahead of him, anyone watching us from the
> cottonhouse can see Jewel's frayed and broken
> straw hat a full head above my own.
> The path runs straight as a plumb-line, worn
> smooth by feet and baked brick-hard by July,
> between the green rows of laid-by cotton, to the
> cottonhouse in the center of the field, where it

> turns and circles the cottonhouse at four soft
> right angles and goes on across the field again,
> worn so by feet in fading precision.[4]

From the evidence of these two paragraphs, we could infer
that Darl is an unusually perceptive observer, verbally and
mentally skilled in ways which distinguish him from other
characters in the novel, particularly from the members of
his family. Some critics have said that Darl faithfully
represents Faulkner's point of view and that skilled intelligence is, by its very nature, a trustworthy consciousness.
But I do not think that we should overgeneralize Darl's consciousness to include an insightful *and adequate* response
to the world. As Cleanth Brooks has observed, Darl is "a
rationalizing and deflating force."[5] His language, in the
passage included above, for instance, suggests a particular
kind of intelligence: it prescribes fixed and substantive
standards for reality, as in the mathematical plotting of
things that exist in space. At the beginning of the novel,
Darl looks at the world, or what he acknowledges as reality
in the world, as if its measurable properties were ultimately
valuable. Hence, he is interested in precise distances:
"I am fifteen feet ahead of him ..."; he is scrupulously
attentive to detail: Jewel's hat is a "frayed and broken straw
hat"; he uses similes as if he thought they were figures of
speech which could give him possession of the thing perceived: "straight as a plumb-line." At other points in this
first passage, Darl's language also reveals a preoccupation
with material causes and a tendency to juxtapose radically
unlike things into relationships of equality. Illustrating
both of these habits of mind, he sets up an odd, disturbing
parallelism of unlike causes: "worn smooth by feet and baked
brick-hard by July...." Consistent with his observation of
things in his first monologue, Darl does not seem to see himself in a participating relationship with his environment.
Hence, he does not report that he actually hears the sound
of the adze blade but says instead that he went into the
house and was "followed by" the sound (p. 5).

Darl's predispositions, as they are revealed in the
language of his first monologue, ask us to raise some fundamental questions about his priorities, questions which become
even more admissible in view of a contrasting example of attitudes which is included as a recollection in Darl's second
monologue. The recollection begins with a comment about
water: it tastes better, Darl says, "when it has set a while
in a cedar bucket" until it has acquired "a faint taste like
the hot July wind in cedar trees smells" (p. 10). Instead
of radical juxtaposition and precise verbal designation, Darl

here records a synesthetic impression and seems to relish its
mystery. Then he pictures the memory:

> I used to lie on the pallet in the hall, waiting
> until I could hear them all asleep, so I could
> get up and go back to the bucket. It would be black,
> the shelf black, the still surface of the water a
> round orifice in nothingness, where before I stirred
> it awake with the dipper I could see maybe a star
> or two in the bucket, and maybe in the dipper a star
> or two before I drank. (pp. 10-11)

For the reader, this is more than sentimental reverie. Darl's
language, in contrast to that in his first monologue, presents
an entirely different way of thinking about things and an
entirely different kind of verbal sensitivity. He entertains
the memory of the experience without asking that it offer
guarantees ("maybe a star or two"). He says, as well, that
motion "stirred it awake." Stillness, in this case, was "a
round orifice in nothingness," a mirror for something else.
Darl's recollection about the water, however, has ironic implications which begin to show us more specifically the nature
of his predicament. The recollection concerns an experience
out of the past, an experience which must have recurred for
Darl, when he was a boy, with some regularity and which he
has continued to remember with satisfaction and pleasure.
As an event in the past, it is very different from the present
events which occur during the course of the novel. Because
it is a completed event, it can be kept whole and intact; it
cannot threaten him with unpredictability. Memory, in other
words, seems to be a manageable phenomenon for Darl; he is
comforted by its stability.

Generalizing from the evidence presented thus far, I
suggest that Faulkner presents Darl as a character who cannot
distinguish between those perceptual faculties which tyrannize
and those which liberate. He is destroyed by his assumption
that the world, in order to exist and have meaning, must conform to his conception of it and be utterly possessed by him.
He is destroyed by pride. The novel may be said to dramatize
his demise, culminating in the "mad" disassociation of self
which occurs in his last monologue. Such a reading would explain why Faulkner keeps us alerted to Darl's intense scrutiny
of tangible details and why he continues to suggest a pattern
in Darl's responses. The implications of the passage about
water in the cedar bucket reappear in these thoughts, for
example:

> I enter the hall, hearing the voices before I reach
> the door. Tilting a little down the hill, as our
> house does, a breeze draws through the hall all

> the time, upslanting. A feather dropped near the
> front door will rise and brush along the ceiling,
> slanting backward, until it reaches the down-turn-
> ing current at the back door: so with voices. As
> you enter the hall, they sound as though they were
> speaking out of the air about your head. (p. 19)

Again, we can sense an unspoken receptivity, an openness, a
willingness to be moved by something, as if the numinous
presences in Darl's surroundings registered on his consciousness. He seems to have the capacity for amazement and is not
impelled to bring things under harness with language. But
irony is functioning here, too: there is nothing in this experience which threatens Darl; he can afford to be gentle
and delicate, since he knows what to expect. As his attention is turned to immediately present events, however, to
situations which have not recurred and whose meanings are
not already known to him, his language displays the possessive
verbal habit, meticulous and precise in its observations. He
cannot deal with situations which are unexpected or unpredic-
table except by wrenching them into rigid categories. Here
is Darl's opening description of the ill-fated river crossing:

> Before us the thick dark current runs. It talks
> up to us in a murmur become ceaseless and myriad,
> the yellow surface dimpled monstrously into fading
> swirls travelling along the surface for an instant,
> silent, impermanent and profoundly significant, as
> though just beneath the surface something huge and
> alive waked for a moment of lazy alertness out of and
> into light slumber again. (p. 134)

Darl is flexible at this point and can accept what he perceives
as something that is not terribly threatening. But by the
time he has reached the end of his version of the crossing,
when chaos has erupted and he is surrounded by uncertain
motion, his language changes:

> For another instant I see him [Cash] leaning to the
> tilting wagon, his arm braced back against Addie
> and his tools; I see the bearded head of the rearing
> log strike up again, and beyond it Jewel holding
> the horse upreared, its head wrenched around, hammer-
> ing its head with his fist. I jump from the wagon
> on the downstream side. Between two hills I see
> the mules once more. They roll up out of the water
> in succession, turning completely over, their legs
> stiffly extended as when they had lost contact with
> the earth. (p. 142)

Darl is looking for visual bearings again. And throughout
most of his monologues, when he finds himself in situations
of risk, he responds in this way. The following passage is
a particularly good example of an unsuccessful attempt to
stabilize the stubborn pressures of external reality with
language:

> *The tilted lumber gleams dull yellow, water-soaked
> and heavy as lead, tilted at a steep angle into the
> ditch above the broken wheel; about the shattered
> spokes and about Jewel's ankles a runnel of yellow
> neither water nor earth swirls, curving with the
> yellow road neither of earth nor water, down the
> hill dissolving into a streaming mass of dark green
> neither of earth nor sky.* (p. 48)

The repetition of the "neither" construction, with its underlying sense of puzzlement, indicates that Darl is confused
(perhaps frustrated) by his inability to name what he sees
or to liken it to any other thing. For him, it remains there,
impalpable and inscrutable.

Darl's monologues also contain evidence of an illuminating
pattern of similes. In the first few pages of *As I Lay Dying*,
Darl's similes could pass for observed "facts" and could be
construed as genuine attempts to establish apt comparisons:
Jewel's eyes are "like wood"; the boards of Addie's coffin
are "yellow as gold, like soft gold" (p. 4); Anse's shoes
"look as though they had been hacked with a blunt axe out of
pig-iron"; Jewel's horse is "a glittering maze of hooves as
by an illusion of wings"; Jewel mounts his horse "in a stooping
swirl like the lash of a whip" and rides him "leech-like on
the withers" (pp. 11-13). Even Darl's most extravagant simile
in the early monologues may be said to draw a credible likeness: Jewel and his horse "are like two figues carved for a
tableau savage in the sun" (p. 12). But as Darl and Jewel
begin the trip to deliver the load of lumber, Darl begins to
force analogies and displays verbal self-consciousness. His
similes become more complex; in many instances, they juxtapose
the animate with the inanimate, implying either that Darl does
not distinguish clearly between the world of organic life and
the world of dead things or that he forces one to meet the
terms of the other. Situations of risk or danger, which Faulkner seems to associate with motion and present time in the
novel, become portentous for Darl. Hence, he likens the rising
sun to "a bloody egg upon a crest of thunderheads" (p. 39).
In the "clairvoyant" description of Addie's death, he says
that Vardaman's "pale face" faded "into the dusk like a piece
of paper pasted on a failing wall" (p. 48), a likeness which

implies that Darl is having to work very hard with language
to particularize the significance of things. Ironically, he
does not discern the truth that he is able to apply to Anse,
whom he imagines at Addie's bedside, "smoothing at the wrinkles
which he made [in the quilt] *and which continue to emerge
beneath his hand with perverse ubiquity ...*" (p. 51; italics
added). In this activity, as narrated by Darl, Anse is using
his hands in much the same way, and with much the same result,
as Darl uses words.

Like the wrinkles in the quilt, the possibility of a
liberated understanding is always present, available to Darl
in one form or another; but he does not see it. Instead, he
moves closer to despair and its disassociating and dislocating
consequences. This development can be traced in his similes.
As he imagines Cash at work on the coffin, he says that "the
chips look like random smears of soft pale paint on a black
canvas. The boards look like long smooth tatters torn from the
flat darkness and turned backside out" (p. 71). The rain runs
down Anse's face "slow as cold glycerin" (p. 74). In the scene
where Addie is loaded onto the wagon, the coffin slips away
from Darl "like a sled upon invisible snow, smoothly evacuating
atmosphere in which the sense of it is still shaped" (p. 92).
Darl looks at Dewey Dell's eyes, and reflected in them he sees
"Peabody's back like two round peas in two thimbles" (p. 97);
Tull's mouth is "bluish, like a circle of weathered rubber"
(p. 152); the eyes of Jewel's horse "*roll in the dusk like
marbles on a gaudy velvet cloth*" (p. 174); Jewel's eyes are
no longer "wooden" but "look like spots of white paper pasted
on a high small football" (p. 203).

In view of the pattern of Darl's similes and what it suggests
about his epistemological expectations, his decision to burn
the barn and to end the journey is a crucial part of the narrative. Philosophically considered, this act is his extreme
attempt to bring situations to heel. Correspondingly, it is
at this point in the novel that he uses his most sharply
polarized comparisons: Jewel "springs out like a flat figure
cut leanly from tin"; Addie's coffin looks "like a cubistic
bug"; the flames of the fire sound "like an interminable train
crossing an endless trestle"; the cow "rushes between us and
through the gap and into the outer glare, her tail erect and
rigid as a broom nailed upright to the end of her spine";
the hallway "looks like a searchlight turned into rain" (pp.
208–11). On one occasion during his description of the fire,
Darl makes no real differentiation between Jewel and a simile
which Darl has just used to "contain" him:

> When we are through the gap he begins to run.
> "Jewel," I say, running. He darts around the corner.

> When I reach it he has almost reached the next one,
> running against the glare like that figure cut from
> tin. (p. 211)

When Darl says that Gillespie and Jewel "are like two figures
in a Greek frieze, isolated out of all reality by the red glare,"
the point is made explicitly. And by the time Darl finishes
describing the fire, it is no longer a fire: it is a "rain
of burning hay like a portiere of flaming beads"; Mack "slaps
at the widening crimson-edged holes that bloom like flowers
in his [Jewel's] undershirt" (pp. 211-12). Ultimately, Darl cannot
distinguish between words and deeds, to use Addie's terms.
He refuses to accept the inviolate uniqueness of unfamiliar
things, and the violation retires him from the world. At the
end of his last monologue, when the disassociation of self
has taken place, he is no longer able to appreciate particularity:

> The wagon stands on the square, hitched, the
> mules motionless, the reins wrapped about the seat-
> spring, the back of the wagon toward the court-
> house. It looks no different from a hundred other
> wagons there; Jewel standing beside it and looking
> up the street like any other man in town that day,
> yet there is something different, distinctive. (p. 244)

Almost pathetically, Darl senses that he has missed something
and offers one final, bizarre explanation:

> There is about it that unmistakable air of definite
> and imminent departure that trains have, perhaps
> due to the fact that Dewey Dell and Vardaman on the
> seat and Cash on a pallet in the wagon bed are eating
> bananas from a paper bag. "Is that why you are
> laughing, Darl?" (p. 244)

The answer to his question--eight times we are told--is "yes."
Darl is laughing because, in spite of himself, he cannot resist
the temptation to try to know things conclusively.

    If I am right about the kinds of problems which are
illustrated in Darl's language, other elements of his experience
should offer corroboration. And they do. His monologues
reveal, as I have said, a growing frustration with the elusive-
ness of the external world and with the tenuousness of events
in present time. They also exhibit a rising cynicism about
teleological meaning. At the beginning of the novel, Darl may
simply be world-weary. His world-weariness, however, alternates
between bitterness and despair; and his view of man seems to
move resonantly close to the King Lear tradition, strongly
suggested, for example, in this glimpse of his sister: "She

sets the basket into the wagon and climbs in, her leg coming
long from beneath her tightening dress: that lever which moves
the world; one of that caliper which measures the length and
breadth of life" (pp. 97-98). Later in the river episode, when
he sees the shape of Dewey Dell's breasts under her wet dress,
he concludes that they are "those mammalian ludicrosities
which are the horizons and the valleys of the earth" (p. 156).
Yielding to predispositions such as these, Darl is driven to
the binding conclusions that come at the end of the novel.
For him, experience has shown that "lives ravel out into the
no-wind, no-sound, the weary gestures wearily recapitulant:
echoes of old compulsions with no-hand on no-strings: in sunset
we fall into furious attitudes, dead gestures of dolls" (pp.
196-97). Unlike Lear, Darl cannot escape into fantasy to find
succor; and although he can divorce himself from the world,
he cannot divorce himself from its stern reluctance to yield
to his conceptions of it. In a sense, he cannot *become* mad.
At the end, therefore, Darl is not simply telling us that
he knows what sodomy is when he mentions the "little spyglass he got in France at the war" that contained a picture
of "a woman and a pig with two backs and no face" (p. 244).
With the devastating appropriateness of the obscene souvenir,
he is telling us what the world is really like to him.

This understanding of Darl makes sense, I think, not
only along broad lines of development in *As I Lay Dying* but
also in selective applications. It gives us, among other
things, another perspective from which to interpret his motivation and his attitudes toward other members of his family.
In the case of Jewel, Darl's taunts about illegitimacy obviously
express his resentment; he is a legitimate son of Addie and
is unloved; Jewel is a bastard son and is loved. At least
that is the way Darl sees it. We should remember, however,
that Darl is constantly talking about Jewel's horse and is
constantly calling our attention to the fact that it is
Jewel's forceful management of the animal which seems to be
the source of envy. For Darl, Jewel owns the horse in a very
real sense; but, in view of Darl's own predilections, that
model of ownership is a provocation, since Jewel seems to have
what Darl wants. Hence, Darl belittles Jewel for whatever
comfort Jewel is able to find in "fooling with that horse"
(p. 11). Perhaps Darl sees in Jewel a kind of violence which
can appropriate the meaning of things, which can render
something manageable and make it a possession, giving it,
in other words, the kind of "is-ness" which Darl thinks about,
at one point, nostalgically: "Beyond the unlamped wall I can
hear the rain shaping the wagon that is ours, the load that
is no longer theirs that felled and sawed it nor yet theirs
that bought it and which is not ours either, lie on our wagon

though it does, since only the wind and the rain shape it
only to Jewel and me, that are not asleep" (p. 76). A passage
such as this one would account for the anomalous mixture of
envy and resentment which appears, typically, in Darl's
references to Jewel's horsemanship: Darl wants what Jewel
has and, simultaneously, hates him for having it. Clearly,
Darl is attracted to Jewel's physical efficaciousness,
particularly to the way in which he is able to accomplish
his objectives:

> *He is down there in the barn, sliding fluidly past*
> *the gaudy lunging swirl, into the stall with it.*
> *He climbs onto the manger and drags the hay down*
> *and leaves the stall and seeks and finds the curry-*
> *comb. Then he returns and slips quickly past the*
> *single crashing thump and up against the horse,*
> *where it cannot overreach.* (p. 174)

The horse, as Darl understands it, is not "just a shape to
fill a lack" (p. 164). Apparently, it gives Jewel a sense
of purpose and dignity; and Darl cannot forgive his "brother"
for having something that is dear. Thus, after Jewel has
lost the horse in Anse's trade for the team of mules, Darl
seems motivated by a vengeance that will not be satisfied
with anything short of Jewel's utter existential defeat:
"*Jewel, I say, Who was your father, Jewel?*" (p. 203). Darl
is the kind of person who, in order to compensate for his
own emptiness, must make other people miserable, specifically,
those people whom he cannot possess or those who have some
degree of mastery over their environments. He will not let
them have an inviolable self; no one, except Darl, can have
a secret. If sanctuaries exist, he will destroy them, even
though he knows--and this makes his position culpable--that
among human beings there is a level of experience which cannot
be possessed or owned but which is simply there to be shared
(unspoken, and perhaps unspeakable). We know that Darl has
this alternate model of experience in his consciousness because of something that he says about himself and Cash: "he
and I look at one another with long probing looks, looks that
plunge unimpeded through one another's eyes and into the
ultimate secret place where for an instant Cash and Darl
crouch flagrant and unabashed in all the old terror and the
old foreboding, alert and secret and without shame" (p. 135).
It is in the context of his recognition of a nonverbal,
intuitive reality that Darl's monologue about Jewel's acquisition of the horse becomes thematically significant. Other
readings of *As I Lay Dying* have neglected this part of Darl's
narrative, except insofar as it provides a background for
Jewel's furious energy; they have not noted its distinctiveness

as an expression of Darl's consciousness. In view of the kinds
of language and the repeated ontological considerations which
characterize his other monologues, Darl's story about Jewel's
nightly visits to Lon Quick's forty acres is interpretively
crucial. It is told in the past tense, a time designation
which links it with the reverie about the water in the cedar
bucket. Along with that reverie, it offers a contrast to the
sense of being adrift in time which we sense in Darl's habit
of describing all present experience as if it were locked into
the continuum of time, unable to become event or deed. Darl's
manner of telling the story, moreover, is not self-conscious.
His diction is simple and unadorned. To note one obvious
divergence from his other monologues, his similes are straightforward, almost cliché: one of them compares Jewel to "a dead
man" (p. 122); another describes Jewel as being "gaunt as a
bean-pole" (p. 124); another likens Vardaman to "a cricket
in the grass, a little one" (p. 129).

As for its content, the story about Jewel's acquisition
of the horse is about a secret, Jewel's secret. It is also
about how the knowledge of the secret was obtained, how the
secret was shared, and how it was preserved as a secret until
Jewel came home one morning, riding the horse which he had
earned by clearing Lon Quick's land. "So we didn't tell," Darl
explains, "not even when after a while he'd appear suddenly
in the field beside us and go to work, without having had
time to get home and make out he had been in bed all night"
(p. 125). Darl's words reveal that there was a time in his life
when he was not frustrated by partial knowledge or driven by
the need to violate (by making public, for example) privacy.
In recounting his mistaken speculations about Jewel's night-
time activity, he says: "And I wondered who the girl was. I
thought of all I knew that it might be, but I couldn't say
for sure" (p. 124). Similarly, in his eye contact with Cash,
there was no compulsion to possess the fleeting and variegated
phenomenon that is present in the living human eyeball, none
of the retinal aggressiveness which prompts Tull to say,
"It's like he had got into the inside of you, someway. Like
somehow you was looking at yourself and your doings outen
his eyes" (p. 119). Darl and Cash looked at each other, Darl
tells us; but Darl was not acquisitive: "I told Cash, and
Cash and I looked at one another" (p. 124). Here is another
illustration:

> And when I saw him I knew that he knew what it was.
> Now and then I would catch him watching Jewel with
> a queer look, like having found out where Jewel went
> and what he was doing had given him something to
> really think about at last. But it was not a worried

> look; it was the kind of look I would see on him
> when I would find him doing some of Jewel's work
> around the house, work that pa still thought Jewel
> was doing and that ma thought Dewey Dell was doing.
> So I said nothing to him, believing that when he
> got done digesting it in his mind, he would tell
> me. But he never did. (p. 126)

This kind of reporting is not typical of Darl; it is certainly not the kind of reporting that characterizes his narrative of the events surrounding Addie's death.

I have concentrated on some of the details in Darl's story about Jewel because I think they encourage us to give critical weight to the conversation which Darl and Cash had, at the time of the episode, about "safe things." They also encourage us to interpret this conversation as a paradigm for an understanding of truth--or, more exactly, of a prosperous perception of reality--that would enable Darl to deal with things in positive and successful terms. Cash begins the conversation by guessing that Jewel is not mixed up with a young girl: "Aint any young girl got that much daring and staying power. That's what I dont like about it" (p. 124). Darl interjects his opinion that a married woman would be safer for Jewel than a girl. Cash replies: "It aint always the safe things in this world that a fellow...." He is not able to say exactly what he means, but Darl catches the drift of the thought and asks a question: "You mean, the safe things are not always the best things?" (p. 125). Then Darl makes his own observations about "safe things":

> When something is new and hard and bright, there ought
> to be something a little better for it than just
> being safe, since the safe things are just the
> things that folks have been doing so long they have
> worn the edges off and there's nothing to the
> doing of them that leaves a man to say, That was
> not done before and it cannot be done again. (p. 125)

In words, Darl advocates a philosophy of risk.

It seems to me that Faulkner, through Darl, is making a comment on the human situations in *As I Lay Dying*. Many of the characters in the novel are looking for, or are already certain that they have (as in the case of Cora Tull), "safe things." Some of them--Anse, for example--are utterly incapable of experiencing a life which will be "new and hard and bright"; they are bound to a ritualized existence that can only adjust passively to outside influences. To rephrase the point, there is no sense of human agency in what they do,

a deficiency which Faulkner keeps before our eyes with frequent references to blamelessness: Anse attributes everything
to luck and will not be "beholden" to any man; and while Cora
makes her promises, she is only interested in herself and
always manages to rationalize her mistakes so that she can
emerge from them "without loss" (p. 9). In the conversation
with Cash, Darl articulates what is fundamentally wrong with
the Bundrens. And, ironically, the judgment also applies to
Darl. In spite of what he understands or has understood in
the past, Darl cannot appreciate things which are "new and
hard and bright." Present time and motion threaten him. Instead of seeing life as a manifestation, as evidence of a
capacity *to become*, he sees it negatively as a condition in
which things are emptied of their essences. For Darl, present
time and motion do not imply a vigorous life possibility;
rather, they paralyze him with overwhelming despair at the
instability of the world. His assumptions are self-defeating,
but they explain why he thinks about being "emptied for
sleep"--why he talks about it that way--and why he expresses
this wish: "If you could just ravel out into time. That would
be nice. It would be nice if you could just ravel out into
time" (p. 198). In a way, the title of the book, taken metaphorically, epitomizes Darl.

   I have used Darl as the organizing center of *As I Lay
Dying* because the patterns in his monologues make a strong
case for authorial indirection as the unifying principle
of the book. While criticism has recognized the experimental
nature of Faulkner's presentation of the story, it has not
reached conclusions which accord with this recognition. Usually,
it has found Cash the moderately well-adjusted and enlightened
"hero" who has the final word. We do Faulkner an injustice,
I think, whenever we try to formulate his position in *As I
Lay Dying* as if it were equal to any of the Bundrens' views
or equal to any of the views of the peripheral characters.
What I have tried to show, in working with Darl, is that
Faulkner is not simply judging the folly or wisdom of the
arduous trip to Jefferson. He is fictionalizing the story of
a group of human beings who perceive the world as if it were
at best something that needed to be "endured."[6] The language
from the "Address upon Receiving the Nobel Prize for Literature" is applicable in this case. *As I Lay Dying* is about
people who do not "prevail" over "the problems of the human
heart in conflict with itself." As narrators, they tell
"not of love but of lust, of defeats in which nobody loses
anything of value, of victories without hope and, worst of all,
without pity or compassion."[7] Through them, Faulkner is writing about the causes and consequences of human bondage; and

he is speaking to all of us who lie dying in our separate
and collective lives.

Whatever hope Faulkner sees in *As I Lay Dying* is expressed
by the Bundrens' unrealized possibilities for "courage and
honor and hope and pride and compassion and pity and sacrifice.
They do not see these possibilities, but we do. We see them
in the alternatives to the ways in which Darl perceives and
understands reality. We see them, as well, in the sequence of
the monologues and, more persuasively, in the chronologically
displaced episodes and reveries, of which Addie's single
monologue is the most extreme example. What I have said about
Darl provides a rationale for this sequence. All of the
chronologically displaced passages in *As I Lay Dying* describe
an act of will in which someone has been emotionally committed
to something: that is, whether he admits it or not, he has
done things which have changed (or will change) the direction
of his life or which have brought him into intimate relationships with other people. By placing these experiences well
into the novel and by having them recur with enough regularity
to help us recognize that they have not been carelessly
misplaced, Faulkner is able to suggest that acts of will--
i.e., decisions--not only have immediate consequences but
also affect, and are contiguous with, those events which
continue to emerge in chronological time. This would mean that
the Bundrens are deceived in thinking that their actions are
not contributing factors in subsequent fortunes or miseries:
actions in the past continue to be influential in the linear
course of human events, continue to "interrupt" them, or are
"reborn" or resuscitated out of the very events which occur
as a result of these actions. If this is so, Faulkner is
showing us how purposeful *life* is, in spite of the Bundrens'
thoughts to the contrary, and how persistently it "prevails,"
even in the face of seemingly irreparable defeat.

NOTES

1. See, particularly, Jack G. Goellner, "A Closer Look
at 'As I Lay Dying,'" *Perspective*, 7 (Spring 1954), 42-54,
and Olga W. Vickery, "The Dimensions of Consciousness: *As I
Lay Dying*," in *The Novels of William Faulkner* (Baton Rouge:
Louisiana State University Press, 1959), pp. 50-65.

2. "Faulkner's Carousel: Point of View in *As I Lay Dying*,"
Laurel Review, 10 (Spring 1970), 74-85. Ditsky says that
Faulkner "argues for the strength and enduring qualities
of man" (p. 75).

3. Elmo Howell, "Faulkner's Jumblies: The Nonsense World of *As I Lay Dying*," *Arizona Quarterly*, 16 (Spring 1960), 70.

4. *As I Lay Dying* (New York: Random House, 1964), p. 3. Hereafter, all references to this edition will be cited parenthetically in the text.

5. *William Faulkner: The Yoknapatawpha Country* (New Haven: Yale University Press, 1963), p. 145.

6. William Faulkner, *Essays, Speeches & Public Letters*, James B. Meriwether, ed. (New York: Random House, 1966), p. 120.

7. Ibid.

8. Ibid.

YOKNAPATAWPHAN BAROQUE: A STYLISTIC
ANALYSIS OF *AS I LAY DYING*

E. Pauline Degenfelder

As I Lay Dying, published in 1930, represents in microcosm Faulkner's encounter with and solution to the problems of the twentieth-century artist.[1] On the one hand, Faulkner acknowledges the modern breakdown of communication and the relative isolation of human experience through his use of the interior monologue. Conversely, by creating the mythical Yoknapatawpha County, Faulkner supplies a vision of cultural unity and a counterstatement to the contemporary dissolution of commonly held beliefs.

This thematic dialectic between isolation and involvement has been amply acknowledged by the novel's commentators. William Van O'Connor, for example, states that the theme divides the characters "into those who accept the bitterness and violence of living and those who do not"[2], Irving Howe labels the novel a blend of "human tragedy and country farce"[3], and Michael Millgate points out that horror and comedy coexist in a "macabre manner" in the work.[4] Melvin Backman extends these comments by attributing the novel's dualities to the "multiple point of view, an ambiguity of theme and symbolism, and a richly suggestive treatment of character and event."[5] The major shortcoming of these analyses, however, is their failure to relate fully the novel's complexity to its variant styles. Irving Howe, for example, acknowledges only one style, indigenous "American lyricism."[6] Although both Olga Vickery and Cleanth Brooks distinguish between the styles accorded to conversation and to interior monologue, and although Mrs. Vickery points to the novel's range from "realistic and colloquial" style to a symbolic mode,[7] such descriptive tags are incomplete and ambiguous. Even an exclusively stylistic study, such as Warren Beck's, which mentions specific features such as "full sentence structure," lapses into qualitative description: "side by side with [the] richly interpretative style there exists ... a realistic colloquialism."[8]

Such subjective comments, in otherwise illuminating
essays, overlook the unique features of Faulkner's style
and point, moreover, to the absence of any generally accepted
procedure in discussing style. As Louis T. Milic has defined
the problem, "stylistics ... has for most scholars still no
method beyond the method of impressionistic description and
a vague use of rhetoric"; a solution to this shortcoming,
also proposed by Milic, consists in describing stylistic
features in "concrete and verifiable terms, which finally
means, in quantitative terms."[9] Consequently, this analysis
of style in *As I Lay Dying* will focus on syntax and diction
and will utilize recent developments in generative and transformational grammars. Such a discussion, in turn, will demonstrate the stylistic differentiation which underlines, and
brings about, the thematic tension between the isolated individual, particularly the artist, and the integrated community.

In general, Faulkner employs two basic styles in the novel,
either separately or simultaneously, depending upon the
identity and complexity of the speaker. To dramatize the
individual's alienation from the community, Faulkner uses
a baroque style; to depict the solidarity of the community's
folk, he utilizes a colloquial mode. Both styles--the baroque
and the colloquial--Faulkner has mentioned implicitly in his
fiction and criticism. The baroque mode, for example, appears
in *Mosquitoes* (1927), where the statue of Andrew Jackson,
"bestriding the terrific arrested plunge of his curly balanced
horse" is characterized as "*baroque* plunging stasis" (italics
mine).[10] Clearly, this peculiar combination of motion and
stasis antedates and foreshadows the baroque style in *As I
Lay Dying*, in which, claims Hyatt Waggoner, the image of Jewel
and his horse provides "the stylistic key to the vision that
shapes the novel."[11] Of the second mode, the colloquial,
Faulkner has been more conscious, acknowledging his debt to
the writer generally considered the exemplar of colloquial
style: "In my opinion, Mark Twain was the first truly
American writer, and all of us since are his heirs, we descended
from him."[12] Furthermore, Faulkner explicitly recognized
the need to diversify styles. In his lectures at the University
of Virginia, he stated that style "to be alive ... must be in
motion.... If it becomes fixed then it's dead, it's just
rhetoric. The style must change according to what the writer
is trying to tell. What he is trying to tell in fact compels
the style."[13] To Faulkner, expression and content are in-
separable. Style, then, is not a matter of linguistic choice;
that is, Faulkner implies that the same thought cannot be
expressed in alternate linguistic constructions, but rather
that the medium is the message.[14] The fact that Faulkner values
the "motion" of style also explains why he assigns his most

perceptive characters a baroque style in *As I Lay Dying*, for
this medium can most effectively reflect the restless energy
of human imagination.

The novel is composed of fifty-nine sections, with a total
of fifteen speeches by varying characters. The distribution of
the sections is varied.[15] The majority of the monologues belong
to the Bundren family, and the second son, Darl, is assigned
the greatest number of sections. This high incidence for Darl
occurs since he is the most articulate, and disturbed, member
of the family, and since he attempts to resolve his dilemma
in terms of language. Cash occupies an intermediate position
in number of sections assigned because he represents a balance
between words and deeds. Jewel and Addie, who claim to eschew
words, are assigned only one section each. Although the community receives only slightly more than a quarter of the sections,
its presence is maintained for several reasons. First, since
men like Samson, Armstid, Moseley, and MacGowan remain fixed
in their respective locations, they help to record the stops
the Bundrens make on their journey toward Jefferson. Secondly,
the community's presence offers absolute norms of value against
which to measure the Bundrens' endeavors. In their outrage
at Addie's putrefying body, for example, the folk place the
odyssey in a comic perspective. Lastly, the communal characters
provide the reader with information the family otherwise distorts or suppresses. Tull, for example, narrates directly and
factually the attempted river crossing. The only other account
is Darl's emotive response which tends to obscure the events.

Chronologically, Tull remains in the novel until the
Bundrens have successfully crossed the river, and the incident
demonstrates the community's willingness to aid the Bundrens.
His wife, Cora, is both community member and Addie's acquain-
tance; hence, her commentary is both representative and personal. These biases appear in her death-watch monologues. In
analyzing Cora's syntax and that of other characters, and in
determining how Cora's utterances constitute the colloquial
mode, I shall use two methods. The first is Francis Christensen's mode of determining grammatic structure by considering
the levels of statement and their constituent constructions.[16]
Layers of structure are indicated by indenting each unit and
numbering the levels. Throughout this analysis, I shall use
the following abbreviations of syntactical structures: SC
(subordinate clause), RC (relative clause), NC (noun cluster),
VC (verb cluster), AC (adjective cluster), A + A (adjective
series), Abs (absolute), and PP (prepositional phrase).

While Cora sits by Addie's bed, her reflections are at
odds with the funereal context. Her paramount concern is
her disappointing failure to sell some cakes a town matron
ordered. These thoughts, in turn, trigger related reflections:

"We could have stocked cheaper chickens, but I gave my promise
as Miss Lawington said when she advised me to get a good
breed, because Mr Tull himself admits that a good breed of
cows or hogs pays in the long run" (p. 6). Using Christensen's
method, the following pattern results.

> (1) We could have stocked cheaper chickens,
> (1) but I gave my promise
>> (2) as Miss Lawington said when she advised
>> me to get a good breed, (SC)
>> (2) because Mr Tull himself admits that a
>> good breed of cows or hogs pays in the
>> long run. (SC)

Structural analysis reveals that the texture of Cora's sentences, and of colloquial sentences in general, is relatively
thin and bare; that is, few levels are added to the main one,
and the nouns and verbs of the main level are not particularly
enriched by the additions that do occur. The plainness of
Cora's style contrasts markedly with the density of Darl's
utterances, which will be analyzed later in this essay.[17]
The thin texture of Cora's sentence likewise corresponds
to a marked superficiality of ideas. The use of "as" implies
that levels (1) and (2) are related in a cause-effect structure, but it is difficult to ascertain the connection between
Miss Lawington's advice (2) and the granting of the promise
(1). One possibility is that Miss Lawington made the first
comment ("We could have stocked cheaper chickens") and that
the promise was made to "Mr" Tull. Another possibility is
that both Mr. Tull and Miss Lawington suggest that Cora
purchase a good breed. The ambiguity of Cora's intention
results from the word "as." Cora seems to use "as" as a
causative which is equated with "because," but "as" could also
function as a time-marker.

This ambiguity is compounded by Cora's jump from point
to point and her disregard for unity of subjects. The passage
remains vague even when other statements in the paragraph
are examined:

> (1) So I saved out the eggs and baked yesterday.
> (1) The cakes turned out right well.
> (1) We depend a lot on our chickens.

The beginning of the paragraph (quoted above) matches the
end--"So I baked yesterday, more careful than ever I baked
in my life, and the cakes turned out right well" (p. 7)--
but without interior development or regard for chronology.
Incoherence is added to circumlocution. The use of "so"
leads the reader to expect a result, but in actuality the
second sentence is the result of the first, and the third

sentence is a tangential comment prompted by the mention of
"eggs" in the first sentence. Yet, Cora's speeches do serve
to reflect the geographical verisimilitude of dialect. Her
passages clearly contain the features commonly associated
with colloquial style:[18] concreteness of diction ("chickens,"
"cows," "hogs"), minimal qualification of nouns ("cheaper,"
"good"); elimination of long words; emphasis on commonplace
words; absence of fresh metaphors ("long run"); repetition
of individual words ("good breed") and of sound ("cheaper
chickens," "get ... good"); and parallel structures. Cora's
passages, an effective simulation of oral and extemporaneous
speech, exemplify colloquial style unrelieved by other modes
and thus help to define the community to which she belongs.

Another method of measuring the complexity of syntax is
to examine what the transformational grammarians[19] call "the
deep structure" of a statement; that is, to determine what
verbal transformations have occurred before the sentence
reaches its final form. I shall show how "embedded sentences"
precede the finished statement by reconstructing the constituents which compose the sentence. In Cora's comments, the
following transformations occur:

> We could have stocked cheaper chickens
> > (the chickens are cheaper)

> ... advised me to get a good breed
> > (the breed is good)

> ... a good breed of cows or hogs pays
> > (a breed of cows is good
> > a breed of hogs is good)

> in the long run
> > (the run is long)

The transformations are few and of the same adjectival ("a
good breed") or conjoining ("cows or hogs") patterns. These
facts account for Cora's lack of linguistic agility. Her use
of the same adjective for chickens, cows, and hogs contributes
to confusion of ideas but is characteristic of the colloquial
conversational tone, which depends partially on repetition for
its effect. Cora's use of the dead metaphor, which requires
a transformation to reveal a once-effective tenor-vehicle
relationship, further indicates her conventionality.

At the other end of the linguistic continuum from Cora
is Darl, whose elaborate and perceptive comments employ a
complex syntax. Observing Dewey Dell, whose secret only he
knows, he remarks, "She sets the basket into the wagon and
climbs in, her leg coming long from beneath her tightening

dress: that lever which moves the world, one of that caliper
which measures the length and breadth of life" (pp. 97-98).
The syntactic structure of Darl's remark has the following
pattern:

> (1) She sets the basket into the wagon and climbs in,
>   (2) her leg coming long from beneath her tighten-
>   ing dress: (Abs, PP)
>   (3) that lever which moves the
>   world; (NC)
>   (3) one of that caliper which
>   measures the length and
>   breadth of life. (NC, PP)

Having accepted the conventions of colloquial dialect which
Faulkner has established in other sections of the novel, the
reader is jarred by Darl's metaphysical speculations. Such
syntax and diction are clearly not a realistic duplication
of untutored rustic speech. Instead, Darl's passage reveals
those features which Morris Croll and T.S. Eliot have defined
elsewhere as baroque.[20] First, Darl's thoughts concerning
Dewey Dell's womanhood are transferred into images ("tightening," "caliper"), so that he is apprehending thoughts sen-
suously, transmuting concepts into sensations.[21] Also
baroque are Darl's startling juxtapositions of opposites
("the length and breadth of life," life and death) and his
facile manipulation of space, whereby he can project himself
into the logically impossible position of observing the world
from the outside ("that lever which moves the world"). Darl's
dense sentence structure is also a baroque feature. It is
composed of numerous additions, these containing within
themselves further substructures. The deliberate asymmetry
of the sentence members reveals not the logical but the
emotional development of the nodal statement. The arrangement,
in fact, conforms to the pattern described by Croll as the
"loose period," a hallmark of baroque prose: the sentence
begins with a statement which is complete in itself, followed
by an absolute participle ("her leg coming long"); the
symmetry of the sentence is further broken, because each addition is dictated by what immediately precedes it, and no
effort is made to recapitulate or restate the opening statement. The purpose of this sentence, and of the loose period
in general, is to express, "as far as may be, the order in
which an idea presents itself when it is first experienced."[22]
A final feature of the baroque sentence is an ending which
frequently presents "a vision of vast space or time, losing
itself in an altitudo, a hint of infinity"[23]; likewise,
Darl's passage progresses from observation of a physical
movement ("climbs," "leg") to a metaphysical speculation

on the progress of life through successive generations.
The open-endedness, the straining toward obscurity, and the
constantly mobile quality of Darl's utterances ally him with
the writhing, contorted figures of seventeenth-century baroque
sculpture.

Besides containing interior complexity, Darl's sentences
achieve considerable variety in their inter-relations. The
example cited is followed by "She sits on the seat beside
Vardaman and sets the parcel on her lap"; the relative rapidity
of action signals the end of Darl's suspended perception.
At least two of the transformations he uses in the first
example are interesting for their departure from "normal"
usage. "Her leg coming long" has been derived from "Her leg +
comes" + a participial transformation, added to "her leg is
long." In constructing his observation, Darl retains something
of the original constituents, because he disregards the
categorical restriction that adjectives do not expand (modify)
verbs or participles. Darl expresses the conjunction of both
motion and description, an effect absent in the possible
alternative, "her long leg coming." These effects are likewise
achieved in the more conventionally grammatical construction
"her tightening dress." In his hypersensitive anxiety, Darl
chooses this phrase over one alternative, "her tight dress,"
because he perceives the world as process, and the course of
Dewey Dell's pregnancy as a continual process.

At points, Darl's contemplation becomes obsessive, and
his syntax reveals a linguistics of madness. Darl records
Dewey Dell's response to his knowledge of her pregnancy thus:
"Her face is calm and sullen, her eyes brooding and alert;
within them I can see Peabody's back like two round peas in
two thimbles: perhaps in Peabody's back two of those worms
which work surreptitious and steady through you and out the
other side and you waking suddenly from sleep or from waking,
with on your face an expression sudden, intent, and concerned" (p. 97).

```
        (1) Her face is calm and sullen,
        (1) her eyes brooding and alert;
                (2a) within them (PP)
            (2) I can see Peabody's back
                (2b) like two round peas in two thimbles; (PP)
                        (3a) perhaps in Peabody's back (PP)
                    (3) two of those worms
                        (3b) which work surreptitious and
                             steady through you and out the
                             other side (SC,PP)
        (1) and you waking suddenly from sleep or from waking
            (Abs, PP)
```

(2) with   an expression (PP)
    (2a) on your face (PP)
          (3) sudden, intent, and concerned.
          (A + A)

The density of structure is further accompanied by the
multiple transformations which have occurred:

her eyes brooding and alert
(her eyes are brooding
          brood + participial transformation,
(her eyes are alert)

you waking suddenly
(you who wake suddenly
     the waking is sudden
     wake + participial transformation)

those worms which work surreptitious and steady
through you
(the work is surreptitious + the work is steady)

on your face an expression, sudden, intent, and
concerned
     (there is an expression on your face
          the expression is sudden,
          the expression is intent,
          the expression is concerned
                              concern + participial
                                   transformation
               express + nominalization trans-
                    formation)

The high incidence of participial transformations and the one
nominalization transformation, all of which are dependent
upon verbs for their node, suggests the hyperactivity of
Darl's mind as he constantly seeks to define, refine, and
advance the thrust of his impressions. His sensibility,
disdaining complacency and ease, displays the contortion
and purposive extravagances (thimble-eyes-worms) characterized
by Morris Croll as baroque traits. The movement from "her"
to "you," indicative of his self-involuted anxiety, signals
his "waking suddenly" from brooding. This tendency to shift
persons, to speak of himself as observer ("you"), becomes
fixed at the conclusion of the novel. In his final speech,
Darl's madness is apparent from third-person references
to himself: "Darl has gone to Jackson. They put him on the
train" (p. 243). Already in the above passage there is syntactic foreshadowing of his breakdown. The third level clause

("two of those worms") receives no predicate; the absolute
("you waking suddenly from sleep or from waking") is obscure
because of the collocation of the two "wakings." Such syntactic
incompleteness and semantic disruption point to Darl's imbalance.

Darl's shift from one level to another and the density
of his structure are hallmarks frequently associated with
Faulkner himself. The similarity between Darl's and Faulkner's
syntax can be ascertained by comparing Darl's section to
section four of *The Sound and the Fury*, in which Faulkner
drops the interior monologues of the three previous characters
to resume his own "voice."

    (1) The day dawned bleak and chill,
       (2) a moving wall of grey light out of the
          northeast (NC)
          (3) which,
             (4) instead of dissolving into moisture,
                (PP)
          (3) seemed to disintegrate into minute and
             venomous particles, (RC)
             (4) like dust that, (PP,RC)
                (5) when Dilsey opened the door
                   of the cabin and emerged, (SC)
             (4) needled laterally into her flesh,
                (5) precipitating not so much a
                   moisture as a substance (VC)
                   (6) partaking of the quality
                      of thin, not quite congealed
                      oil.

Faulkner's "voice" shares some of the features of Darl's
speeches, notably the suspension of forward movement and
return to previous levels (the movement of 3 and 4) and the
packing of several structures within one layer. Cleanth
Brooks, in discussing the changes of the characters' rhetoric
in *As I Lay Dying*, states that "This is one of the conventions
which must be accepted in a reading" of the novel,[25] but does
not offer a rationale for the practice of this convention.
Faulkner intrudes in almost all the characters' sections,
with the possible exception of Cora's speeches. Evidently
his purpose is not to achieve complete verisimilitude, but
rather to aid his characters to communicate insights they
might feel but be incapable of articulating. Hence, the
relativity achieved by syntactic perspectivism, variety
in style, and shifting points of view is modified. Sometimes
Faulkner is the omniscient narrator who appears in the guise
of his characters. In this capacity he is the omnipresent

artist-player who, like his counterpart in *Flags in the Dust*, simply provides names for the pawns in his game.   As Richard Chase comments about *As I Lay Dying*, "a multiple point of view, if it is multiple enough, of necessity becomes simply the point of view of the omniscient author."   Thus, while the novel evidences linguistic perspectivism by the use of differing styles and multiple points of view, at certain points Faulkner's presence is discernible in syntax and diction.

Darl, whose abnormality is consistently noted by others, is a character whose style, and thus identity, sometimes approximates Faulkner's. By this similarity, Faulkner suggests the familiar theme of madness allied to genius, a topic he commented on at the University of Virginia: "who can say just how much of super-perceptivity ... a mad person might not have? ... it's nice to think that there is some compensation for madness. That maybe the madman does see more than the sane man. That the world is more moving to him."[28] Paradoxically, however, if one assumes that Faulkner remains relativistic in technique in *As I Lay Dying*, he is implying through Darl's madness the inadequacy of verbal forms to order and reflect reality, a view which allies Faulkner also with Addie and, by inference, Jewel.

As Cash comments, Darl's insanity is a relative matter, in actuality based on the presumptions of others. He recognizes that although perception and judgment are subjective, yet when a sufficient number of interpretations coincide, the phenomenon is considered certitude:

> Sometimes I think it *aint* none of us *pure* crazy and
> *aint* none of us *pure* sane until the balance of us
> talks him *that-a-way*. It's like it *aint* so much what
> a fellow does, but it's the way the majority of
> *folks* is looking at him when he does it. (p. 223;
> emphasis added)

The community's indictment of Darl is as much the product of verbal constructs as are Anse's concept of love or Cora's convictions on sin. As if to underscore the basic subjectivity of judgment, Faulkner assigns to Cash comments on the motif of insanity which are expressed in colloquial dialect (italicized) and diction connoting uncertainty ("sometimes," "it's like"). Furthermore, Cash uses his carpenter's terminology and his standards of craftsmanship to judge Darl's burning of the barn. Accordingly, Cash condemns Darl's act because "there just *aint* nothing justifies the deliberate destruction of what a man has built with his own sweat and stored the fruit of his sweat into" (p. 228). Even when Cash ignores the morality of his brother's crime, he uses the craftsman's standards to designate Darl's poor execution of the arson: "A *fellow* cant *get away from* a shoddy job" (p. 227).

Cash's statements carry the significant form of surface symmetry expected of the artisan. In explaining the reasons for bevelling the coffin, he first imposes order on disparateness by numbering the reasons:

I made it on the bevel.

1. There is more surface for the nails to grip.
2. There is twice the gripping-surface to each seam.
3. The water will have to seep into it on a slant. Water moves easiest up and down or straight across.
4. In a house people are upright two thirds of the time. So the seams and joints are made up-and-down. Because the stress is up-and-down.
5. In a bed where people lie down all the time, the joints and seams are made sideways, because the stress is sideways.
6. Except.
7. A body is not square like a crosstie.
8. Animal magnetism.
9. The animal magnetism of a dead body makes the stress come slanting, so the seams and joints of a coffin are made on the bevel.
10. You can see by an old grave that the earth sinks down on the bevel.
11. While in a natural hole it sinks by the center, the stress being up-and-down.
12. So I made it on the bevel.
13. It makes a neater job.   (pp. 77-78)

Cash balances the statements against each other, both in structure and appearance, through the reiterative diction. "There is more surface for the nails to grip" is paired with "There is twice the gripping-surface to each seam." "To grip" in the first sentence has an equivalent in the participial transformation "gripping." The structurally similar statements 4 and 5, which are concerned with life, receive their antithesis in statements 9, 10, and 11, which are concerned with the position of coffins. His recapitulation of the topic in statement 12 matches his original statement ("I made it on the bevel"), thus rounding out and completing his analysis. This feature of his syntax allies Cash with the colloquial mode; likewise, his diction displays colloquial features-- use of dialect, of simple words, of nouns which receive only

minimal qualifications, and elimination of long words and
emotive words. In addition, Cash's diction and syntax evidence marks of the baroque style--obscurity ("Animal magnetism," "Except"), pictorialism (through numbering), and
deliberate asymmetry, both in varying length and grammatical
form of the members which constitute this statement.

Cash's championing of the principle of balance against
surrounding chaos appears most dramatically in his use of
mirror-image statements. The loading of the coffin into the
wagon Cash reconstructs thus:

> "It wont balance. If you want it to tote and
> ride on a balance, we will have--"   (1)
> "Pick up. Goddamn you, pick up."   (2)
> "I'm telling you it wont tote and it wont ride
> on a balance unless--"   (3)
> "Pick up! Pick up, goddamn your thick-nosed
> soul to hell, pick up!"   (4)
> It wont balance. If they want it to tote and
> ride on a balance, they will have   (5)
>   (p. 90)

Here again, Cash blends the colloquial and baroque styles.
The verbal and syntactic identity between statements 1 and
5 and 2 and 4 match the parallelism and repetition associated
with the colloquial mode, the use of pictorialism to rein-
force the meaning of a concept, in this case, "balance,"
is, as Austin Warren states in his discussion of the emblem,
a characteristic of the baroque mode.   Despite the structural
correspondence, tension and disorder impinge on and break down
the surface symmetry of Cash's utterance. The erratic para- ·
graph indentation, the incompleteness of statements, the
alteration of the spoken statement (1) to the inarticulated
one (5), and the shift from "we" to "they" indicate that
Cash's principle of balance has not been unanimously accepted,
that it remains functional only for him.

As the novel progresses, it is Cash who imposes order on
the family journey, and in the end he acts as its spokesman.
As an artist, he likewise matures, acquiring the powers of
articulation and clairvoyance and developing, as Olga Vickery
points out, "a more comprehensive understanding of himself
and his world."[30] Unlike Darl, who is totally alienated from
his community, and who expresses his isolation in a baroque
style, Cash realizes that he must exist both as an individual
and as a member of a larger community. Hence, as has been
shown, his style is a balance between baroque and colloquial.
Cash's position midway between stylistic extremes seems to be
one that Faulkner himself advocated. In his lectures at the
University of Virginia, he describes himself as a carpenter

who recommends careful craftsmanship and conscious choice,
just as Cash does in his enumerated reasons for bevelling.
Faulkner explains his general aesthetic in terms of carpentry:
"he [the writer] uses his material from the three sources
[imagination, observation, and experience] as the carpenter
reaches into his lumber room and finds a board that fits
the particular corner he's building"; and Faulkner parallels
his authorship of *As I Lay Dying* with the carpenter's job:
"Now there was the need to use symbolism which I dug around,
scratched around in my lumber room, and dragged out."[31]

As the novel proceeds, Faulkner increasingly identifies
Cash as the sane artist. Conversely, he increasingly pairs
Darl with Vardaman, perhaps to indicate Darl's regression to
a more immature state of mind. In fact, Darl begins his final
speech ("Darl has gone to Jackson") by echoing Vardaman's
immediately preceding comments about the train ride to and
confinement in Jackson ("*He had to get on the train to go to
Jackson*"). Unlike Darl, however, Vardaman avoids insanity.
In his lectures, Faulkner confirms Vardaman's sanity, although
Vardaman is temporarily unable to distinguish between illusion
and reality.[32] Yet Vardaman works out a satisfactory solution
to his shock. When first confronted with the fact of his mother's
death, he attributes it to Peabody's intervention:

   (1) I can hear the bed and her face and them
   (1) and I can feel the floor shake
      (2) when he walks on it (SC)
         (3) that came and did it. (RC)
         (3) That came and did it (RC)
            (4) when she was all right (SC)
         (3) but he came and did it. (RC)

                                (p. 52)

The child's reaction to the recent event is necessarily confused. His initial apprehension comes through sensory associations. Then, as Vardaman exercises selection over his sensations, the shaking of the floor particularizes Peabody as the
focal and instrumental individual. Through effective verbal
ambiguity, Faulkner has Vardaman link "it" (floor) to "it"
(death). The core of anxiety appears in the thrice-repeated
clause, which spills from one sentence to another without
control. The embedding of the clause "when she was all right"
explains the process of Vardaman's horrifying conclusion of
Peabody's agency. Like Darl, Vardaman freezes reality. The
passage begins in the present tense, for Vardaman is experiencing what is actually a past event as if it were occurring in
the present. When he realizes that Addie has somehow changed
status, that she is no longer "all right," he shifts to past
tense. What at first seems like complex thought because of

the presence of several layers of specificity is offset by
the monotony of the monosyllables and the lack of variety in
the phrasing itself. In attempting to account for the unfathom-
able phenomenon of his mother's death, Vardaman acquires certainty through reiteration.

Vardaman's speech likewise demonstrates how a state of
agitation impedes transformation and, hence, expressivity.
The constituent "that came and did it" is derived from either
"he came" and "he did it" or "it came" and "it did it."
Vardaman's use of the ambiguous relative "that," which can
function colloquially as referent for either "he" or "it,"
reveals his initial uncertainty. After the observation of his
mother's health, however, Vardaman's perplexity disappears
with the onset of "he came and did it." The cause having been
determined, Vardaman seeks to account for the effect, the
disappearance of his mother. The style here is somewhat calmer:

> (1) *My mother is not in the box.*
> (1) *My mother does not smell like that.*
> (1) *My mother is a fish*

(p. 187)

The uniformity of structure-subject ("*mother*" thrice-repeated),
verb, predicate/complement—is a verbal reassurance of his
mother's continuing existence. Vardaman's rejection of the
adult explanation of the phenomenon, indicated by the negative
and emphatic morpheme "*not*," is followed by the emotionally
satisfying assertion "*My mother is a fish*". The declaration
itself is almost syllogistic and causes certitude. Now
Vardaman speaks not metaphorically or symbolically of the
fish as surrogate for his mother but of what is for him a
psychological reality.[33] The texture of these sentences is
bare, because Vardaman has already resolved his dilemma. The
process of his reasoning is delineated in the comparatively
convoluted sentence which precedes:

> (1) *She got out*
>   (2a) *through the holes I bored,* (PP, RC)
>   (2b) *into the water* (PP)
> (1) *I said,*
> (1) *and*
>   (2) *when we come to the water again* (SC, PP)
> (1) *I am going to see her.*

Thus Vardaman, by boring holes in the coffin, sees himself
as his mother's quasi-savior. In his mind, Addie's liberation
results in a change of form to fish, a feasible explanation
which helps Vardaman retain his sanity.

As if to underline Addie's persisting life, Faulkner
introduces her only once, after the trial by water which

she has survived. Addie's speech, immediately following Cora's,
is significantly placed, for it shows Cora's erroneous judgment in two matters. First, throughout the book, Cora mis-
interprets Darl's intensity as love for Addie. Yet the reader
learns that Darl abandons the coffin and that Jewel and Cash
remain with it during the river-crossing. Hence, Cora's
comment on Darl--"him the only one of them that had sense
enough to get off that wagon" (p. 145)--is an ironic praise
of expediency, not love. Secondly, the placement allows Addie
to answer the indictment of pride, vanity, and blindness which
Cora has levelled at her. Addie, the proponent of deeds,
"responds" by discussing her relationship with Anse. Her
comments, however, are equally applicable to Cora, because
both Anse and Cora depend upon mere verbal forms, like "love"
and "salvation" to conceal their hollowness. Addie evaluates
Anse's use of language thus:

> (1) He had a word, too.
>   (2) Love, he called it. (NC)
> (1) But I had been used to words for a long time. (RC)
>   (2) I knew that that word was like the others: (RC)
>   (3) just a shape to fill a lack; (NC)
>   (2) [I knew] that (RC)
>   (3) when the right time came, (SC)
>   (2) you wouldn't need a word for that anymore
>   than for pride or fear. (RC, cont'd., PP)
>   (p. 164)

Addie then abruptly dismisses Anse's views, as if they
merited no further comment.

As if to underscore the psychic distance between Addie
and Anse, Faulkner casts their utterances into different
dialects, as is demonstrated by the following examples:

Anse	Addie
it want no luck	It *was not* over
hisself	himself
I *reckon*	I would *think*
strove	tried
It not *done* raining	it *was over*
I *knowed* you are not sick	I *knew* that living
	was terrible
I *got* a little property	I *have* people
I *aint* got *none*	You *haven't* got *any?*

These differences in pronunciation, vocabulary, and grammar
are due to Addie's superior education, her town (rather than
country) background, and her greater intelligence. Her section
is marked by clarity in thinking, variety in structure, and

adeptness in syntax. Even the syntactical transformations she
uses conform to her philosophical distrust of words and thus
delete excess verbiage. "I knew that that word was like the
others: just a shape to fill a lack" is derived from "that
word was just a shape" + "a shape fills a lack." A further
distinction between Addie and Anse is Addie's ability to
employ more than one mode of expressivity. Colloquial features
in her section appear in the use of parallel structure and
the marked repetition of certain words and their variants,
as in the passage which discusses her relationship with
Whitfield (pp. 166-167)--"I believed" (twice), "I would
think" (five times), "terrible" (three times), "sin" (eight
times). At the same time, baroque characteristics occur in
Addie's pictorialism to express her state of "unvirginity"
and her appropriating the doctrine of the divine Incarnation[34]
to her own situation; for her the defective word "love"
becomes flesh and is consequently redeemed in the persons of
her favored children, Cash and Jewel. Lastly, Addie's frequently complex sentence structure evinces the baroque
characteristics of syntactical asymmetry, of a thought progression by which the first member is a logically self-con-
tained statement and subsequent members extend the statement
imaginatively, and of obscure conclusion:

> (1) I would lie by him in the dark,
>> (2) hearing the dark land talking of God's love
>>   and His beauty and His sin; (VC, VC)
>> (2) hearing the dark voicelessness in which
>>   the words are the deeds, (VC, RC)
>>> (3) and the other words that are not deeds, (RC)
>>>> (4) that are just the gaps in peoples'
>>>>   lacks, (RC)
>>>>> (5) coming down like the cries of
>>>>>   the geese out of the wild dark-
>>>>>   ness in the old terrible
>>>>>   nights, (VC, PP)
>>>>> (5) fumbling at the deeds like
>>>>>   orphans to whom are pointed out
>>>>>   in a crowd two faces and told,
>>>>>   (VC, RC)
>>>>>> (6) That is your father, your
>>>>>>   mother. (RC)
>>>>>>>   (p. 166)

Despite the fact that Addie ostensibly rejects words as
a sign of duplicity and emptiness, her section reveals that
she, too, exploits language. Not only is her section comparatively lengthy, but she, who shuns words, uses "word"/"words"
twenty-two times in her passage. She argues that her exclusive

love for Cash and Jewel is justified since they are the word
become flesh through deeds. In reality, her division among
her children is coldly calculating: "I gave Anse Dewey Dell
to negative Jewel. Then I gave him Vardaman to replace the
child I had robbed him of. And now he has three children that
are his and not mine" (p. 168). This passage suggests that
Addie herself is responsible for the schizophrenia within
the family. Darl is the child most disastrously affected by
this family environment. When he is born, Addie repudiates
him and then rejects Anse by asking to be buried among her
own people in Jefferson. Like Quentin Compson in *The Sound
and the Fury*, Darl, who is victimized by lack of mother love,
states, "I cannot love my mother because I have no mother"
(p. 89); furthermore, he is the only character in the novel
who clearly perceives Addie's deceitfulness, the gap that
separates her words and her deeds.

In her relationship with her husband, Addie's assessment of Anse seems fair, especially since it is supported
by the community's comments on his lassitude and his abuse
of his children. Anse's own sections are filled with self-
seeking concerns, platitudes, and rationalizations. Yet,
there is some evidence that Addie has unmanned Anse. She
is a rustic Delilah who orders her Samson to get sheared:
"If you've got any womenfolks, why in the world dont they
make you get your hair cut?" (p. 162).[35] Addie declares
that when she married Anse he died, and she may be another
example of Faulkner's domineering and enervating females.
In *Flags in the Dust*, similar phrasing occurs to describe
Bayard Sartoris' submission to women: "He had been so neatly
tricked by earth, that ancient Delilah, that he was not
aware that his locks were shorn, was not aware that Miss
Jenny and old Bayard were wondering how long it would be
before they grew out again. He needs a wife was Miss Jenny's
thought. Then maybe he'll stay sheared" (pp. 195-196). Addie's
linguistic adeptness furthers her insidious influence over
her family, making her a formidable character indeed.

Addie's passage is followed by that of Whitfield.
Addie's evaluation of him as a person for whom salvation
is a matter of words is verified by Whitfield's peroration.
His style, basically oratorical, is a substyle of the
colloquial and is marked by those characteristics which
Bridgman states are common to oratory and colloquialism--
exclamations, repetitions, accumulations of synonyms, and
rhetorical emphases.

> (1) "Just let me not perish
>> (2) before I have begged the forgiveness of the
>> man (SC)

                    (3) whom I betrayed," (RC)
    (1) I prayed;
    (1) "let me not be too late;
    (1) let not the tale of mine and her transgression
        come
        (2a) from her lips (PP
        (2b) instead of mine. (PP)
                (3) She had sworn then that she would
                    never tell it, (RC)
                (3) but eternity is a fearsome thing
                    to face:
                    (4) have I not wrestled
                        (5) thigh to thigh with Satan
                            myself? (Abs, PP)
    (1) let me not have also the sin of her broken vow
        upon my soul.
    (1) Let not the waters of Thy Mighty Wrath encompass me
        (2) until I have cleansed my soul (SC)
            (3) in the presence of them (PP)
                (4) whom I injured." (RC)

                                        (p. 170)

The highly wrought structural formality of the opening clauses
is disrupted by the asymmetry created by the interior clauses,
making visible the presence of two counter-movements. Whitfield
easily falls into the repetitive pattern of Bible-belt exhorta-
tion, whose lulling effect obscures the real cause of his concern, i.e., the fear that Addie may break her vow, compounding
the crime of their infidelity by the revelation of his duplicity.
Like Dimmesdale in Hawthorne's *The Scarlet Letter*, Whitfield
reasons that only when publicly articulated does the crime have
final verification. The passage is both oratorical and baroque,
and incorporates the differences which Croll points out between
the two styles.[37] The oratorical strain appears in the carefully
revised, circular arrangement, whereby subsequent members
refer back to and emphasize the central member, "Just let me
not perish," by means of repetition and parallel structure.
The interior members, however, display baroque characteristics
since they differ structurally from previous members and
since they give the illusion of advancing without premeditation,
each addition being the response to the previous member and
not to the central thought. The break in the formal tempo and
syntax into the baroque imbalance reveals the source of Whitfield's anxiety. The statements concerning Addie are structurally subordinate, corresponding to the concealment of their
relationship. Also subordinate are "whom I injured" and "whom
I betrayed." This placement, along with the insistent use of
the hortative "let me" and the morpheme "not," discloses that
Whitfield's approach is dictated by fear of punishment rather

than by a genuine desire to repair his transgressions. While
Whitfield tries to conceal himself in language, his syntax
and diction give him away. His use of a phrase like "thigh
to thigh with Satan" is a ludicrous confusing of sexual and
spiritual diction, just as his religion has disguised his
sexual relationship with Addie. Whitfield's speech is a parody
of confessional phrasing. Likewise, his journey through water
is a parody of the similar ordeal the Bundrens have endured.

Whitfield's volubility and lubricity are calculated to
deflect the thrust of his statement from his own guilt to admiration of his rhetorical virtuosity. The ending of his
peroration, revealed through transformations, attests to his
linguistic skills and accounts for his ability to move an
audience:

> Let not the waters of Thy Mighty Wrath [Thy Wrath
> is compared to water; Thy wrath and water are
> mighty; the wrath is Thine] encompass me until
> I have cleansed my soul [the soul is mine, in con-
> trast to the wrath which is Thine] in the presence
> of them whom I injured [I injured them, they will
> be present].

The high incidence of pronouns reveals Whitfield's sense of
self-importance and his presumption of an intimate relationship with God. However, the syntax also contributes to Whitfield's intense awareness of the distance between himself
and God--the understood "you" and "Thy" are contrasted with
"me," "I," "my," thus increasing the sense of God's justice
and the devolution of guilt upon himself.

Although his passage is highly moving, even the community
recognizes Whitfield's speciousness. Vernon Tull, in commenting on Whitfield's sermonizing, says, "His voice is bigger
than him. It's like they are not the same. It's like he is
one, and his voice is one" (p. 86). Whitfield's theatrical
effects are to be contrasted with the oratory of Reverend
Shegog, the Negro preacher in *The Sound and the Fury*: "the
voice consumed him, until he was nothing and they were nothing
and there was not even a voice but instead their hearts were
speaking to one another in chanting measures beyond the need
for words" (p. 367). Whereas Whitfield exalts his own personality, Shegog abnegates his identity. Whereas Whitfield's
exploitation of language results in the dissociation of
sensibility within himself, Shegog's use of language produces
an authentic fusion of hearts with his audience.

The syntactic aspect of linguistic forms has two functions
in *As I Lay Dying*. On the one hand, the structure of an individual's utterances reflects the manner in which he confronts
and arranges the formlessness of reality in a pattern most

useful and significant to him. Thus, the characters who are able to construct significant forms through imagery, such as Darl and Cash, approach the position of the artist. On the other hand, structure is also partially determined by the form that a preconstructed language imposes upon the character, thus forcing him to build his interpretation of reality within the limitation of the language itself. Hence, the structure of a human being's language influences in part the manner in which he views reality. Characters like Cora and Whitfield allow language to control them; Cash and Addie are able to manipulate the language suitable to their views. Darl is both controller and victim of language, and the tensions contained in his syntax are probably the closest approximation in the novel of the artist's problem of expression through, and control by, language. In general, baroque syntax indicates the character's complexity, originality, emotiveness, and alienation. Colloquial style, dependent on predetermined forms, usually marks its practitioners as simple, conventional, complacent, and integrated into the community.

A character's choice of diction, as of syntax, is likewise dependent upon the resources of language, revealing his degree of linguistic control and his perspective of reality. Conversely, diction reveals the extent to which language imposes reality on the character. Cora displays the latter tendency to an extreme. Her rigidity of thought is determined by and reflected in needless repetition and verbal sloppiness. The passage quoted at the beginning of this essay comes from a paragraph in which "so" appears eleven times, with a total of three distinct meanings: "So [therefore] after they were going to cost *so* [degree] much more than Mr Tull thought, and after I promised that the difference in the number of eggs would make it up, I had to be more careful than ever because it was on my final say-*so* [approval] we took them" (p. 6; emphasis added). These prosaic thoughts, juxtaposed with Addie's grim languishing, violate the reader's sense of what lexical fields are appropriate to the decorum of a death-watch. Cora's choice of diction renders her pose of good Christian neighbor a travesty.

Because her religious motives are suspect, the exposition of her religious convictions takes on a duplistic character:

> Because it is not us that can judge our sins
> or know what is sin in the Lord's eyes. She has
> had a hard life, but so does every woman. But you'd
> think from the way she talked that she knew more
> about sin and salvation than the Lord God Himself,
> than them who have strove and labored with the sin

>in this human world. When the only sin she ever
>committed was being partial to Jewel that never
>loved her and was its own punishment, in preference
>to Darl that was touched by God Himself and con-
>sidered queer by us mortals that did love her. I
>said, "There is your sin. And your punishment too.
>Jewel is your punishment. But where is your salva-
>tion? And life is short enough," I said, "to win
>eternal grace in. And God is a jealous God. It is
>His to judge and to mete; not yours."   (pp. 159-160)

Cora's diction, highly derivative and unoriginal, is, in
fact, a cliché-ridden evangelical interpretation of Addie's
condition. Looking at the contentive words, and disregarding
the function words, we find that "sin" appears five times;
"punishment" three times; "judge," "mete" and "know" five times;
and "salvation" and "eternal grace" three times. Clearly,
Cora considers sin the dominant aspect of reality. For her,
life, consisting of "laboring" and "striving" against sin,
is inexorably followed by eternal condemnation or reward.
Cora makes a strong distinction between temporality and
eternity, allowing no blending of the two time-schemes. Like
Mr. Coldfield in *Absalom, Absalom!*, Cora values benevolent
actions not because they serve humanity in present time but
rather because they contribute to a spiritual account redeemable
in the after-life. Hence, the temporal constrictions and the
materialism of Cora's religion are reiterated in her oftheard
refrain, "I'm bounding toward my God and my reward."
    In the quoted passage, the nature of the addresser-
addressee relationship is ironic: Cora is advising Addie that
the fallibility of human beings impedes a true knowledge of
the nature of sin. Yet, by the end of the section, she appro-
priates to herself the divine function of judging Addie's sin.
The incidence of "I said," giving the sense of Cora's reporting her own speech, points to Cora's self-righteous approba-
tion. Addie, whose ethical code is independent of traditional
religion, also can exploit orthodox rhetoric to her own uses.
Thus she adjusts Cora's faulty perception by giving Cora's
statements to a highly personal application: Addie, too, will
experience a "cross" and "salvation," but her savior through
water and fire is Jewel.
    The affinities between Cora's and Whitfield's notions of
reality are reinforced by the similarity in their lexical
fields. In his section, Whitfield, a manipulator of language,
displays superior adeptness and chicanery, in his use of
variants of "sin"--"lie," "outrage," "deception," "betray,"
"erring," "transgression"--and of "salvation"--"true light,"
"guidance," "peace," "love," "forgiveness," "mercy," "grace."
In fact, the collocates of "sin" define more sharply its

nature. However, Brother Whitfield's elaboration, shifting
from the harsh "sin" and "lie" to the final variant "erring,"
euphemistically mitigates and almost dissipates his self-
condemnation. He interprets Addie's timely death as a sign
of God's mercy and favor toward the sinner.

Although Darl seeks, like Cora, to establish a clear
distinction between life and death, his diction is infinitely
more complex. For him, states of consciousness are posited
only on physical existence:

> In a strange room you must empty yourself for
> sleep. And before you are emptied for sleep, what
> are you. And when you are emptied for sleep, you are
> not. And when you are filled with sleep, you never
> were.... Yet the wagon *is*, because when the wagon
> is *was*, Addie Bundren will not be. And Jewel *is*, so
> Addie Bundren must be. And then I must be, or I could
> not empty myself for sleep in a strange room. And
> so if I am not emptied yet, I am *is*.   (p. 76)

Darl's distinctions between life and death center linguistically
around the synonymous "is," "are," and "fill" and their
philosophical contrast in "was" and "empty." Perhaps because
of the need to assure himself of his own existence, he has
developed a hypersensitive interpretation of the persons and
events surrounding him. He claims that "I cannot love my
mother because I have no mother," a rational explanation supposed-
ly based on Addie's disembodiment. Yet, Darl is unsuccessful
in imposing stasis on form. He discovers that verbal constructs
are ineffective in controlling reality. Though Darl would like
to consider Addie dead ("Addie Bundren will not be"), Addie
persists through Jewel ("Jewel *is*, so Addie Bundren must
be"). Still later, through a highly complex association,
Darl infers that "Jewel's mother is a horse" (p. 89). The
movement in the above passage from concrete to abstract diction conveys Darl's inability to fix death or life as physical
facts. Though logically reasoned, the utterance, an echo
chamber in which Darl loses himself in metaphysical speculation, proves the inadequacy of his linguistic logic.

Since Darl is father to the thought of Addie's death,
Faulkner allows him, though distant, to construct the deathbed scene. Given Darl's clairvoyance (for example, it is he
who discerns Addie's deceit in according Jewel privileges),
the reader grants the account plausibility. Furthermore, the
descriptions of the absent Darl and the present Peabody coincide, increasing the reader's sense of credibility. Shortly
before Addie's death, Peabody describes her eyes as "lamps
blaring up just before the oil is gone" (p. 44) and her
voice, calling Cash, as "harsh and strong" (p. 45). In Darl's

account, Addie calls Cash, her voice "harsh, strong, and
unimpaired," and at the moment of death,

> ... her eyes, the life in them, rushing suddenly
> upon them; the two flames glare up for a steady
> instant. Then they go out as though someone had
> leaned down and blown upon them.   (p. 47)

The similarity in the descriptions points to a similarity
between their spokesmen. Both recognize, despite Darl's efforts
to the contrary, that death is not "a phenomenon of the body"
but "merely a function of the mind--and that of the minds
of the ones who suffer the bereavement" (p. 42). This overlapping between Darl's and Peabody's comments may indicate
the presence of the omniscient author. If Faulkner's repetition in these passages is intentional, the similarity between
Peabody and Darl suggests Faulkner's metaphysical ability
to impose unity on disparateness, to discover identities
between a sane and an insane man, thus bringing the accuracy
of these verbal categories into question. The sameness also
reinforces the essential loneliness of the characters, for
they finally fail to communicate their shared philosophy
to each other.

Darl's speech reflects his effort to retain sanity by
pigeon-holing aspects of time ("was"-"is") and thus being
(life-death) into separate verbal categories. His effort
resembles Anse's dichotomy between stasis and movement.
According to Anse's notions of decorum, man is allied with
trees and houses, static objects, but not with the road, which
symbolizes a fluid existence. He claims that "the road" has
disrupted his order. Presumably "the road" has deflected
Cash's occupational interest from farming to carpentry. In
commenting on Darl, Anse blames Darl's mobility on the almost
anthropomorphic power of the road:

> I says to them, he was all right at first, with his
> eyes full of the land, because the land laid up-and-
> down ways then; it wasn't till that ere road come
> and switched the land around longways and his eyes
> still full of the land, that they begun to threaten
> me out of him....   (pp. 35-36)

Characteristically Anse blames his own misfortunes not on his
indolence, nor his son's confusion on the effect of a
schizophrenic family environment, but sees his trials as the
particular consequences of living by the road. Unlike Darl,
however, Anse can freeze reality. In this respect, his reso-
lute preference for stasis and temporality is personally
adequate.

Addie, of course, sees no such dichotomy between stasis and flux, between death and life. For her life and death are so continually blending that "the reason for living [is] to get ready to stay dead a long time" (p. 161). Addie regards the living and the dead in the same terms. When Anse fumblingly proposes to her, he hints that her relatives might object to their marrying. Addie answers,

> "But they'll be hard to talk to.... They're in the cemetery."
> "But your living kin," he said. "They'll be different."
> "Will they? ... I dont know. I never had any other kind." (p. 163)

Addie discovers that the artificial distinctions of verbal formulation severely restrict an individual's vitality. Hence Anse, who is already death-in-life, uses words like "love" indiscriminately, to fill a void in his character. Addie expresses the Laurentian concept that words prevent authentic relationships among individuals, that it is only through sensuous relationships such as *Blutbruderschaft* that artificial verbal barriers collapse. The schoolchildren she whips are the first to partake in this blood knowledge. Later Cash and Jewel, Addie's treasures, enter her circle and share a physical consanguinity. For Addie words are characterized by the vertical stasis of which Anse approves: she says that "words go straight up in a thin line" (p. 165). Conversely, Addie sanctions deeds, for "doing goes along the earth, clinging to it" (p. 165). She makes a choice in favor of life's fluidity. Addie's distinctions between "words" and "doing," between "stasis" and "mobility," illuminate. Addie's recognition of this polarity ("after a while the two lines are too far apart for the same person to straddle from one to the other") could serve as a metaphoric diagnosis of Darl's condition.

Addie's refusal to accept life as stasis extends, as in Darl's case, to the use of verb tenses which Faulkner assigns to her. I should like to focus on the particular use of the verb "to lie" to demonstrate Addie's view of life as a continuum. The words in the novel's title, "as I lay dying," pose several possibilities. "As" is a conjunction whose use normally implies a continuous action; it suggests, moreover, an incompleteness, a dependence upon other statements and, in fact, the entire book, for its meaning. Furthermore, the verb "lay," considered in standard dialects as the past tense of "lie," cannot be taken as an indicator of an entirely completed action in this novel for several reasons. First, when coupled with "dying," a present form, the verb takes on a distinctly different quality from an alternative like "when

I lay dead." Secondly, throughout the novel the Yoknapatawpha
County dialect allows "lay" to function as an alternate
form of "lie." This confusion of "lie" and "lay" may be an
indication of the cultural lag in the County, because it is
a holdover from nineteenth-century usage whereby the intransi-
tive use of "lay" was considered standard.[38] Tull, in recounting
his mother's death, says, "she ... laid down on the bed and
pulled the covers up and shut her eyes" (p. 29). The fish, later
a surrogate mother, was "laying in the dust" (p. 30); Anse ad-
vises Addie to "Lay still and rest" (p. 36). It might be objected
that since Addie is a teacher her usage of "lie" would differ,
and in fact, except for one expression ("I would lay with
Anse again"), all occurrences of the verb in Addie's section
are standard. But given Addie's peculiar concept that all of
life is a preparation for death, the interpretation of the
verb "lay" as present is not implausible. In fact, the time
distinctions signalled by verbs are really non-operative
for Addie: she "lies" with Anse, a "dead" man, in order to
create life. This coincidence of "lie" and "marriage" suggests
an interesting historical sidelight on the novel. In "A Modern
View of Language," P.K. Saha points out that the word "licgan,"
from which "lie" is derived, orginally meant "to lie down" in
the marriage bed.[39] This folk etymology could be applied to
As I Lay Dying. Not only does Anse "die" when he marries, but
Addie also regards marriage as a type of death. Hence, for
her the title could also mean "as I lay in marriage, I underwent death in life." The novel, then, as its title suggests,
can be interpreted as Addie's quasi-biography. Since Addie
manipulates language to her own ends, her life consists of
"lying," of deception. Yet, since she advocates deeds ("doing
goes along the earth"), all of life is "lying," i.e., movement
in a horizontal direction. For Addie, time is a flux in which
past, present, and future mingle. Time in *As I Lay Dying*
(1930) is Faulkner's fictional parallel to T.S. Eliot's similar statement in *Four Quartets* (1936):

> Time present and time past
> Are both perhaps present in time future.
> And time future contained in time past.
> ("Burnt Norton")

The metaphysical quality of seeing the world in flux is
a baroque characteristic which partially explains Faulkner's use
of certain images. Again, I should like to concentrate on
Darl's perception of objects as reflective of his increasing
tension between stasis and dynamism. Darl has the ability to
suspend continuous motion, to freeze a fluid perception. As

has been pointed out, this characteristic Faulkner labels
"baroque" in *Mosquitoes*. Early in *As I Lay Dying*, Darl
describes Jewel's encounter with the horse thus: "Then they
are *rigid*, *motionless*, terrific, the horse back-thrust on
stiffened, quivering legs, with lowered head.... They *stand*
in *rigid* terrific hiatus" (p. 12; emphasis added). The incidence of words implying stasis (italicized) and their juxtaposition with diction describing movement increase in the
barn-burning episode. Darl, we later learn, has set fire to
the barn. His motivation, deliberately ambiguous, is subject
to several interpretations. As Olga Vickery states, he may,
like the townspeople, be outraged by the putrefaction of his
mother's body and the delay of her burial.   But having observed his hostility toward his mother and his readiness to
describe her death, one hesitates to see him as entirely
disinterested. I should like to propose also that Darl considers
Addie's disappearance necessary to retaining his sanity. The
immolation of the body will allow him to replace objects and
events in rigid, fixed order, and thus effect a distinct
separation between life and death. Faulkner also locates the
source of Darl's madness in his inability to impose stasis
on objects and persons: "He got progressively madder because
he didn't have the capacity--not so much of sanity but of
inertness to resist all the catastrophes that happened to the
family" (italics mine).

Increasingly, Darl sees Addie, as does Vardaman, in anthro-
pomorphic terms; he believes that he is communicating with
Addie, who wants God "to hide her away from the sight of man"
(p. 204). His burning of the barn would be justified by
Addie's wishes and would be conducive to restoring order.
Accordingly, the coffin must be destroyed, because it represents
Addie. When Jewel saves it from the fire, Darl's tension increases. The coffin is subjected to Darl's static perception.
It is "isolated out of all reality" (p. 211), set in a Greek
frieze or a proscenium. Then the peacefulness of the scene
dissolves with the coffin's manifestation:

> It looms unbelievably tall, hiding him: I would not
> have believed that Addie Bundren would have needed
> that much room to lie comfortable in; for another
> instant it stands upright while the sparks rain
> on it in scattering bursts as though they engendered
> other sparks from the contact. Then it topples for-
> ward, gaining momentum, revealing Jewel and the sparks
> raining on him too.... This time Jewel is riding upon
> it, clinging to it, until it crashes down and flings
> him forward and clear....   (p. 212)

The animation of the coffin and Jewel's victory in affirming
existence over annihilation convince Darl of the impossibility
of arranging reality in static forms. Fluidity, in form as
well as in time, constantly impinges upon him.

Other examples of baroque transmutation occur in Darl's
association of Addie, Jewel, and Cash with wood. Early in the
novel he describes Jewel as a cigar-store Indian with wooden
eyes, and the reader's first glimpse of Cash, through Darl,
is that of the carpenter standing in a litter of chips. But
especially for Darl, forms defy fixation. The "soft gold"
boards of the coffin, "bearing on their flanks in smooth undulations the marks of the adze blade" (p. 4), assume their
own "volition" later. Peabody, who describes Addie as a
"bundle of rotten sticks" (p. 43), nevertheless accords her
dignity. But Darl, like the nihilistic Mr. Compson of *The
Sound and the Fury*, thinks of all human endeavors, including
the saving of his mother, as the "dead gestures of dolls"
filled with sawdust (p. 197).

Other characters also display the poetic ability to create
images. Addie associates herself with the wild geese; Cash
describes the second Mrs. Bundren as a "duck-shaped woman"
(p. 249). In view of the obvious differences between the
strong-willed Addie and the more domesticated second wife,
this bird imagery effectively characterizes their personalities.
Sometimes there is a progression from a metaphoric comparison
to a literal statement. At the beginning of the novel, Jewel
describes Cora and the other death-watchers as harpies
("buzzards"); later, on the journey, buzzards surround the
coffin. Addie describes Anse as "a tall bird hunched in the
cold weather" (p. 162). After Anse's visit, Samson discovers
Anse's bird-counterpart in his house:

> When I walked into the hallway I saw something.
> It kind of *hunkered up* when I come in and I thought
> at first it was *one of them got left*, then I saw
> what it was. It was a buzzard. It looked around
> and saw me and went on down the hall, spraddle-
> legged, with its wings kind of hunkered out watch-
> ing me first over one shoulder and then over the
> other, *like a old baldheaded man.*   (p. 112, italics
>   mine)

Again, the use of similar imagery by different characters
indicates Faulkner's presence. Yet, the imagery is suited
to rural life, and each character stamps his individual
imprint on the images, facts which suggest that the narration retains relativity.

A somewhat similar baroque manipulation of form occurs
in several instances whereby characters visualize, instead

of verbalizing their reflections. Since Addie claims to distrust
words, it is not surprising that she expresses her physical and
emotional violation by Anse as a graphic blank on the page:
"The shape of my body where I used to be a virgin is in the
shape of a   and I couldn't think *Anse*" (p. 165). In
Vardaman's last speech, blanks suggest the auditory
effects of silence before sound and the emptiness in
the square after the cow lows: "I hear the cow a long
time, clopping   on the street. Then she comes into the
square. She goes across the square, her head down   clopping
. She lows. There was nothing in the square before she
lowed.... She goes on, clopping   . She lows" (p. 241).

   If, as Arnold Hauser states elsewhere, "All art is a game
with and a fight against chaos,"   it is Darl who succumbs
to chaos and madness and who thus represents the unsuccessful
artist. Cash emerges victorious because he successfully effects
a compromise between the horizontal and the vertical aspects
of reality, between movement and stasis. He advocates bevelling (slanting) as a principle of craft and of life style.
Through this perspective, life and death, actuality and mysti-
cism, words and deeds, are constantly blending. Appropriately,
Cash is the family's final spokesman. At the end of the novel,
order has been restored. Cash has a vision of the family
gathered around the gramophone with their new mother, and
this circularity suggests a modified stasis. Yet, concomitant
with circularity is the open-endedness of continuing dynamic
processes. Dewey Dell's pregnancy suggests that life replaces
death in a never-ending cycle. As artist, Cash replaces Darl,
who, desperately erecting static form and time, had always
to witness their breakdown. Hence, through Darl and Cash,
Faulkner suggests that the artist must both retain his private
interior vision and must partake of community with other men.
Throughout the novel, the repetitiveness and the resultant
unity of colloquial speech are counterpoised with the explosive,
contorted exuberance of the baroque mode. Faulkner, relativistic in his refusal to endorse a single mode of expressivity, nevertheless can contain and blend disparate styles
in an artistic equilibrium.

NOTES

1. All references to *As I Lay Dying* are to the Random House Vintage Books edition, 1964.

2. *The Tangled Fire of William Faulkner* (Minneapolis: University of Minnesota Press, 1954), p. 53.

3. *William Faulkner: A Critical Study* (New York: Random House, 1952), p. 191.

4. *William Faulkner* (New York: Grove Press, 1971), p. 34.

5. *Faulkner: The Major Years* (Bloomington: Indiana University Press, 1966), pp. 51-52.

6. *William Faulkner: A Critical Study*, p. 189.

7. Olga W. Vickery, *The Novels of William Faulkner* (Baton Rouge: Louisiana State University Press, 1964), p. 51; Cleanth Brooks, *William Faulkner: The Yoknapatawpha Country* (New Haven: Yale University Press, 1963), p. 146.

8. "William Faulkner's Style," In *Faulkner: A Collection of Critical Essays*, ed. Robert Penn Warren (Englewood Cliffs, New Jersey: Prentice-Hall, 1966), pp. 58, 61.

9. "Metaphysics in the Criticism of Style," Paper read before the annual meeting of the Conference on College Composition and Communication, Denver, Colorado, March 25, 1966.

10. *Mosquitoes: A Novel* (New York: Liveright, 1951), pp. 14, 49. That Faulkner may have been influenced by baroque sculpture in writing *Mosquitoes* is indicated in the description of an unfinished statue in the novel: "As you entered the room the thing drew your eyes: you turned sharply as to a sound, expecting movement. But it was marble, it could not move...: motionless and passionately eternal the virginal breastless torso of a girl, headless, armless, legless, in marble temporarily caught and hushed yet passionate still for escape, passionate and simple and eternal in the equivocal derisive darkness of the world ... something to trouble the very fibrous integrity of your being" (p. 11).

11. *William Faulkner: From Jefferson to the World* (Lexington: University of Kentucky Press, 1959), p. 70.

12. *Lion in the Garden: Interviews with William Faulkner, 1926-1962*, ed. James B. Meriwether and Michael Millgate (New York: Random House, 1968), p. 137.

13. *Faulkner in the University*, ed. Frederick L. Gwynn and Joseph L. Blotner (New York: Random House, 1965), p. 279.

14. For a presentation of the existing approaches to style, see P.K. Saha, "A Linguistic Approach to Style," *Style*, 11, 1 (Winter 1968), 7-31.

15. The distribution of the sections is as follows: Darl, nineteen; Vardaman, ten; Tull, six; Cash, five; Dewey Dell, four; Cora and Anse, three each; Peabody, two; Samson, Addie, Whitfield, Armstid, Moseley, MacGowan, Jewel, one each.

16. Francis Christensen, "A Generative Rhetoric of the Sentence," *Contemporary Essays on Style*, ed. Glen A. Love and Michael Payne (Glenview, Illinois: Scott, Foresman, & Co., 1969), pp. 27-36.

17. The criteria for this discussion of texture are those of Christensen, who states that few additions to nouns, verbs, or main clauses result in a "thin" texture and a "plain or bare" style. Conversely, frequent or many additions result in a "dense or rich" texture (*ibid.*, p. 31). Faulkner employs varying densities to individualize his speakers and their *Weltanschauung*.

18. For a discussion of the colloquial style of American writers other than Faulkner, see Richard Bridgman, *The Colloquial Style in America* (New York: Oxford University Press, 1968). These features are noted on pp. 12, 79, 99, 103, 121.

19. For fuller discussions of transformational grammar, see Owen Thomas, *Transformational Grammar and the Teacher of English* (New York: Holt, Rinehart and Winston, Inc., 1965), and Richard Ohmann, "Literature as Sentences," *Contemporary Essays on Style*, ed. Glen A. Love and Michael Payne (Glenview, Illinois: Scott, Foresman and Company, 1969), pp. 149-157.

20. See Morris Croll, "The Baroque Style in Prose," and T.S. Eliot, "The Metaphysical Poets," *Seventeenth Century Prose and Poetry*, ed. Alexander M. Witherspoon and Frank J. Warnke (New York: Harcourt, Brace & World, Inc., 1963).

21. The colloquial and baroque styles both employ images but in distinctive methods and for different purposes. When Cora mentions "hogs," "chickens," etc., the referent is a concrete, unambiguous object. When Darl refers to an object, he immediately transforms and then embroiders it into a metaphor; thus Dewey Dell's leg becomes a lever, a caliper. Such ingenious elaboration of a figure of speech suggests Darl's tendency toward metaphysical conceit and the humor resulting from such exaggeration. When Dewey Dell, for example, emerges from the river, Darl describes her breasts as "those mammalian ludicrosities which are the horizons and the valleys of the earth" (p. 156).

22. Croll, pp. 1071-1075. Bridgman, in characterizing sentences of colloquial prose, also uses the term "loose" to describe this example from *The Adventures of Huckleberry Finn* (p. 122): "Every lady with a lovely complexion, and perfectly beautiful, and looking just like a gang of real sure-enough queens, and dressed in clothes that cost millions of dollars, and just littered with diamonds." If Christensen's approach is applied to this sentence, the following pattern emerges:

    (1) Every lady with a lovely complexion,
        (2) and perfectly beautiful, (AC)
        (2) and looking just like a gang of real
            sure-enough queens, (VC, PP)
        (2) and dressed in clothes that cost millions
            of dollars, (VC, PP)
        (2) and just littered with diamonds. (VC, PP)

This configuration differs significantly from the pattern described by Croll as "loose," since all additions in this sentence refer back to the first level, since they are all coordinate structures, and since they markedly avoid subordination.

23. Croll, p. 1075.

24. *The Sound and the Fury* (New York: Random House, 1966), p. 330.

25. *William Faulkner: The Yoknapatawpha Country*, p. 160.

26. New York: Random House, 1973, pp. 369-370.

27. *The American Novel and Its Tradition* (Garden City, New York: Doubleday & Company, 1957), p. 207.

28. *Faulkner in the University*, p. 113.

29. "Baroque Art and the Emblem," *Seventeenth Century Prose and Poetry*, p. 1080. In fact, some of the Bundrens have their own "emblems"--Cash, his tools; Jewel, the horse; and Vardaman, the fish.

30. *The Novels of William Faulkner*, p. 57.

31. *Faulkner in the University*, pp. 103, 109. For additional explicit parallels Faulkner makes between writing and carpentry, see pages 49-50, 68, 72, 84, 120, 168, 257.

32. *Ibid.*, pp. 110-111.

33. Faulkner is, of course, aware that the fish, in Christian symbology, represents Christ, the Christian, and eternal life, and in archetypal symbology, fecundity and re-generation. His use of the fish in *As I Lay Dying* illustrates

both his instinctive choice of the appropriate "symbol" and the creation of distance between the author and the narrator, Vardaman. Vardaman, unconscious of symbolism, reaches the conclusion that his mother survives in the form of a fish because this meaning evolves from his actions and his natural surroundings; Faulkner employs the fish because it suggests the wider Christian symbolism and archetypal patterns which underlie this novel.

34. Austin Warren notes that during the Counter-Reformation the Catholic Church used the doctrine of the incarnation to justify the sensuousness of baroque art as a "sanctification of the body and the senses" ("Baroque Art and the Emblem," p. 1079).

35. I am indebted to P.K. Saha for calling my attention to this allusion.

36. *The Colloquial Style in America*, p. 13.

37. "The Baroque Style in Prose," p. 1073.

38. See Thomas Pyles, *The Origins and Development of the English Language* (New York: Harcourt Brace Jovanovich, Inc., 1971), pp. 214-215.

39. P.K. Saha, "A Modern View of Language," *Case Western Reserve Law Review*, XXIII, 2 (Winter 1972), p. 337.

40. *The Novels of William Faulkner*, pp. 58, 59.

41. *Faulkner in the University*, p. 110.

42. *The Social History of Art*, II (New York: Alfred A. Knopf, 1951), p. 94.

PRIDE AND NAKEDNESS:
AS I LAY DYING

Calvin Bedient

The force of *As I Lay Dying* is in its opacity. Faulkner's
novel has the particularity of real experience, and this is
so rare a quality in modern art that we have forgotten how
to appreciate it. So untranslatable, so irreducible to symbol
and idea is the detail of the novel that one looks for
analogies in painting and music; and even the sporadic ex-
plosions of reflective rhetoric in the book convey little
more than a momentary and frustrated impulse to the "universal":
they remain essentially opaque. For example, the construction
"How do our lives ravel out into the no-wind, no-sound, the
weary gestures wearily recapitulant: echoes of old compulsions
with no-hand on no-strings: in sunset we fall into furious
attitudes, dead gestures of dolls"[1] has no value whatsoever
as literal statement or meaning, particularly in the context,
where it lies disconnected, florid, and obtrusive, like a
bouquet found abandoned in the dust. These words function,
instead, precisely as "furious attitude," as an expressive
verbal gesture, a mood-painting; they are as immediate in
interest as the sudden clenching of a hand or the swirls in
a Van Gogh cypress.

In the sense intended by William Golding in *Free Fall*,
As I Lay Dying is patternless, "translating incoherence into
incoherence,"[2] from life to art. The novel has a wonderful
immunity to schematization; it is innocent of both a moral
and a morality, and it seems to breathe out rather than posit
a world view. Faulkner's novel does have, to be sure, a
narrative movement and structure--a movement that, considering the fragmentation of narrative method, is remarkably
steady, and a structure that is timeless, that answers to
some unchanging psychological need: the journey undertaken
and, despite great perils, completed. And yet, regardless
of this, the book is open, both in the sense of making room
for the incidental (indeed, the trivial[3]) and in the sense
that it does not understand itself: it is essentially spectacle.

As I Lay Dying is to be "seen," not understood; experienced, not translated; felt, not analyzed. The malignity it portrays, both of the land and sky and of man is aesthetic. Here suffering is above all a spectacle—to us, to the neighbors of the Bundrens (the chorus to the collective protagonist), and even to Anse Bundren, who looks upon each new misfortune as a show of the Opponent's ingenuity, the staging of Destiny. Is there, indeed, an organizer behind the spectacle? The novel does not help us to an answer. What it unfolds before us is simply the autonomy of misfortune: the brutal fact of its monotonous regularity and astonishing variety, of its farcical absurdity, of its tragedy; and questions of cause are not raised—they are extraneous. There is thus in the novel a fundamental silence that is truly terrible. For what is more mysterious, finally, than immediacy? Explanations tranquilize wonder, and *As I Lay Dying* contains no explanations.

The nakedness of form in this novel is the aesthetic equivalent of an act of courage; and despite its strong element of farce, the book is like tragedy in its refusal to mediate between destructive contradictions. The openness of *As I Lay Dying* is thus almost morally exhilarating; and yet it is appalling, too. For like its own Darl Bundren, the novel lacks defenses; it takes the world upon its flesh like a rain of arrows. Can one imagine a Faulknerian utopia? His books do not hold their heads so high as hope. *As I Lay Dying* is a prolonged cry of astonishment; everything within it is recorded as if with a soundless gasp. "Outrageous," say the neighbors when they are assailed by the odor of the rotting corpse; and the word echoes and expands until it has embraced everything in the book.

One could argue that *As I Lay Dying* is patternless to a fault—that it is, in places, confused and self-destroying. The crucial monologue of Addie Bundren, for instance, is a marvel of dazzling unintelligibility. Why does she call herself "three" (herself, Cash, and Darl) when, as she says, Darl is her husband's child and not her own? By Cash's birth, she remarks, her "aloneness had been violated and then made whole again by the violation: time, Anse, love, what you will, outside the circle" (p. 164). But if Cash is still inside the circle with Addie, is her aloneness truly intact? Very often, the illogic of the characters is extreme, grotesque; it is not merely puzzling, but dizzying, and throws the mind down. And yet this grotesquerie possesses a kind of beauty— the beauty of opacity. Like the pyrotechnic rhetorical reflections, the logical absurdities have a stubborn and assertive density that makes them analogous to the squiggles and clots of paint on modern canvasses; the book is entirely of a piece, opalesque all through.

It is for this reason that the thematics of *As I Lay Dying*
are difficult to approach—or better, that it is questionable
to speak of a thematics at all. At any rate, there is clearly
no Ariadne's thread that will lead one through the labyrinth.
But of course it is far from my intention to claim—what
would after all be self-defeating—that the book cannot be
discussed. The problem is that it can be discussed endlessly,
since its patternlessness results, not in emptiness, but precisely in a continuous, turgid thickness of meaning, the significant indefiniteness of life itself. My purpose is simply
to explore one of the dialectics of the novel as this is
manifested in both the content and the form. I shall be bolder
and assert that this dialectic is at the center of the book—
not its theme, but its axis; not what the novel is "about,"
but a significant part of its substance and the determining
principle of its form.

II

In *As I Lay Dying* life is conceived as the antagonist,
living is "terrible," the protagonist self is alone: a naked
and isolated consciousness in a broad land. This nakedness,
this dreadful isolation, is already a kind of defeat, a form
of abjectness, so that the utmost to be expected from the
mind in its continual conflict with the world is simply a
capitulation without dishonor: a surrender of everything,
if need be, except pride. It is true that there are or appear
to be, in the Faulknerian world, other "answers"[4] to aloneness—
for example, Vardaman's mental revision of a reality his emotions cannot accept, and the physical "violation" of Addie's
aloneness that comes with childbearing. Yet Vardaman's answer
is transparently desperate, and Addie's seems to have the
effect, not of breaking through her aloneness, but of ex-
panding it; the circle of isolation remains inexorable. Thus
the third term of this existential dialectic, the solution
which remains after all others have failed, is pride, for
pride is the only answer that stands upon, rather than attempts
to evade, our inescapable nakedness.
The most remarkable quality of the very remarkable
Bundrens—country people who feel their difference from
"town folk"—is their fierce, their unexpected, their mag-
nificently sustaining pride. Even Anse Bundren really seems
to believe that he would be "beholden to none" (p. 218)—
though in truth, of course, he often is. Like wounded animals
that have instinctively found the herb that will cure them,
the Bundrens have discovered pride; and each is typical, each
is "universal," precisely in bearing, not as an idea but as

a fact, the wound of nakedness, the solitary confinement and essential impotency of conscious being.

The fact and awareness of isolation is the very bedrock in Faulkner; it is given out direct as an odor. And it is the strength and beauty of *As I Lay Dying* that the form of the novel itself amplifies, that it is an aesthetic equivalent for, this truth. For each of the numerous monologues constitutes a new demonstration of the obvious: the fundamental isolation inherent in the very structure of consciousness.

Now let us take note of an apparent contradiction in the form and, at the same time, of its echo in the content. Obviously, each monologue is implicitly isolated, hermetically sealed from the others; yet the result of their grouping is, nonetheless, an appearance of mutual co-operation. *As I Lay Dying* is a composite narrative, a kind of unwitting group enterprise; and undeniably this apparent aspect of the form is as expressive as the actual technique of the accretion of fragmentary monologues. Considered as a whole, the novel expresses, through its form, Faulkner's profound feeling for the human group, above all for the family, which is presented as constituting its own fate: a kind of involuntary and inescapable group confinement, the inexorable circle in expanded form.

Human coherence in Faulkner, whether of the family or of the larger community, is presented chiefly as a response to the onslaughts of an opposing world. In the Bundrens, Faulkner lays bare the most primitive of the motives to community: society as a principle of survival. Shy and aloof as a herd, the Bundren family is held together, not by love, but by pride, which is its instinctive response to danger, including unfavorable public opinion. And if this herd is self-destructive, still it prefers its cannibalism to exposure to the world, to a nakedness synonymous with defeat.

The Faulknerian family is thus a kind of exacerbating protective covering, a hair shirt, to the "abject nakedness" of the individuals composing it. This accounts for the fact that family ties are so horrendously tense in Faulkner: they are the crackling bonds of a bitter necessity. At bottom, the Faulknerian family is a compulsive effort to end, to disguise, nakedness; but since nakedness is inescapable, this effort issues in hate. Thus if nakedness leads to community, it is also true that community leads to an aggravation of nakedness. The effort returns upon itself. Like the aesthetic form of the novel, the family only *appears* to transcend or resolve the fundamental isolation of the individual; in actuality, it is a terrible and frustrating unit of interlocking solitudes, atomic in structure like a molecule.

Yet the family is no more, if no less, terrible than nakedness. In the absence of other consolations, it may afford at least an illusion of "confidence and comfort"--words Darl uses when he defines the meaning that the coffin has for Addie (p. 5). Let us note that the coffin and the family are analogous forms, or better, that a dreadful yet desired confinement and covering is the form that accounts for both. Peabody helps us to this perception when, seeing Anse and Addie together, he observes of the latter:

> She watches me: I can feel her eyes. It's like she
> was shoving at me with them. I have seen it before
> in women. Seen them drive from the room them coming
> with sympathy and pity, with actual help, and cling-
> ing to some trifling animal to whom they never were
> more than pack-horses. That's what they mean by the
> love that passeth understanding: that pride, that
> furious desire to hide that abject nakedness which
> we bring here with us...[and] carry stubbornly and
> furiously with us into the earth again. (pp. 44-45)

This little-noticed but important passage obviously extends into a paradigm of the behavior of the Bundrens on the journey to Jefferson, for they too, in their furious desire to hide their abject nakedness, drive from them those coming with sympathy and pity. More subtly, it explains the importance to Addie of the coffin, over the construction of which she attends, from her bedroom window, with an anxious and severe observation. To her, the coffin is a substitute for her family; it represents but a change of coverings.

Of course, for a while after death Addie clings to the family itself, and it is in this sense that she is not yet dead, that the entire journey takes place while she still lies "dying." Through her magnificent will, which is the instrument of her pride, she is thus doubly protected on her way to the grave, even in death covering her nakedness in the fierceness of her "modesty," which is but the pride, as it were, of her privacy. "For an instant," as the coffin is loaded on the wagon, "it resists, as though volitional, as though within it her pole-thin body clings furiously, even though dead, to a sort of modesty, as she would have tried to conceal a soiled garment that she could not prevent her body soiling" (p. 91). It is as if even death could not conquer Addie's pride, though it constitutes the final and absolute nakedness. By means of the promise Addie exacts from her family to bury her in Jefferson, she prolongs even into death their customary relationship to her while she was living, which was to protect her, to encircle her with "her own flesh and blood." She is thus not so much carried as

attended to Jefferson. Nor does she "die" until she is placed
in the ground. Then at last she is abandoned and--as she might
have foreseen--immediately forgotten, replaced at once by
a new "Mrs Bundren." By that time, however, she has punished
her family just as she had intended[5]--punished it by keeping
it to herself a little longer, and in suffering, and for the
reason that she had needed it, just as, in the instance of
the deceit she practices for Jewel, she hated him "because
she had to love him so that she had to act the deceit" (p.
123).

In Faulkner, then, pride binds but at the same time lacer-
ates; there is a distance between people which, except in rare
instances, cannot be closed, which, indeed, is maintained by
pride itself. For pride is an expression of the aggressive
instinct, a response and counterantagonism to the antagonism
of destiny, to the painfully naked structure of being. The
community that pride creates is at best an illusory one--
the Bundrens on the road to Jefferson. And this deceptive
community, overlaying a stark and irremediable personal
nakedness, is mirrored in the form of the novel, which is
real in its parts--its lonely monologues--but illusory as a
"whole." In both the characters and the form that presents
them, it is isolation that is basic and substantive.

                              III

Turning from the relationship of form to content, let us
consider the two characters of the novel who embody the extreme ends of Faulknerian being: Darl Bundren, in whom nakedness has an absolute form, and his brother Cash, in whom pride
attains to a constructive, humane, and stabilizing limit.

Alone among the Bundrens, Darl lacks the ingredient, the
enzyme, of pride. Stricken in his very being, he is a demonstration of our natural emptiness, of a nakedness powerless
to hide itself behind an "I." What is more, the vacuum of
identity in Darl, unlike that of the mystic or the artist,
cannot be seized upon and converted into a positivity; for
although Darl is invaded by others as the mystic is inundated
by God and the novelist possessed by his characters, those who
occupy Darl do not replenish him, and naturally his consciousness deteriorates by a law of diminishing returns. Hopelessly
open and undefended, at times even plural and familial, Darl's
mind leaps barriers of space and flesh, flowing everywhere
like the floodwaters of the river--but flowing because un-
formed, because it has no home in itself, no principle of
containment.

This bitter gift and fatality, this plurality of being,
Darl carries like a cross. If he is a freak, he is also a

victim, and knows with characteristic lucidity what has made
him the casualty he is. When Vardaman says, "But you *are*,
Darl," the latter replies: "I know it.... That's why I am not
is. *Are* is too many for one woman to foal" (p. 95). The
point is that, unlike Jewel (whose "mother is a horse"),
Darl has never been a foal, that is, sponsored; and as he
here observes to Vardaman, it is his fate to be everyone
except himself. He is *de trop*, a consciousness inhabiting
the world as a kind of excess, baseless, and, as a result,
pitilessly empowered to trespass upon the privacy of others.

Darl exists, but, because he is unloved, he cannot become
himself; at least this is the explanation that he himself
seems to favor. As Ortega has noted, love is choice in its
very essence, a vital preference of this being over that one,
a corroboration of the beloved;[6] and Darl knows that he has
never been affirmed. "Jewel *is*," Darl thinks at one point,
"so Addie Bundren must be" (p. 76); for the created postulates
the creator. But Darl maintains that he has no mother, and
the absence of the creator throws into doubt the reality of
the created:

> In a strange room you must empty yourself for
> sleep. And before you are emptied for sleep, what
> are you. And when you are emptied for sleep, you
> are not. And when you are filled with sleep, you
> never were. I dont know what I am. I dont know if
> I am or not. (p. 76)

By thus equating being with consciousness, which sleep
annihilates, Darl removes from existence its stability, giving
it the flickering reality of a dream. "And so," he concludes,
"if I am not emptied yet, I am *is*." Only on that condition.
For Darl has, he feels, no identity ("I dont know what I am")
and thus no cord of continuity capable of withstanding
the unraveling power of sleep. So the ending of the monologue falls with the force of a metaphor: "How often have I
lain beneath rain on a strange roof, thinking of home."

Further, Darl's consciousness, in this passage, casts
upon the world itself a desubstantiating shadow, so that
for him objects too may appear suddenly orphaned:

> Beyond the unlamped wall I can hear the rain shaping
> the wagon that is ours, the load that is no longer
> theirs that felled and sawed it nor yet theirs that
> bought it and which is not ours either, lie on our
> wagon though it does, since only the wind and the
> rain shape it only to Jewel and me, that are not
> asleep. (p. 76)

More than this, their being is also subject, like his, to
abrupt cancellation: "And since sleep is is-not and rain and

wind are *was*, it [the load] is not" (p. 76). And although
for the present the wagon "*is*," it too will surrender its
reality when it has carried Addie Bundren to Jefferson: "when
the wagon is *was*, Addie Bundren will not be" (p. 76). For
Darl, then, being springs from the mother ("Jewel *is*, so
Addie Bundren must be"); disjoined from Addie, the world and
Darl appear equally unauthored, existing without authentica-
tion, hovering on the verge of extinction.

Mercilessly unclouded by egoism, Darl's mind is the per-
fect mirror of what surrounds him, which it reflects with a
terrible clarity. It is only his own identity that is obscure
to Darl--the failure of the mirror to reflect itself. In this
novel, shapelessness is the condition against which the
characters must define themselves, and Darl cannot find his
own shape. It is thus his destiny to be, not himself, but the
world. Since Darl neither acts (he is called "lazy"), nor
possesses anything that he can call his own, nor is loved,
he must fall back upon introspection to give him identity.
But, as Husserl observes, consciousness is itself empty; we
must be conscious *of* something to be conscious at all;[7] and
when Darl turns in upon himself, he finds nothing there.
Tragically, Darl is not made present to himself as an *object*
until he is acted upon, literally apprehended by the world
and conducted to the insane asylum at Jackson (for, to be
acted upon, one must exist). But the Darl then given birth
is a monster, a belated and violent creation, who rightly
laughs at the brutal comedy of his birth, and who, with heart-
breaking irony, is at last all affirmation: "Yes yes yes yes
yes" (p. 243). At this parturition, the suspected absurdity
of the world finally declares itself unequivocally. Appallingly,
it answers to expectation. And yet to be so well served is,
after all, a kind of mercy. For Darl has at last discovered
certainty: "Yes yes yes yes yes."

If, on the one hand, Darl remains, even to the end, a
transparent perceiver, he has become, on the other, a pure
opacity. It is true, of course, that Darl was never perfectly
transparent; earlier there is in him, for instance, the darkness of the body ("I could lie with my shirt-tail up, ...
feeling myself without touching myself, feeling the cool
silence blowing upon my parts" [p. 11]), and what appears to
be an incestuous feeling for Dewey Dell asserts itself,
through metaphor, on the train to Jackson. Ethereal as he
is, moreover, Darl possesses, in addition, that subterranean,
savage charge of energy which is necessary for life itself:
"he and I look at one another," Darl says of Cash, "with ...
looks that plunge unimpeded ... into the ultimate secret
place where for an instant Cash and Darl crouch flagrant and
unabashed in all the old terror and the old foreboding, alert

and secret and without shame" (p. 135). Yet Darl *is* abashed
at this naked core: that is his tragedy. Limitless, unclaimed,
despairing of attaining shape, his very being longs to be
undone: "If you could just ravel out into time. That would
be nice. It would be nice if you could just ravel out into
time" (p. 198). This decreation, however, is not permitted
to Darl, whose fate it is to *see*, and who must endure even in
madness a perception as pitiless as it is crystalline.

There is, of course, one point at which Darl *acts*: his
setting fire to the barn that contains his mother's corpse.
When this attempt fails, Darl is found, in tears, lying on
the coffin, his passivity resumed, his mind more hopeless than
ever. Darl's laughter at his seizure by the asylum authori-
ties, Cash's insight, "This world is not his world; this
life his life" (p. 250), and the tearful resurrender to non-
entity over the putrescent body of his mother, taken together,
suggest how unbearable the world must appear to a being ab-
solutely naked to it, between whose capacity to suffer and
the power of the world to inflict pain no selfhood and no love
have intervened.

Though Darl's consciousness is so attentive and catholic
that it seems at times to be a form of love, it is, for the
most part, as neutral as photographic film. For Darl loves
no one--except perhaps, in an unspeakably tormented way,
Addie Bundren (as the barn-burning obscurely suggests)--
and, until the end, he affirms nothing at all. On those few
occasions when he displays strong feeling toward others, he
is barbed and vindictive; for even he has a component of egotism, though only so much as is requisite for suffering. And
just as he bitterly resents the woman who has caused his
emptiness, so he resents those of her children who are enviably
intense and narrow with their own being: Jewel and Dewey
Dell. If Darl taunts them, he does so because they are so
self-absorbed, because they *can* be self-absorbed, and from
his aggressive insinuations one may understand that he would
like to induce in them a portion of his own pain. Jewel and
Dewey Dell, both truly flagrant and unabashed, are equally
exposed to Darl, the first through the inexpressible intensity
of his feeling for his mother, which renders him rigid, and
the second, who is pregnant, through the unwelcome violation
of her aloneness. Nor is it by chance that Darl gains and
wields like a weapon secret knowledge of each: his clairvoyance is sharpened by his envy. At the end, when these two
throw themselves upon Darl with ferocity, they are simply
reasserting the privacy of their identities. The very fact
that they have identities to defend proves their existential
superiority to Darl; a battle between unequal opponents,
the scene is cruel.

Perhaps Darl is finally a standing condemnation of the
world. If "[t]his world is not his world; this life his life,"
is it not because it is unloving where he wants its love,
random where he wants its reason, savagely obtuse where he
needs its understanding? Darl is not better than the world,
only--by a kind of ontological error--more generous: though
he receives nothing from his surroundings, he gives himself
to them, just as he lends his eyes to the land that fills
them. Doubtless, Cash is being sentimental when he says,
"Sometimes I think it aint none of us pure crazy and aint
none of us pure sane until the balance of us talks him that-
a-way" (p. 223); and yet clearly this is true of Darl. Until
he is seized, he is not truly insane; but then, sitting on
the ground and laughing, bitter and manic, he does grant
the world its victory and surrenders to the unreason at its
heart. In his last monologue, which is tantamount to a
ferocious, uncontrollable parody of all those earlier monologues in which his mind had seemed to belong to the family
itself, he watches and attends "our brother Darl" (p. 244)
on his departure to Jackson, and is puzzled by his laughter.
Now that he sees "Darl," now that Darl exists for him, he
cannot comprehend him. And perhaps he senses, as he speaks
of our brother Darl in his cage in Jackson, that ultimately
such laughter is beyond understanding.

It is against this dreadful nakedness that pride, in
Faulkner, assumes its value. If Darl is our innate nakedness
in extremis, impotent to defend itself, Cash exemplifies
the pride that saves us and is itself the substance of identity; for the identity a man asserts is simply that part
of himself he thinks well of.

As I Lay Dying brings to mind Conrad's *Heart of Darkness*,
not only in the land that shapes "the life of man in its
implacable and brooding image" (p. 44) and in the tensions
it establishes between the shaped, moral surfaces of the mind
and subterranean psychic energies (tensions aggravated,
moreover, by a journey through a violent land), but also
in its cautious celebration of the worker as hero. For Cash,
like Marlow, is man defining himself, declaring his human
dignity through the perfection of his work. Both heroes labor
precisely in order to avoid being shaped by the violent land,
or better, to avoid being shapeless; and in work each discovers the reality of himself. Whereas Marlow knows that work
is man's defense against himself, a noble self-avoidance,
Cash senses merely that the man is the work--an important
but lesser insight. What Marlow tries to defend himself
against is the darkness in himself; the darkness in Faulkner's
novel, by contrast, is of the world. It is more than human,
though it encompasses the human; and Cash is heroic (un-

assumingly and narrowly heroic) not so much in mastering
himself as in contesting the amorphousness, the appalling
anonymity, of existence itself.

For in the world depicted in Faulkner's novel, the hero's
role must be to shape and to define. We see in Cash literally
a rage for efficiency as he labors at the coffin, "his face
sloped into the light with a rapt, dynamic immobility above
his tireless elbow" (p. 72), working on into the night and
the rain unfalteringly, as if "in a tranquil conviction that
rain was an illusion of the mind" (p. 73). But neither at
this time nor any other (a truth not generally grasped) does
Cash's devotion to the perfection of his work dehumanize him:
he is never the equivalent, say, of Conrad's Chief Accountant,
whose books are kept in dazzling yet mean order only yards
above a grove of death. On the contrary, Cash is always a
figure nearer to Marlow, provincial and less profound, but
humane and wise. Cash builds the coffin where his dying mother
can see him because he loves her, as Jewel jealously perceives
("It's like when he was a little boy and she says if she had
some fertilizer she would try to raise some flowers and he
taken the bread pan and brought it back from the barn full of
dung" [p. 14]); and such dogged, mechanically rationalized,
and in the circumstances impractical efficiency indicates
that his labor is basically an act of pride, the purpose
of which is to assert the human in the teeth of its negation--
the nothingness awaiting life, the shapelessness surrounding
it. After Addie's death, when Cash (his ears deaf to the
practical words of his father, his face composed) stands
"looking down at her peaceful, rigid face fading into the
dusk as though darkness were a precursor of the ultimate
earth, until at last the face seems to float detached upon
it, lightly as the reflection of a dead leaf" (p. 49), he
takes in at once what he and his mother are up against and
returns immediately to work. Against such dematerialization
of the human, the construction of the coffin, which looks
so merely mechanical, is actually a passionate protest, a
fierce assertion of human value. Built under the inimical
pressure of time, but nonetheless perfected beyond practical
reason, the coffin is to death what *As I Lay Dying* itself
is to the artless world: a product of love, a preserving
form, and in its craftsmanship a predication of human dignity.

From first to last Cash is the most human of the Bundrens--
and also the most humane. The notion that Cash develops during
the course of the narrative--"from unimaginative self-con-
tainment to humane concern"[8]--has taken hold despite obvious
objections: the gross improbability of such a development
in a man in his late twenties within a nine-day period and,
more important, the textual evidence to the contrary.[9] "The

increasing range of Cash's awareness," writes Olga Vickery,
"is suggested by his growing sympathy with Darl."[10] But, on
the contrary, the point to note is that Cash's sympathy with
Darl, which was strong from the first, actually meets with a
check as the novel progresses: it comes up against a moral
judgment.

For though Cash's pride is not in itself dehumanizing,
it necessitates, as a safeguard, a morality that is inevitably
rigid. Of the kinds of strength represented in the novel--the
violence of feeling in Addie and Jewel, the imperturbable,
maudlin self-centeredness of Anse, the wild-seed egoism of
Dewey Dell, the rational stability of Cash--it is only the
latter which is moral in tendency, leading to the correction
of life by mind. The strength of Cash is ultimately the
strength of conviction. When he declares that men who cannot
"see eye to eye with other folks" must be considered crazy
(p. 223), clearly he is assuming a kind of tacit social contract, according to which men work and construct their build-
ings and shape their lives with the understanding that others
will not hinder them or destroy the fruits of their labor.
Those who fail to honor this contract are morally blind, that
is, "crazy." "I dont reckon nothing excuses setting fire to
a man's barn and endangering his stock and destroying his
property," Cash says. "That's how I reckon a man is crazy"
(p. 223). What Cash opposes is not simply the destruction of
material property, for property is never simple. There is always
the man *in* the property to take into account, the value it
possesses from having absorbed part of the human life that
shaped it: "there just aint nothing justifies the deliberate
destruction of what a man has built with his own sweat and
stored the fruit of his sweat into" (p. 228).

Like Marlow, then, Cash values a good job because it
creates human value, or rather, it is valuable because it is
a human creation. The meaning of work is that it is an essentially human expression; and its value is that it allows a
man to be proud of himself as a creator. But where Marlow also
values work for its binding effect--workers become brothers--
Cash, an American very much on his own, prizes work solely
as a source of human identity and pride. Life as it gets lived,
certainly as the Bundrens live it, is a "shoddy job" (p. 227),
a judgment that includes not only Darl's burning of the barn,
but also the attack made upon Darl by Jewel and Dewey Dell. To
Cash, a neat job does more than testify to man's capacity for
shaping; it is also a symbol of discipline and decency, of a
renunciation of aggression. Thus for Cash, life, like the
building of a barn, is what you make of it, and the shameful-
ness of the present, its shoddiness, really stems from a failure
of pride, of man's imagination of his value. Only recently,

Cash implies, have people moved away "from the olden right teaching that says to drive the nails down and trim the edges well always like it was for your own use and comfort you were making it" (p. 224). Why is this teaching "right"? Because a man defines himself, not by what he builds, but by the way he builds it: "it's better to build a tight chicken coop than a shoddy courthouse, and when they both build shoddy or build well, neither because it's one or tother is going to make a man feel the better nor the worse" (p. 224). And if ultimately the self-definition of man matters, it is because, naked as man is, he has nothing else to claim as his own.

Both Marlow and Cash are forced to judge as evil the actions of men of whom they almost feel themselves to be accomplices, for just as Marlow acknowledges the "fascination of the abomination,"[11] so Cash had thought more than once that "one of us would have to do something" (p. 223) to get rid of the corpse. In noble contrast to the vicious men around them, each judges with a sense of necessity, in the name of civilization, and at real cost to himself. But it is precisely here that we come up against the negative limits of pride; for the final relationship of Cash to Darl is one of unbending (though not insensitive) pride to abject nakedness. The response the book itself makes to Darl's nakedness, the response it elicits from the reader, is that of a disarmed compassion unadulterated with judgment. "It was bad so," Cash says of Darl's laughter. "I be durn if I could see anything to laugh at. Because there just aint nothing justifies ... deliberate destruction..." (p. 228). The point is not that Cash is incapable of perceiving abject nakedness, for it is this that he describes when he says, "It's like there was a fellow in every man that's done a-past the sanity or the insanity, that watches the sane and the insane doings of that man with the same horror and the same astonishment" (p. 228). What is significant is that Cash cannot *afford* his own insight into abjectness. For compassion dissolves pride, it is utterly passive--at its fullest, it is a recognition of man's ultimate, existential defeat. On the other hand, though the novel carries us beyond Cash into the impotent heart of understanding, into a compassion beyond social principle and responsibility, it will not allow us to judge pride, either. What it says, rather--even through the fact that Cash, the technician, has broken his leg for the second time and lies helpless as Darl is apprehended--is that finally the world is too much even for the proud and that there is no limit to the demand life makes upon our compassion.

IV

Let us return to our examination of the relationship between form and content in Faulkner's novel. We have noted

in the subject matter a polarity of nakedness and pride,
and in the aesthetic form an answering nakedness. Let us
now see whether there is also, in the technics of the novel,
a complementary pride.

   As I Lay Dying is primarily naturalistic in technique.
The device of the narrative soliloquy is a means of present-
ing the mind in its immediacy, and in this sense it directly
serves the ends of realism. Let us acknowledge, further,
that the basic impulse underlying the book is unmistakably
a yearning for reality. And yet it would be untrue to claim
that Faulkner's novel lacks all traces of the dehumanization
often observed in modern art. In his seminal essay on this
trend, Ortega pungently remarked that all style involves
dehumanization, for style necessarily deforms reality; and
it was the aim of modern poetry, as Ortega saw it, to substitute style for reality.[12] I have remarked already upon the
turgidity and opacity of Faulkner's rhetorical style. Now
let us take this observation to its limit: Faulkner's metaphorical prose is, at its densest, not so much a mimetic instrument as the preening expression of the pride of the imagination in itself. This is to say that Faulkner's very language
is proud, and proud precisely as a defiantly "free" response
to the threat always present in the perilous nakedness of the
self and the world.

   When, for example, Darl says of the vultures that they
hang in the sky "in narrowing circles, like the smoke, with
an outward semblance of form and purpose, but with no inference of motion, progress or retrograde" (p. 216), or when
Peabody defines death as "no more than a single tenant or
family moving out of a tenement or a town" (p. 43), the
language gets in the way of the reality it describes, or
better, the language here secretly flouts and overcomes
reality, achieving a proud independency. Or consider the
description of Vardaman's face at his mother's death: "From
behind pa's leg Vardaman peers, his mouth full open and all
color draining from his face into his mouth, as though he has
by some means fleshed his own teeth in himself, sucking"
(p. 48). It is the simile that is primary, and the reality
referred to exists principally as a pretext for the image:
an image which is, in truth, not a description but an inven-
tion, a subjective idea. In all these instances, Faulkner's
prose is distended to make room for the imagination. And the
result is a style at once grotesque, as though somehow
maimed, and proud, as if totally free to make of itself what
it will.

   The very grotesqueness of the style is a demonstration
that language is not free, that it is governed by certain
laws. And as a rule Faulkner's language bends, if not bows,

to necessity, admitting the authority of reality. But plainly
Faulkner's style is impatient of law, and harbors a resentment toward the duty of mimesis. In its attempts to liberate
itself, it moves toward its own self-defeat, at times failing
to convey any meaning at all. Proud as it is, it represents,
like Cash's pride, an ambiguous triumph over nakedness: its
strength is at the same time an impotence, a refusal to admit,
and perhaps an inability to tolerate, the naked power of the
world. As in the polarity, then, between proud and naked being
in the novel, there is between the openness of the form and
the opacity of the style an unremitting tension, a contradiction that testifies, on the one hand, both to man's hunger
for reality and to his nerve for the truth, however invidious
it may be, and, on the other, to his proud and imaginative
spirit--to his ambition to create an object, whether a building or a prose, that is his own.

NOTES

1. William Faulkner, *As I Lay Dying* (New York: Random
House, 1964), pp. 196-97.

2. London: Faber and Faber, 1959, p. 8.

3. For example, the final words of Samson's monologue:
"I have known him [MacCallum] from a boy up; know his name
as well as I do my own. But be durn if I can say it" (p. 113).

4. In using this term, I have in mind Addie Bundren's
comment: "And when I knew that I had Cash, I knew that living
was terrible and that this was the answer to it" (p. 163).

5. "But then I realised that I had been tricked by words
older than Anse or love, and that the same word had tricked
Anse too, and that my revenge would be that he would never
know I was taking revenge. And when Darl was born I asked
Anse to promise to take me back to Jefferson when I died..."
(pp. 164-65).

6. José Ortega y Gasset, *On Love: Aspects of a Single
Theme*, trans. Toby Talbot (New York: Meridian Books, 1957),
pp. 17-18.

7. See Edmund Husserl, *Ideas* (New York: Macmillan, 1952);
Jean-Paul Sartre, *Being and Nothingness* (New York: Philosophical
Library, 1956), p. li.

8. Irving Howe, *William Faulkner*, rev. ed. (New York:
Vintage, 1962), p. 188.

9. See pages 124–25, where Cash is shown to be extraordinarily sensitive and sympathetic, and surprisingly worldly-wise, at a period that antedates the present time of the novel.

10. "The Dimensions of Consciousness: *As I Lay Dying*," in *William Faulkner: Three Decades of Criticism*, ed. Frederick J. Hoffman and Olga W. Vickery (East Lansing: Michigan State University Press, 1960), pp. 239–40.

11. Joseph Conrad, "Heart of Darkness," in *Youth and Two Other Stories* (Garden City, New York: Doubleday, Doran, 1923), p. 50.

12. *The Dehumanization of Art and Other Writings on Art and Culture*, Doubleday Anchor Book (Garden City, N.Y., 1956), pp. 23, 32.

DARL BUNDREN'S "CUBISTIC" VISION

Watson Branch

On ne peut pas porter partout *avec soi le cadavre de son père.*--Guillaume Apollinaire

Darl Bundren's experience "in France at the war"[1] had a major role in determining both the substance and the mode of his vision of reality. Though Darl's French experience is never described in *As I Lay Dying*, it was as important to him as was the unmentioned but obviously traumatic experience of war to Nick Adams in "Big Two-Hearted River." In Nick's case his total effort is directed towards reordering his life to regain control of himself so he can operate with grace under whatever pressures may arise in the future. This effort is apparent in Nick's deliberate and ritualistic behavior, and it seems successful to a high degree even though the symbolic fishing of the swamp is left for another day. The structure of Nick's thoughts and actions, embodied in the style Hemingway chose to portray them, reveals through contrast the nature of his wartime experience: reasonable order is the antidote for maddening chaos.

Darl, however, makes no obvious effort to counteract the wartime experience. In fact, what Darl saw in France has so marked his view of life and his mode of vision that Faulkner reveals it through identity: dislocation and disorientation are the reflection of maddening chaos.

Because the journey to France is never narrated, its nature can only be hypothesized, but internal evidence in *As I Lay Dying* points emphatically toward two basic aspects. First, the war showed Darl absurd and wasteful death (and, by extension, absurd and wasteful life) on a scale unimaginable to him had he remained at home in Yoknapatawpha County. Second, the exposure to contemporary movements in the plastic arts--especially Cubism, which had been prevalent in Paris for a decade before American soldiers got there--provided Darl with a mode for conceiving reality commensurate to the disorientation he felt.

The most fundamental cause of Darl's present anguish, as has been so often noted,[2] is located in his relationship with his mother, Addie Bundren. The rejection Darl felt as an unwanted and unloved child has left him without a sense of identity. In the night he ponders his own "is-ness," and in the day he reacts to the living members of his family, especially his brother Jewel, on the basis of feelings centered around Addie's relationship to each of them. But the war, too, had a most important effect on Darl, especially on his sanity. Faulkner once said that "Darl was mad from the first,"[3] but this was in response to a specific question regarding the possibility that Darl became mad in the course of the book. Darl is mad in the opening section, though he is certainly more in control of himself than he will be in the closing sections. But he is not mad in the flashback scene (pp. 121-29) in which he describes Jewel's working to buy his horse, a section that predates the wartime trip to France.[4]

As Ronald Sutherland points out, the change in Darl's personality from this flashback to the present action of the story has two main causes. First is the discovery at the end of that section of the special relationship between Jewel and Addie. This explains Darl's fascination with Jewel and his preoccupation with family ties. The second cause is Darl's journey away from "his native soil":

> Darl has been overseas during the World War, which
> undoubtedly played havoc with his sensitive nature,
> broadening his awareness and deepening his sensi-
> bilities, creating a problem of readjustment to
> the temporarily forgotten crudeness of home life--
> a grotesque kind of crudeness which the atmosphere
> of the novel vividly impresses upon the reader. It
> is significant that Faulkner had Darl avoid men-
> tion of the war until the last, when, on the train
> to Jackson, he is rapidly losing his grips on sanity
> and is speaking of himself in the third person....[5]

The traumatic experience of war puts Darl in the company of other characters Faulkner created during this early period of his writing, characters such as Bayard Sartoris III, Donald Mahon, and Elmer Hodge.[6] They return home from war unfit to cope with life as they find it, and they escape it one way or another.

Images of the horror and confusion that could have twisted the consciousness of young American soldiers like Darl are contained in the first two paragraphs of Faulkner's recently published essay "Literature and War": the "sqush and suck" of the duck-boards in the mud, the "casual dead rotting beneath dissolving Flemish skies," the "dreadful

smell of war---- a combination of uneaten and evacuated
food and slept-in mud and soiled and sweaty clothing,"
in that ambiguous land where hillsides dissolve in the rain
"until the very particles of earth rise floating to the top
of the atmosphere," and where "air and earth are a single
medium in which one tries vainly to stand."[7] Michael Millgate
suggests that the essay, though undated, "is certainly to be
associated with the thinking about the First World War which
produced such poems as 'November 11' ... and which led eventually to *Soldiers' Pay*." And he later remarks "the extra-
ordinary persistence with which the First World War pervades
Faulkner's work both as subject-matter and as theme--as a
point of reference, a gauge of morale, a phenomenon at once
physical and psychical *with which his characters must come
to terms*."[8] In his listing of Faulkner's works in which the
First World War plays a major or minor role, Millgate does
not specifically include *As I Lay Dying*, but the change in
Darl's character from his prewar portrait to the disoriented
individual seen in the balance of the book is strong evidence
that once again Faulkner is representing the ravages of war
upon the mind of a sensitive young man.

Of equal importance for Darl's character is the hypothetical exposure in France to European art, especially to
Cubism and related movements like Vorticism and Futurism.
Faulkner makes no specific mention of Darl's ever having seen
art works in France, but the internal circumstantial evidence
points in that direction even more strongly than it does regarding the war. Such an exposure would provide Darl with a
realistic source for certain imagery--imagery that is the
major qualitative feature that sets his language apart from
that of the other characters. Allusions to Greek friezes and
Cubistic bugs, to carved tableaux and painted canvases, seem
highly inappropriate for a country boy and have led even so
astute a critic as Olga Vickery to say, "The images are not
derived from Darl's experience but rather snatched from some
region beyond his knowledge and comprehension."[9]

Except for these and similar images drawn from the world
of art, Darl's language differs from that of the other characters only in the quantity of figuration and abstraction,
stylistic modes which pervade the book. The minds of many of
the characters tend toward abstraction, and Darl is not unique
in his use of figurative language--he simply uses it more
often and draws his images from a wider set of experiences,
including particularly his trip to France. The quantity of
metaphorical expression assigned each character depends, obviously, on the space or number of sections allotted him;
but more important, as an aspect of character development, the
quantity depends on the basic sensitivity of his nature and

sometimes on the level at which his consciousness is operating at the moment.[10] Faulkner gives sensitive characters like Vardaman, Dewey Dell, Addie, and Peabody figurative language as poetic as Darl's, so their sections contain highly expressive and profound images while those of Cash, Jewel, Anse, and most of the non-Bundrens usually do not.

There is no question that the language of many of these country folk is often beyond their intellectual capabilities and is therefore unrealistic. Faulkner probably intended it to be a verbal recreation of, or metaphor for, the person's vision of reality and his state of mind. Yet for all this lack of verisimilitude, the images--though not all the abstract words--are drawn from the life and experience of the particular character. Darl is no exception because his trip to France could well have provided him with the experience of those art objects which he uses as images to embody his vision of life in Yoknapatawpha County.

The exposure to art in France also gave Darl a new *way* of seeing reality: he has the eye of a plastic artist, particularly that of a Cubist. And this aspect of Darl's characterization, like some of his images, was probably a product of Faulkner's own trip to France after the war.

In mid-August 1925, Faulkner arrived in Paris, "that merry childish sophisticated cold-blooded dying city to which Cezanne was dragged by his friends like a reluctant cow, where Degas and Manet fought obscure points of color and line and love, cursing Bougereau [*sic*] and his curved pink female flesh, where Matisse and Picasso yet painted."[11] He stayed first at a hotel in Montparnasse but soon moved to his more permanent quarters at 26 Rue Servandoni, near the Luxembourg Gardens, where he could watch toy boats being sailed on the pond, and the Luxembourg Galleries, where he could see Post-Impressionist and other modern painting. As Joseph Blotner noted, "There were also many small galleries in the Quarter, some of them showing the work of artists rejected by the Salon. There was a wide range of exhibitions to see, from the cubist paintings of someone like André Lhote to the strong nudes of Jules Pascin."[12] Letters home from Paris indicate that he had plenty of time to look at paintings, for, Faulkner wrote, "When it rains-- as it has for a week almost,--I go to picture galleries." One day he told of going to "a very very modernist exhibition" of "futurists and vorticists," and in September he managed to see the works of Matisse and Picasso in two private collec- tions, as well as, in his words, "numberless young and struggling moderns."[13]

It is highly probable that Faulkner was aware of movements such as Dada and Surrealism, whose techniques in great measure grew out of Cubism. Though Dada, which had been born in Zurich

in 1916, had pretty much run its course by the twenties, many
of its elements and its members had been absorbed by the
Surrealist movement. In fact, André Breton had published his
first *Manifeste du surréalisme* in Paris the year before
Faulkner arrived, and during Faulkner's stay there in 1925
two extremely important events in the history of Surrealist
painting took place: the first one-man show of Paul Klee in
Paris, from October 21 to November 14 at the Galerie Vavin-
Raspail, and the first group show for Surrealist painters,
the *Exposition, La Peinture Surréaliste*, from November 14 to
25 at the Galerie Pierre.[14] The show included works by Jean
(Hans) Arp, Max Ernst, André Masson, Joan Miró, Man Ray, and
Pierre Roy, as well as Klee, Giorgio di Chirico, and Picasso,
though the last three were not considered part of the movement per se: di Chirico's exhibited paintings were from the
prewar period and Picasso's were definitely Cubist. Faulkner
did not mention going to this show, but it would be somewhat
surprising if he missed so important an exhibition. His
photographer friend, William C. Odiorne, who did a series of
portraits of Faulkner in November, probably would have been
aware of a show that displayed Man Ray's works.

The fame of Dada and Surrealism was widespread thanks to
the groups' penchant for contrived public demonstrations,
disruptions, and soirées, their wild and well-attended
"manifestations," and—because they were guided by writers
rather than painters—their publications, especially *Littérature*
and *La Revolution Surréaliste*. The latter proclaimed in 1925
that Le Bureau Central de Recherches Surréalistes would be open
every evening from 4:30 to 6:30 at 15 Rue de Grenelle—just a
few blocks from Faulkner's room in the Rue Servandoni.

Because Faulkner was himself a graphic artist, he must
have been strongly affected by the new things being done by
these "moderns." The rejection of the curvilinear and decora-
tive style of Art Nouveau by the Cubists and their followers
probably shocked an artist whose drawings, such as those in
the University of Mississippi yearbook a few years before, so
resembled that earlier style. And Faulkner acknowledged his
admiration for the progenitor of Cubism when he wrote to his
mother on September 21, "And Cezanne! That man dipped his
brush in light like Tobe Caruthers would dip his in red lead
to paint a lamp-post."[15] In his speculations on the influence
of Cézanne and of Impressionists and Post-Impressionists in
general on Faulkner's writing, Richard P. Adams cites a 1958
University of Virginia interview during which Kraig Klosson
asked Faulkner

> to comment on the theory of a critic "who is of the
> opinion that on your first trip to France you became

familiar with the works of several of the French
impressionists, and especially Cézanne, and who
has found a similarity in your use of color in your
books and Cézanne's use of color in his paintings."
Faulkner said, "I think that criticism probably has
a great deal of merit in it. As I was saying before,
a writer remembers everything he ever reads or ever
sees and then when he needs it, he draws upon his
memory and uses it." Mr. Klosson pressed for a more
definite statement: "Then, Sir, when you were in Paris
you did go to the art galleries and did see and
remember the paintings of Cézanne?" Faulkner said,
"Yes, that's right."[16]

But Cézanne's use of color was not of paramount importance,
as Adams recognizes when he determines the Impressionist and
Post-Impressionist influence on Faulkner to be "also a matter
of how the artists go about building the structures of the
works." He sees Cézanne's method as having been one of "laying
on patches of color" and filling his canvas "until the forms
emerged," a method demanding that the viewer "enter into the
process of constructing the picture along with the painter,
to recapitulate and bring to life the painter's experience
of the scene." The manner of composition, Adams asserts--
though he does not attempt to prove it here--is similar to
Faulkner's method of writing.[17]

   This technique, common to Impressionists and Post-Impressionists alike, was not the most revolutionary feature of
Cézanne's painting. The aspect that most influenced the painters in Paris in the earliest years of the twentieth century--
and which must have been available to Faulkner the graphic
artist, who, as Adams says, "always looked at things with a
painter's eye"[18]--was Cézanne's ability to conceive and to
form, out of temporary and fragmentary visual sensations, a
permanent and unified plastic structure. The emphasis then
is not on the object represented nor, as with the Impressionists,
on the act of perceiving the object. Instead it is on the
form created on the surface of the painting itself. As Albert
Gleizes and Jean Metzinger, themselves Cubist painters, wrote
in 1913 of Cézanne, "His work, a homogeneous mass, shifts
under the glance, contracts, expands, fades or illuminates
itself, irrefragably proving that painting is not--or is no
longer--the art of imitating an object by means of lines and
colors, but the art of giving our instinct a plastic consciousness."[19] They contrasted the "superficial realism" of the
Impressionists to this "profound realism" of Cézanne, which
plunges "into the profoundest reality, growing luminous as
it forces the unknowable to retreat."[20]

There has been a tendency, as John K. Simon observes, to
invoke "Pictorial comparison" when dealing with Faulkner's
work,[21] but in the case of Darl, Faulkner has created a
character whose particularly painterly vision appears marked
by the Cubist imagination with its large and admitted debt
to Cézanne. Specific Cubist images appear in *Mosquitoes*,[22]
the novel Faulkner began while in Paris and then put aside
in favor of "Elmer" only to complete it upon his return to
the United States. While it seems appropriate for the New
Orleans artists of *Mosquitoes* to see things in painterly
terms, it is unusual for a country boy from Yoknapatawpha
County to envision reality as a Cubist artist might, but
that is exactly what Darl is presented as doing.[23]

Several critics have called Darl an artist or poet,
and one of his passages has been compared to Post-Impressionist
painting.[24] Darl's vision of reality, as portrayed in his
own words, has much in common with that of the Cubists and
Post-Cubists, as manifested in their paintings--paintings
seen by Faulkner in Paris in 1925. Darl often exhibits
specific Cubist techniques in the verbal constructs by which
he expresses his view of the world: geometric patterns of
juxtaposed forms, multiple points of view, collages, emphasis
on two-dimensional surface rather than three-dimensional depth,
and dislocation and disorientation of forms in space.

The vision and the technique are certainly Cubist in
Darl's picture of Gillespie's barn bursting into flames:

> The front, the conical façade with the square
> orifice of doorway broken only by the square
> squat shape of the coffin on the sawhorses like
> a cubistic bug, comes into relief. (pp. 208-09)

Not only does Darl make an explicit verbal allusion to Cubism,
he also creates a Cubist painting by reducing the three-
dimensional barn to geometric shapes--conical and square--
flattened to the two-dimensional surface of the façade with
the coffin and sawhorses brought up to the plane of the empty
doorway.[25] Much the same effect is created by the way Darl
presents the opening scene in the first two paragraphs of
the book:

> Jewel and I come up from the field, following the
> path in single file. Although I am fifteen feet
> ahead of him, anyone watching us from the cotton-
> house can see Jewel's frayed and broken straw hat
> a full head above my own.
>   The path runs straight as a plumb-line, worn
> smooth by feet and baked brick-hard by July, between
> the green rows of laid-by cotton, to the cotton-
> house in the center of the field, where it turns

> and circles the cottonhouse at four soft right
> angles and goes on across the field again, worn
> so by feet in fading precision.   (p. 3)

Critics have already noted the geometric precision of this
description,[26] and while surface geometry is one obvious
quality of Cubist painting, other elements of Darl's vision
here may be compared to the very clear and direct Synthetic
Cubist still lifes Picasso, Braque, and Gris were doing in
the teens and early twenties. The green rows of cotton are
divided by the earth-colored path, and the square brown
cottonhouse is centered in the field where it is circled
by the path's right angles to create a geometric pattern
of juxtaposed masses of color.

Another element of Darl's Cubistic vision in this scene
is his development of a multiple point of view. First he
opposes his own position to that of "anyone watching" from
the cottonhouse who would see the brothers coming up the
path with Darl superimposed on Jewel. Then he presents the
scene from both a horizontal perspective parallel to the
earth's surface and a vertical one perpendicular to it, allowing the reader to see the path and the cottonhouse *simultaneously* from ground level where the rough logs and opposing
windows show and from above where the right angles of the
path and the centrality of the cottonhouse become apparent.
And in the paragraph immediately following the two quoted
here, Darl's clairvoyance permits him yet another point of
view as he "sees" Jewel's "wooden face"[27] (p. 4) inside
the cottonhouse though there is no window in the side for
him to see through.

Multiple point of view is apparent in Cubism from its
earliest, Analytical period for the purpose of representing
"profound" reality, reality as it is conceived by the mind,
the senses operating in conjunction with the memory and
imagination, rather than as it is perceived by the eye,
from one fixed viewpoint at one instant in time. Gleizes and
Metzinger described the method as "moving around an object
to seize several successive appearances, which, fused in a
single image, reconstitute it in time." The theoretical
basis for this technique was grounded in the belief, probably
derived from Bergson, that

> There is nothing real outside ourselves; there is
> nothing real except the coincidence of a sensation
> and an individual mental tendency. Be it far from
> us to throw any doubt upon the existence of the
> objects which impress our senses; but, rationally
> speaking, we can only experience certitude in
> respect of the images which they produce in the
> mind.[28]

Darl unites his multiple points of view, which combine sight, memory, and imagination,[29] to conceive the scene before him. Instead of imitating the "superficial" reality through detailed photographic description, he creates the "profound" reality by defining the spatial relationships among the forms conceived, embodying that reality in arrangements of simple and generic words that refer to the simple though particular forms that he sees.[30]

One of the most obvious techniques of Synthetic Cubist paintings was collage, the process of pasting paper and other materials onto the picture surface, and Darl often describes objects as if they were composed in this manner. In one of his clairvoyant visions, Darl sees Vardaman's face at the moment of his mother's death "fading into the dusk like a piece of paper pasted on a failing wall" (p. 48), and later he describes Jewel's eyes as looking "like spots of white paper pasted on a high small football" (p. 203). Dadaist and Surrealist artists assumed the collage technique as part of their anti-art campaign. Their purpose was to discredit paintings by including found, real-life objects and materials incompatible with aesthetic beauty, and the parodic effects they achieved were not unlike those created by Darl when he describes Tull's mouth as "bluish, like a circle of weathered rubber" (p. 152), or Mack Gillespie in the middle of the barn fire with "his eyes and mouth three round holes in his face on which the freckles look like English peas on a plate" (p. 210), or the eyes of Jewel's horse as they "*roll in the dusk like marbles on a gaudy velvet cloth*" (p. 174).

When Darl prepares the cement to fix Cash's leg, he presents the action in terms of an artist creating a mixed-media work. First he mixes the cement in the can, "stirring the slow water into the pale green thick coils" (p. 197), to which he adds some sand and then applies it to Cash's leg from which "the sawdust is running out" (p. 197) as if Cash were a broken doll. The addition of the wooden splints and the cords, with the cement moving along them in "thick pale green slow surges" (p. 198), creates a work more Dadaist than Cubist: the cast becomes an ironic and negative parody of a true cast, similar to the way in which the collage and constructionist techniques of the earlier movement were used by Dada to make absurd and nihilistic statements against art itself.[31]

Darl's vision is specifically painterly rather than sculptural or constructional in one of his earlier, clairvoyant sections: "Upon the dark ground the chips look like random smears of soft pale paint on a black canvas. The boards look like long smooth tatters torn from the flat darkness and turned backside out" (p. 71). Here Darl displays

the Cubist technique--taken from the Impressionists and Post-
Impressionists--of applying paint to canvas in smears that
seen close up are no more than patches of paint but when
viewed from what the earlier generation of painters would
regard as the proper distance give the illusion of the object
represented. The Cubists, rather than treating the surface
of the painting as a window through which to see imitated
reality, kept the emphasis on the brushstrokes of paint as
one more means of focusing the viewer's attention on the
surface itself.

Darl has taken this Cubist step forward from Impressionism
by concentrating on the smears of paint and by lifting up the
horizontal dark ground spread before his clairvoyant eyes
until it becomes the vertical black canvas of the picture plane.
In keeping with the Cubist emphasis on the picture surface,
Darl turns the black canvas into the ultimate reality of
the scene: the boards, which in the three-dimensional yet
"superficial" reality of his clairvoyant sight lie on the
dark ground, are conceived by Darl as tatters torn from the
surface of the canvas itself--the canvas that has become the
two-dimensional but "profound" reality of his vision--and
turned backside out so that the strips of white, unpainted
canvas contrast with the black surface.[32]

This emphasis on surface is related to Darl's and the
Cubists' de-emphasis of the importance of the object viewed
in favor of its conceived, "profound" reality. The aesthetic
principle here grows out of a common vision of the nature of
things outside the mind. A breakdown in the integrity of
objects, their dislocation and disorientation, is explicit
in Darl's description of the stream, road, and hill that he
watches as Jewel tries to repair their broken wagon. He sees
colors dissociated from the forms of which they ought to be
accidental concomitants: *"about Jewel's ankles a runnel of
yellow neither water nor earth swirls, curving with the yellow
road neither of earth nor water, down the hill dissolving into
a streaming mass of dark green neither of earth nor sky"*
(p. 48). The similarity of this passage to Faulkner's
description of Henri Barbusse's writing about the war, cited
above, makes clear the underlying emotion that creates such
a vision, but certainly the terms of its presentation here are
more painterly. Darl depicts, with a muted palette of yellow
and green, the disintegrating forms as they fade and blend
into each other, no longer holding their individual shapes
and colors. The same effect of ambiguity, though visually more
prismatic and fragmented, is achieved by Picasso, Braque,
and even Gris in their work between 1910 and 1912, leading
the art critic Jacques Rivière in March of the latter year
to condemn the "inexplicable continuum"[33] of Cubism that con-

fused and welded together objects and the space that separated
them.

Later Darl, mesmerized by the flowing surface of the
river[34] which seems to him "peaceful, like machinery does
after you have watched it and listened to it for a long
time," senses his own disintegration, as though "the clotting
which is you had dissolved into the myriad original motion"
(p. 156). The metaphorical association of river and
machinery and its connection with the dissolution of the
human person, and of rivers and machinery, into "the myriad
original motion" indicate a consciousness on Darl's part of
the reduction of the whole universe to a basic principle of
dynamic energy. This principle, for which Bergson was usually
given credit, was commonly held by painters and sculptors of
diverse movements during the teens and twenties, though most,
whether Cubist or not, depended on the technical innovations
of Cubism for the expression of it. The fascination with what
the Futurists in their 1910 "Technical Manifesto" called
"universal dynamism"[35] led to the depiction of innumerable
and varied metamorphoses as the integral distinctions among
objects--animate and inanimate--broke down under the weight
of the discovery of their essential nature of motion or flux.[36]

Many twentieth-century artists--and Darl is like them in
this respect--attempted to encompass in a single static image
or work of art all the energy and flux of an object in its
spatial environment. He often tries to contain in a single
verbal construct the "dynamic immobility" (p. 72) he envisions
in the world. Faulkner himself spoke of the aim of every
artist "to arrest motion, which is life, by artificial means
and hold it fixed so that 100 years later when a stranger
looks at it, it moves again since it is life."[37]

The concepts of motion and time and particularly their
relationship to artistic creation are among many Faulkner
shared with the painters and writers of the teens and twenties.
In *As I Lay Dying*, Darl's mode of vision and Faulkner's mode
of composition reflect these and other shared ideas: dislocation, disorientation, fragmentation, juxtaposition, simultaneity, ambiguity, conception rather than perception. Alfred
Kazin said that Faulkner represents,

> like the surrealists, like the anxious and moving
> search for spiritual integrity in so much of con-
> temporary poetry, the loneliness of the individual
> sensibility in a period of unparalleled dissolution
> and insecurity; and ... even more vividly a reac-
> tion against a literature of surface realism that
> merely records the facts of that dissolution.[38]

Ultimately, the ideas Faulkner shares with Cubist and Post-Cubist painters are more important than the specific influences of those artists' works that he saw while in Paris in 1925 or saw or heard about earlier in New Orleans or New York City. Faulkner obviously never approached the literary Cubism of Gertrude Stein in some of her portraits or in *Tender Buttons* or of Guillaume Apollinaire in poems like "Zone."[39] But as Juan Gris said in an interview published in Paris a few months before Faulkner arrived there, "Cubism is not a manner but an aesthetic, and even a state of mind; it is therefore inevitably connected with every manifestation of contemporary thought."[40]

Darl Bundren, though not even a would-be artist like Elmer Hodge to whom he bears a "family" and experiential resemblance, often sees with the eye of and conceives with the mind of a Cubist or Post-Cubist painter, indicating something more specific in his characterization than a general expression of "contemporary thought." Faulkner, when he wrote *As I Lay Dying*, was remembering and using the contemporary art he saw in Paris in 1925 in the same manner as he was using Cézanne's paintings. He created a character whose vision reflects directly, by specific allusions, and indirectly, by a mode of conceiving reality that tends toward the creation of painterly images, the influence of Cubist art.

NOTES

1. William Faulkner, *As I Lay Dying* (New York: Random House, 1964), p. 244. All subsequent citations from *As I Lay Dying* refer to this corrected edition and are included within parentheses in the text.

2. For readings of the relationship of Darl and Addie, see Calvin Bedient, "Pride and Nakedness: *As I Lay Dying*," in this volume, pp. 95-110; André Bleikasten, *Faulkner's "As I Lay Dying*," trans. Roger Little (Bloomington: Indiana Univ. Press, 1973), pp. 87-91; Cleanth Brooks, *William Faulkner: The Yoknapatawpha Country* (New Haven: Yale Univ. Press, 1963), pp. 145, 158; Charlotte Goodman, "The Bundren Wagon: Narrative Strategy in Faulkner's *As I Lay Dying*," *Studies in American Fiction*, 7 (Autumn, 1979), 237-38, 240-41; William J. Handy, "*As I Lay Dying*: Faulkner's Inner Reporter," *Kenyon Review*, 21 (Summer 1959), 447-51; Robert Hemenway, "Enigmas of Being in *As I Lay Dying*," *Modern Fiction Studies*,

16 (Summer 1970), 137-38, 140-42; Michael Millgate, *The Achieve-
ment of William Faulkner* (New York: Random House, 1966), pp.
104-07; John K. Simon, "What Are You Laughing At, Darl?:
Madness and Humor in *As I Lay Dying*," *College English*, 25
(November 1963), 105-06, and "The Scene and the Imagery of
Metamorphosis in 'As I Lay Dying,'" *Criticism*, 7 (Winter
1965), 18; Ronald Sutherland, "*As I Lay Dying*: A Faulkner
Microcosm," *Queen's Quarterly*, 73 (Winter 1966), 543, 546-
47; Olga W. Vickery, *The Novels of William Faulkner* (Baton
Rouge: Louisiana State Univ. Press, 1964), pp. 53, 54, 58-60;
and Edmond Volpe, *A Reader's Guide to William Faulkner* (New
York: Farrar, Straus & Giroux, 1964), pp. 133-34, 137-38.

3. *Faulkner in the University*, ed. Frederick L. Gwynn
and Joseph L. Blotner (New York: Vintage Books, 1965), p.
110. Though Addie gives both Dewey Dell and Vardaman as well
as Darl to Anse so that "he has three children that are his
and not mine" (p. 168), the two younger ones do not lose
their sanity as their brother does. For an examination of the
sources of Darl's madness, see Simon, "What Are You Laughing
At."

4. The time of the action is not stated in the book, but
internal evidence points to 1919 or 1920 as an approximate
date. This was the time of the action in *Soldiers' Pay* and
Flags in the Dust, which also have to do with men returning from
World War I. Dewey Dell says she is seventeen (p. 190). It is
probable that Addie "gave Anse Dewey Dell to negative Jewel"
(p. 168) fairly soon after Jewel was born. Cash says he and
Darl were "born close together," but it was "nigh ten years
before Jewel and Dewey Dell and Vardaman begun to come along"
(p. 224). That would mean Jewel is about 18, Cash 27, and
Darl 25 or 26. Vardaman, from his behavior, seems to be 11
or 12. If the time of the present action is 1919 or 1920,
Darl's flashback section (pp. 121-29) takes place in 1916
or 1917, when Jewel "was fifteen" (p. 121). If the present
action is much later than 1920, Darl and Cash would have to
be older than they logically seem to be, and the span of
years between Cash and Jewel greater than Cash says.

5. Sutherland, pp. 543-44.

6. Bleikasten (p. 90) also mentions Quentin Compson and
Horace Benbow as examples of "those wounded heroes (literally
or figuratively) who appear so often in Faulkner's early
novels."

7. The essay is published in full and discussed by
Michael Millgate in "Faulkner on the Literature of the First
World War," *Mississippi Quarterly*, 26 (Summer 1973), 387-93.

Faulkner is discussing here the writings of Siegfried Sassoon and Henri Barbusse.

8. Millgate, "Faulkner," pp. 387, 391; emphasis added.

9. *"As I Lay Dying," William Faulkner: Two Decades of Criticism*, ed. Frederick J. Hoffman and Olga W. Vickery (East Lansing: Michigan State College Press, 1951), p. 197. Also, see Vickery's *The Novels of William Faulkner*, pp. 50-51. For examples of other attempts to deal with the "inappropriateness" of Darl's language, see Bleikasten, p. 41; Warren Beck, "William Faulkner's Style," *William Faulkner: Three Decades of Criticism*, ed. Frederick J. Hoffman and Olga W. Vickery (1960; rpt. New York: Harcourt, Brace & World, 1963), p. 149; Brooks, pp. 146, 160; Richard Chase, *The American Novel and Its Tradition* (Garden City, N.Y.: Doubleday, 1957), p. 207; Joseph M. Garrison, Jr., "Perception, Language, and Reality in *As I Lay Dying*," in this volume, pp. 49-62; Irving Howe, *William Faulkner: A Critical Study* (New York: Random House, 1952), pp. 137-38; Joseph W. Reed, Jr., *Faulkner's Narrative* (New Haven: Yale Univ. Press, 1973), p. 98; and Sutherland, pp. 542-46. Some parts of Stephen M. Ross's theoretical essay, "'Voice' in Narrative Texts: The Example of *As I Lay Dying*," *PMLA*, 94 (March, 1979), 300-310, treat the problem of "appropriate" language. (See especially p. 303.) Coincidentally, Ross closes his essay by comparing the effect mimetic and textual "voices" create in *As I Lay Dying* with the effect Cubistic modes create in painting.

10. For comments on style as an indication of levels of consciousness, see Vickery, *The Novels*, p. 51, and Volpe, p. 128. A thorough analysis of language and style in *As I Lay Dying* can be found in Bleikasten, pp. 21-43.

11. William Faulkner, "Elmer," ed. Dianne L. Cox, *Mississippi Quarterly*, 36 (Summer 1983), 432. Joseph Blotner reads "Monet" for "Manet" and "life" for "line" when he quotes the same passage in *Faulkner: A Biography* (New York: Random House, 1974), I, 460.

12. Blotner, p. 453. The documented facts regarding Faulkner's activities in Paris are taken from chapters 25 and 26 of Blotner's biography.

13. *Selected Letters of William Faulkner*, ed. Joseph Blotner (New York: Random House, 1977), pp. 14; 13; 24.

14. Information about these shows may be found in the "Chronology" prepared by Irene Gordon and published in

William S. Rubin, *Dada, Surrealism, and Their Heritage* (New York: Museum of Modern Art, 1968), p. 205.

15. *Selected Letters*, p. 24. This phrase echoes one Faulkner wrote the preceding April in a sketch for the New Orleans *Times-Picayune*, in which he remarked to the painter William Spratling, with whom he was to make his trip to Europe in a few months, "how no one since Cezanne had really dipped his brush in light" (*New Orleans Sketches*, ed. Carvel Collins, rev. ed [New York: Random House, 1958], p. 46). Faulkner's interest in Cézanne may have developed through Sherwood Anderson, as Thomas L. McHaney speculates, or possibly through reading Clive Bell and Elie Faure, whose books he has Elmer Hodge take on his cruise to Europe ("The Elmer Papers: Faulkner's Comic Portraits of the Artist," *Mississippi Quarterly*, 26 (Summer 1973), pp. 301–2). Bell, in his 1913 *Art* (New York: Frederick A. Stokes, n.d.), says that "Cézanne inspires the contemporary movement" (p. 199). His collection of reprinted essays, *Since Cézanne* (New York: Harcourt, Brace, 1922) discusses the Cubists in some detail and devotes one whole essay to "Matisse and Picasso." The fourth volume of Faure's *History of Art*, trans. Walter Pach (New York: Harper, 1924) is devoted to "Modern Art." He gives Cézanne considerable space in the chapter on "The Contemporary Genesis" and also discusses Picasso and mentions a number of other Cubists. Faulkner probably knew something of contemporary movements of painting before his trip to Paris. He may have gotten firsthand reports of the famous 1913 Armory Show, and his stay in Greenwich Village in the autumn of 1921 certainly exposed him to avant-garde art (see Blotner, p. 319). Marcel Duchamp was in New York City at that time, and both Francis Picabia and Man Ray had lived and worked there, the latter moving to Paris in July 1921. Faulkner said in another *Times-Picayune* piece (8 February 1925) that "planes of light and shadow were despair for the Vorticist schools" (*New Orleans Sketches*, p. 16).

16. Richard P. Adams, "The Apprenticeship of William Faulkner," *Tulane Studies in English*, 12 (1962), 128.

17. Adams, pp. 128–29. McHaney (pp. 295, 299, 301–04) discusses the influence of Post-Impressionist art on Faulkner in much the same terms Adams uses, but with detailed attention to "Elmer." In regard to Faulkner's other early novels, McHaney notes a pattern of structure composed of "equal parts juxtaposed" to make up "a whole which constitutes a post-Impressionistic novel of the generation after the war" (p. 304). And in particular the fifty-nine sections of *As I Lay Dying* create an "almost pointillist" composition (p. 304).

18. Adams, p. 127.

19. Originally published in *Du Cubisme* (Paris: Figuière, 1912), this translation is from *Cubism* (London: Unwin, 1913) as reprinted in Herschel B. Chipp, *Theories of Modern Art: A Source Book by Artists and Critics* (Berkeley: Univ. of California Press, 1968), p. 209.

20. Chipp, pp. 208, 209.

21. Simon, "The Scene," p. 2n. For a number of pictorial comparisons regarding *As I Lay Dying*, see Bleikasten, pp. 12, 37, 69, 109, 125.

22. William Faulkner, *Mosquitoes* (1927; rpt. Garden City, N.Y.: The Sun Dial Press, 1937). An early description of Jackson Square in New Orleans pictures the cathedral "cut from black paper and pasted flat on a green sky" (p. 14), and later the sculptor, Gordon, sees the warehouse and dock as "a formal rectangle without perspective," and the masts of a freighter as flat "as cardboard, and projecting at a faint motionless angle" above the warehouse (p. 47).

23. A clue to Darl's painterly vision may be found in the similarities between him and Elmer Hodge, the aspiring painter who is the main character in Faulkner's unfinished novel. In "Elmer," the protagonist's past is disclosed in flashbacks to "reveal that experience has *gradually* shaped the young American into a would-be artist" (McHaney, p. 301), and his youth has much in common with that of Darl, whom André Bleikasten (p. 90) calls "Faulkner's portrait of the artist as a young madman." As Blotner (p. *68*, n. 455.26) notes, "Elmer's family suggests the Bundrens"—both families are poor and live in the South; Elmer's shiftless father is much like Anse; his sister's name, Jo-Addie, "suggests that of Addie Bundren," (McHaney, p. 284n); and her peculiar relationship with Elmer resembles that between Dewey Dell and Darl, particularly as shown in the scenes deleted from *As I Lay Dying* where "mutual empathy" (Blotner, p. 637) is expressed between the two Bundren children. Also the two mothers die in the course of the novels, Elmer's before and Darl's after the army experience they have in common. And both men come from that experience unfit for the old way of life.

24. Bedient, p. 95. Also see Bleikasten, p. 90; Blotner, p. 635; Brooks, pp. 145-46; Handy, p. 445; Donald M. Kartiganer, *The Fragile Thread: The Meaning of Form in Faulkner's Novels* (Amherst: Univ. of Massachusetts Press, 1979), pp. 30-32; Reed, p. 90; and Simon, "What Are You Laughing At," p. 108.

25. Juan Gris said in a lecture printed in the *Transatlantic Review* the year before Faulkner came to Paris, "the only true pictorial technique is a sort of flat, coloured architecture"; reprinted in Daniel-Henry Kahnweiler, *Juan Gris: His Life and Work*, trans. Douglas Cooper (New York: Harry N. Abrams, [1969]), p. 197.

26. Millgate, p. 104; Simon, "What Are You Laughing At," p. 106, and "The Scene," p. 6.

27. Darl's often repeated description of Jewel's wooden features suggests the carved wooden masks from Africa that Picasso and other Cubists so admired when the movement was beginning in 1906-1908, and it suggests the masklike faces on the portraits the Cubists did under the influence of those African carvings.

28. Chipp, pp. 216, 214.

29. Darl's clairvoyance--and his telepathy--can be equated to poetic imagination. See Faulkner's remarks on Darl's madness and poetic vision in *Faulkner in the University*, p. 113.

30. The geometric pattern of juxtaposed masses and the multiple views of forms that Darl composes into his opening vision resemble in technique the angular Synthetic Cubist paintings Faulkner might well have seen in Paris in 1925, ranging from the simplicity of Gris's "Grapes" (1921, Kunstmuseum, Basel) to the ambiguity of Picasso's "Still Life in a Landscape" (1915, private collection of H. Berggruen, Paris), in which the ambiguity arises as much from the arrangement of the forms on the canvas as from the representation of the forms themselves, some of which are quite clear in their reference to objects. The essence of Darl's verbal picture is like the essence of painting as Gris stated it in 1924: "painting is the expression of certain relationships between the painter and the outside world, and ... a picture is the intimate association of these relationships with the limited surface which contains them" (Kahnweiler, p. 201).

31. The Dada-Surrealist artist Max Ernst sometimes constructed collages by fixing wooden slats and twine dipped in paint to the surface of his canvases, and he combined pieces of painted wood and metal within a frame to represent "Fruits of a Long Experience" (1919, Penrose Collection, London). The Cubists also worked with these mixtures of material to achieve constructions that could be called, as Alexander Archipenko did, "Sculpto-painting," like his "Médrano" (1915, Tate Gallery, London), made of painted tin, glass, wood, and oilcloth, or Picasso's "Still Life" (1914, Guggenheim Museum, New York), which combines painted wood, cut to represent objects, with upholstery fringe.

32. In the scene of the finishing of the coffin, Darl's imagination brings the background towards him, cutting it off with a plane close behind his subject as the Cubists did with their pictures from the very beginning, following Cézanne's example. The air behind Cash and Anse is for Darl an "impalpable plane" upon which "their shadows form as upon a wall"

(p. 72). In another scene, Darl's sense of inviolable surface
makes it seem to him that the river has severed the bodies
of Jewel and Tull who wade in it because "they do not appear
to violate the surface at all" (p. 156). He uses the word
three times in one sentence to describe the flooding river:
"the yellow *surface* dimpled monstrously into fading swirls
travelling along the *surface* for an instant, silent, imperma-
nent and profoundly significant, as though just beneath the
surface something huge and alive waked for a moment of lazy
alertness out of and into light slumber again" (p. 134;
emphasis added).

33. First published in *Revue d'Europe et d'Amérique*
and quoted in Nicholas Wadley, *Cubism* (London: Hamlyn, 1970),
p. 54. The late works of Analytical Cubism, such as Picasso's
"Portrait of Daniel-Henry Kahnweiler" (1910, Art Institute
of Chicago) or "Ma Jolie" (1911-12, Museum of Modern Art,
New York), Braque's "Man with a Guitar" (1911, Museum of Modern
Art, New York) or "Le Portugais" (1911, Kunstmuseum, Basel), and
Gris's "Portrait of Picasso" (1912, Art Institute of Chicago),
portray the same dissolution of forms and the muting of colors,
the merging of objects which spread and invade the space
around them and simultaneously dissolve into the background
until objects, space, and background become undifferentiated,
reduced to the plane of the picture surface.

34. Darl's imagination turns the river's "thick soiled
gouts of foam" (p. 134) into lathering sweat of a driven horse,
and a surging, foam-draped log becomes Christ (p. 141): objects
grow ambiguous, move, and are transformed into strange new
beings. His surreal vision of life suggests, in its ambiguity
regarding the appearance of things, Picasso's nonillusionist
Cubist paintings of the twenties such as "The Three Musicians"
(1921, Philadelphia Museum of Art) and his "Mandoline and
Guitar" (1924, Guggenheim Museum, New York) in which the elements of the still life seem arranged on the flat plane of
the canvas to form a death's head. The hallucinatory paintings
Surrealists drew forth from the subconscious, such as Miró's
"The Tilled Field" (1923-24, private collection of Mr. and
Mrs. Henry Clifford, Radnor, Pa.), Masson's "Woman" (1925,
private collection of Dr. and Mrs. Paul Larivière, Montreal),
or Ernst's Dove Series, the *frottage* (rubbed) pictures begun
in 1925, depict strange juxtapositions and stranger metamorphoses, imaginative constructs similar to what Darl envisions
at the river and elsewhere in the book. Bleikasten (p. 106)
equates Darl's picture of men and beasts in "identical attitudes and expressions" of "common terror" when faced by death
and disaster at the river to Picasso's "Guernica" (1937,
Museum of Modern Art, New York), painted in response to the
destruction of that Basque town in April 1937.

35. The manifesto, originally published in Milan as a pamphlet, was translated into English for the first London exhibition of Futurist painting and is reprinted in Chipp, pp. 289-93. Gleizes and Metzinger said in *Cubism* (Chipp, p. 209) that Cézanne "teaches us to overcome the universal dynamism."

36. Writing of these prewar years in *From Baudelaire to Surrealism* (New York: Wittenborn, Shultz, 1950), Marcel Raymond said,

> We seem to be confronted with two opposite currents--
> on the one hand, the poets attempt to adjust them-
> selves to positive reality, to the "mechanical"
> world of our era; on the other hand, they desire to
> shut themselves up in the enclosure of the self,
> in the world of dreams.... Moreover ... a whole
> era of contemporary facts supplies ample justifica-
> tion for the reconciliation of the real and the
> imaginary, the positive and the irrational, life
> and dreams, and in the light of these facts the
> opposition of the two attitudes just defined be-
> comes a mere abstraction. (p. 221)

Machines--those inanimate embodiments of speed and power and energy--and the relationship of machines to men and to other animate creatures were of special interest to the artists of the period, such as Fernand Léger and Raymond Duchamp-Villon. The latter's bronze "Horse" (1911, Museum of Modern Art, New York) depicts the state of transition between animal and machine, an image of metamorphosis and dynamism very like the one Darl creates when, in one of his clairvoyant scenes, he sees Cash, machinelike, at work on the coffin (pp. 72-73).

37. Interview with Jean Stein Vanden Heuvel in *Lion in the Garden: Interviews with William Faulkner, 1926-1962*, eds. James B. Meriwether and Michael Millgate (New York: Random House, 1968), p. 253.

38. Alfred Kazin, *On Native Grounds* (1942; rpt. Garden City, N.Y.: Doubleday, 1956), p. 362.

39. Raymond (p. 234) said this poem "belongs to the genre of so-called cubist, synthetic, or 'simultaneist' poems. Here, on a single plane, without perspective, without transition, and often without any apparent logical relationship, we find heterogeneous elements, sensations, judgements, memories intermingled just as in the flux of psychological life."

40. Kahnweiler, p. 202.

FATE AND MADNESS: THE DETERMINIST VISION
OF DARL BUNDREN

Charles Palliser

As I Lay Dying is a novel of remarkable technical complexity and it is therefore understandable that much of the
critical attention which it has attracted in recent years
should have been concentrated on a number of puzzling and
apparently obscure elements in the book. The major difficulties
derive from the enigmatic nature of Faulkner's conception
of the central character, Darl Bundren. It is not easy to
establish whether the author intended him to be interpreted
as being supernaturally endowed with clairvoyant powers or
not. Again, the nature of his insanity and even the question
of whether he is in fact insane, are not easy to determine.
Above all, the novel leaves to be inferred the connection,
if any, between these two attributes of Darl. Most commentators on the book have accepted, as the novel seems to require,
that Darl is actually clairvoyant. The nature of his insanity
and its connection with his alleged clairvoyance have received
little attention.[1]
    The argument of the present article is that the central
theme of the novel is the determinist nature of Darl's vision.
When this is understood then a supernatural explanation of
his insight is not required, the question of his madness
becomes clearer, and the relationship between it and his
apparent clairvoyance is explained. For the determinist outlook which, apparently, endows Darl with clairvoyant gifts
is responsible for making him insane, or appear to be so. The
ambiguity is part of Faulkner's meaning, for the arbitrari-
ness of the conventional distinction between sanity and madness is an important aspect of the novel's concern with the
inevitable subjectivity and solipsism of perception. Faulkner
brings into conflict in the book a number of different kinds
of philosophical and spiritual vision. Consequently, the
nature of Darl's perspective must be examined in the context
of the religious beliefs of his society, and the latter is
an important aspect of the novel which has been largely ignored by critics.[2] The present article will begin by stressing

the fact that Faulkner was obviously anxious to make it clear
that the religious ethos of the novel is a strain of Southern
Baptism which, in its emphasis on the inexorability of the
workings of divine providence, is specifically Calvinist.
In the stated view of the Bundrens, their friends, and their
neighbors, the lot of mankind is a continuous struggle against
sin for possession of the soul in a world in which God ordains
the existence of evil in order to test the individual's faith.
This philosophy is succinctly expressed by the Mottson druggist,
Moseley, whose help in procuring an abortion Dewey Dell tries
to enlist. Throughout the novel the inevitability of her
giving birth despite her attempts to the contrary is a reminder of the inexorability and the cruelty of fate. Moseley
reflects on the harshness of the life that a girl from such
an environment must lead, but his initial temptation to pity
her gives way to the rigorous Calvinist concept of life as
a necessarily cruel testing-ground. So, deciding that her pregnancy is a manifestation, however inexplicable to human eyes,
of divine providence, he reaches this conclusion:

> ... life wasn't made to be easy on folks: they
> wouldn't ever have any reason to be good and die.
> "Look here," I said. "You get that notion out of
> your head. The Lord gave you what you have, even
> if He did use the devil to do it; you let Him
> take it away from you if it's His will to do so."
> (p. 192)[3]

For Moseley adversity and even evil are an essential part of
God's design, and man's duty is passively to accept his lot.
However, considerations of commercial prudence combine in
this instance with the piety of the above sentiments to enjoin
passive acceptance of fate, and Moseley refuses to take the
risk of helping the girl to thwart Providence at the peril
of his soul and his business.

Numerous examples could be cited from the novel to
demonstrate that Moseley's views on Providence are characteristic of those expressed by most of the important figures
in the book--particularly Anse, Cora, and Whitfield. But it
is essential to see that Faulkner directs toward these people
an irony which makes it clear that they merely pay lip service
to the idea that the divine purpose is fulfilled through
everything that occurs, evil as well as good, in ways in-
comprehensible to human beings. On the contrary, they consistently anthropomorphize and trivialize what they pretend
to believe to be far above human concerns or understanding,
taking it upon themselves to interpret events in ways which
support their prejudices or flatter their vanity.

First there is the frequent assumption that God's purpose and the speaker's own advantage coincide. This kind of arrogance, which is particularly characteristic of Anse, is often exposed by Darl; so his description, for example, of his father's reaction to Addie's death lays bare the egotism beneath Anse's apparent piety: "'God's will be done,' he says. 'Now I can get them teeth'" (p. 51). Whitfield similarly assumes that what is to his advantage is necessarily in accordance with the designs of Providence, and he therefore attributes to God's intervention his having safely crossed the swollen ford: "It was His hand that bore me safely above the flood, that fended from me the dangers of the waters" (p. 170). Similarly he concludes that it was God's will that Addie should die without confessing to their adultery.

The same temptation to interpret the divine will is apparent in cases where the speaker's own interests are not directly concerned. Tull recounts his wife's remark that it was no mere accident that the log struck the Bundrens' wagon as it was crossing the ford: "'Log, fiddlesticks,' Cora said. 'It was the hand of God'" (p. 145). And in relation to the same incident Cash similarly assumes that God was intervening in order to destroy Addie's corpse and thereby bring the funeral journey to an end: "... it seemed to me that when Jewel worked so to get her outen the river, he was going against God in a way" (p. 223). He therefore wonders whether Darl's action in firing the barn was not to some extent justifiable. And in his single monologue even the unreflective Jewel in his imagination arrogates God's authority to himself, questioning His fitness to wield supreme power: "If it had just been me when Cash fell off of that church ... because if there is a God what the hell is He for" (p. 15). Jewel's characteristically incoherent words imply that if he were God he would not pass up opportunities to kill the other members of his family. The motive for Jewel's murderous desires is his unwillingness to share his mother, for in his fantasy about her, "It would just be me and her on a high hill and me rolling the rocks down the hill at their faces...."

On the occasions when these people do express their incomprehension of God's purpose it is not with reverence and awe but irritably or self-righteously. It is with a mixture of arrogance and irritation that Anse, implicitly drawing a parallel between himself and Job that is buttressed by his comical imitation of Biblical language, reflects: "I am the chosen of the Lord, for who He loveth, so doeth He chastiseth. But I be durn if He dont take some curious ways to show it, seems like" (p. 105). Similarly Tull, reflecting on the outrage of Vardaman's desecration of his mother's corpse while drilling holes into her coffin, thinks: "If it's

a judgment, it aint right.... Because He said Suffer little
children to come unto Me dont make it right, neither" (p. 70).
And Cora invokes God's will in order to rebuke the iniquity
of a woman who has injured her financially: "The Lord can see
into the heart. If it is His will that some folks has different
ideas of honesty from other folks, it is not my place to
question His decree" (p. 8). But her aggrieved tone shows
that she is clearly querying God's judgment and is far from
the fatalistic acceptance of the mystery of Providence that
her religious beliefs in theory require of her.

Darl is entirely free from this tendency to anthropomorphize God's will, for in marked contrast to the people
around him he never comments on or questions events, whether
human or providential. At first sight there is a contradiction between the apparent clairvoyance which seems to allow
him to forecast the future and the fact that he refrains from
interpreting or even commenting on God's designs. But this
contradiction arises from a misunderstanding, for Darl actually
has no supernatural gifts and there is a rational explanation for his supposed clairvoyance; all that he knows is the
result of guesswork based on his knowledge of the past. Since
the use of the supernatural should, by the application of
Occam's Razor, only be attributed to a writer when no other
explanation is satisfactory, in order to demonstrate that
Darl is not clairvoyant it is only necessary to show that
everything he seems to know by supernatural means could
equally be known by the exercise of ordinary powers.

The evidence of Darl's supposed clairvoyance appears to
suggest that he has access to three kinds of supernatural
means of perception: prophecy, in that he appears to be able
to foresee the future; telepathy, in that he is apparently
able to read the thoughts of other people; and "second sight,"
in that he seems to be able to describe in detail events
which are taking place simultaneously but in his absence.
In fact, Darl does not exercise these three supernatural
faculties: his percipience derives solely from the complete-
ness of his acceptance of the operation of destiny, a complete-
ness which means that his insight into the motives and actions
of his family is accurate but, in its extreme fatalism,
disabling to himself.

Throughout the novel Darl constantly predicts accurately
what is going to happen. But most of these "prophecies"
are forecasts of the behavior of other members of his family
and are simply based on his knowledge of their past behavior.
Darl is particularly sensitive where Jewel is concerned,
and so a typical example of one of his alleged prophecies
is the incident when Jewel insists, in opposition to Anse,
on bringing his horse with the funeral party. Cash and Anse

assume that he will stay behind, but Darl guesses the truth:
"'He'll catch us,' I say. 'He'll cut across and meet us at
Tull's lane'" (p. 98). And, as we learn in the following
section, this is precisely what happens. Again, after the
loss of the family's team of mules during the crossing of
the ford, Darl guesses that Anse will sell Jewel's horse to
buy another team. This is indicated typographically by the
italicization of every reference to the horse in Darl's monologue: "*When I looked back he was leading the horse into the
barn* he was already talking about getting another team, and
by supper time he had good as bought it. *He is down there in
the barn...*" (p. 174). The unitalicized clauses refer to
Anse, already preparing to sell Jewel's horse, while Darl's
thoughts pursue his brother and the animal into the barn.
Similarly, it is presumably Darl's intuitive understanding
of his mother that enables him to predict correctly to Dewey
Dell that Addie will die while he and Jewel are delivering
the load of wood (p. 27). Darl, then, foresees nothing that
is not dependent on human will or, like his forecast of the
rain-storm (p. 17) and of the moment when his mother will
die, predictable on rational or experiential grounds.

The fact that Darl's apparent ability to foretell the
future by supernatural means is really based on his knowledge
of how his family will react to predictable circumstances is
proved by those cases in which he either predicts wrongly
or completely fails to foresee something. For Darl is wrong
in precisely those instances where the unforeseen occurrence
is beyond human control or not predictable on a rational
judgment of the factors involved. For example, he says that
he and Jewel will get back from delivering the load of wood
by sunset the next day, failing to foresee the accident to
the wagon which delays them (p. 19). Similarly, he fails to
foresee that the wagon will be struck by a log while crossing
the ford. Above all, he does not foresee his own committal
to an asylum--the one act on the part of his family which
is totally unexpected. Clearly Faulkner did not intend that
Darl should be seen as gifted with supernatural prescience.

Most of the examples of Darl's supposed telepathic ability
are in relation to Dewey Dell and Jewel, and it is significant
that they are the two who most dread an imminent and unavoidable event and intensely resent Darl's pointing out to them
its inevitability. For Faulkner implies that Darl's ability
to guess the thoughts of his brother and sister derives from
his acute sense of fatalism and of the pointlessness, therefore, of their resistance to the inexorability of events. So
on the occasions when Darl penetrates their minds there are
allusions to the unavoidability of what each of them most
fears and resists: Jewel the death of his mother, and Dewey
Dell the birth of her child.

Each of these events is associated with the inexorable
progress of the traveling wagon as a symbol of the relentless
approach of the future. In the imagery of the novel, as will
be seen below, a sense of fatality is frequently conveyed
through images of circular movement: repetitious, preordained,
and circumscribed. And so in the scene when Darl, fetching
a load of wood on the wagon with Jewel, taunts his brother
by telling him that their mother is dying, his view of the
wagon's movement is conveyed through the image of a ribbon
winding on to a spool. He is mocking Jewel's passionate
resistance in the face of what he, Darl, knows to be inevitable:

> "Jewel," I say. Back running, tunnelled between
> the two sets of bobbing mule ears, the road vanishes
> beneath the wagon as though it were a ribbon and
> the front axle were a spool. "Do you know she is
> going to die, Jewel?"
> It takes two people to make you, and one people
> to die. That's how the world is going to end.
> I said to Dewey Dell: "You want her to die so
> you can get to town: is that it?" (p. 38)

The relevance of the sudden reference to Dewey Dell is explained
by the fact that Darl's thoughts in this passage are moving
from one example of inevitability to another, each symbolized
by the spool image: Addie's death, birth and death generally,
the eventual apocalypse, and finally the imminent funeral
journey to Jefferson and Dewey Dell's desire to get there
in order to obtain an abortion. Darl's ability to intuit his
brother's and sister's thoughts is clearly associated here
with his acute sense of fatality.

In Dewey Dell's own monologue as she is traveling on the
wagon with Addie's coffin, her sense of despair at the relent-
lessness of the passing of time that is bringing closer the
birth of the child that she dreads is vividly rendered in an
image which brutally links the two ideas together: *"That's
what they mean by the womb of time: the agony and the despair
of spreading bones, the hard girdle in which lie the outraged
entrails of events"* (pp. 114-115). And her awareness of
Darl's eyes stripping her naked--a graphic and concrete image
of the way she feels that he can penetrate her secret thoughts--
is counterpointed against her sense of the inexorability of
events of which she is reminded by the "unhurrying mules."
It is from his apprehension of this inevitability that Darl
derives his uncanny insight: "The land runs out of Darl's
eyes; they swim to pin-points. They begin at my feet and
rise along my body to my face, and then my dress is gone: I
sit naked on the seat above the unhurrying mules, above the
travail" (p. 115). There is a vivid contrast throughout this

section between Dewey Dell's passionate despair at the growth
of the foetus within her and the calmly inexorable progress
of the wagon.

The spool image is symbolic not simply of inexorability
but also of pointlessness and closed options--suggested by
the idea of movement from one spool to another. It is an
example of the way in which Darl sees humanity as deprived
of initiative and condemned to meaningless repetition. The
implications of this image are brought out in a meditation
of his which follows a reference to his intuition. He makes
a remark that indicates to his sister that he knows that she
has been unsuccessful in her attempt to obtain an abortion
(using the pretence that she was trying to sell Cora's cakes)
and that she will therefore be condemned to have the child:

> "You had more trouble than you expected, selling
> those cakes in Mottson," I say. How do our lives
> ravel out into the no-wind, no-sound, the weary
> gestures wearily recapitulant: echoes of old com-
> pulsions with no-hand on no-strings: in sunset we
> fall into furious attitudes, dead gestures of dolls.
> Cash broke his leg and now the sawdust is running
> out. He is bleeding to death is Cash. (pp. 196-197)

This is a vivid image of the tragic sense of determinism
from which Darl's supposed telepathy in fact derives. Again,
the image of threads, here the strings of broken puppets,
suggests the metaphysical constraints on human beings. Darl's
vision of his family as puppets, inspired by the sight of
Cash lying with his broken leg encased in cement and covered
with sawdust, brings together two of his principal convictions. First there is the idea that human actions are predetermined as a consequence of the pressure of the past. Darl
sees his fellow men as puppets controlled by external forces:
history, genetic inheritance, conventions, and rituals. These
are all "echoes of old compulsions" which exert their influence
within a godless and meaningless universe--"no-hand on no-
strings." For although Darl's metaphysical outlook appears
to share the predestinarian vision of extreme Calvinism,
there is no suggestion that he accepts any of its theological
tenets. Indeed, one of the ironies of the book is that in
this respect his position is the precise reverse of that of
most of the pious believers around him. Secondly, because
of his acute awareness of the inevitability of death--"in
sunset we fall into furious attitudes, dead gestures of
dolls"--Darl believes that there is no clearly defined distinction between life and death. Again, there is an ironic rever-
sal of the beliefs of his family, for just as they see the
dead mother, Addie, as in some sense still alive up to the

moment when her body is finally buried, so Darl sees living
people as in a sense already dead.

The most important examples of Darl's apparent "second
sight" are Sections 12 and 17 when, while far away with
Jewel fetching the wood, he describes the scene back at the
farm during and shortly after Addie's death. The above demonstration that Darl's apparent gifts of prescience and of
telepathy in fact derive from his determinist outlook applies
also to these sections. Darl's accounts are no more than
hypotheses about what is happening based on his knowledge
of his family's past behavior. The broad outlines of these
hypothetical accounts--the arrival of Peabody, the death of
Addie, the making of the coffin, and the onset of the rain-
storm before it is finished--are corroborated by other characters' accounts, nothing is contradicted, and a few of the
details are confirmed. For example, in a passage within Darl's
first hypothetical section which is italicized and in which
the tense shifts from the present to the future, both devices
are intended to indicate that what Darl is reconstructing as
a hypothesis is not happening simultaneously but will take
place in the future, and his guess is later shown to be
accurate. In this passage Darl conjectures that Dewey Dell
will silently plead with Peabody for help with an abortion
and that he will fail to understand her: *"She will go out
where Peabody is ... looking at him, saying You could do so
much for me if you just would"* (p. 50). All of this is confirmed
in Dewey Dell's next monologue which actually opens with a
reference to Peabody in the words: "He could do so much for
me if he just would" (p. 56).

Darl's apparent "second sight," then, like his supposed
prescience and telepathy, is nothing more nor less than the
exercise of intuition based on past knowledge of his family
combined with an extraordinarily complete and all-pervasive
acceptance of determinism. Indeed Faulkner gives, at one point
in the novel, a clear hint that Darl's insight into his family
is to be interpreted as deriving from his understanding of
them rather than from any supernatural powers. At the end of
the monologue in which Darl recounts how Jewel worked stealthi-
ly at night during one summer in order to earn the money to
buy his horse, he describes finding Addie weeping over the
sleeping Jewel after learning his secret. The possessive
mother is partly jealous of her son's love for the horse
which, throughout the novel, is shown to be regarded by him
as a kind of surrogate for her, although one which he sacri-
fices for her sake. But, as Darl realizes, Addie is also weeping
over Jewel's deception which in a number of respects resembles
her own secret adultery. The incident makes Darl aware of the
peculiar mixture of antagonism and love which Addie feels

towards Jewel as the only person to have engaged her emotions
deeply: "... she felt the same way about tears she did about
deceit, hating herself for doing it, hating him because she
had to" (p. 129). It is at this moment that Darl guesses the
secret of Jewel's paternity: "And then I knew that I knew.
I knew that as plain on that day as I knew about Dewey Dell
on that day." It is thus clear that Darl's insight into the
clandestine pregnancy of both his mother in the distant past
and of his sister in the present derives solely from his sense
of the way in which similar events are inexorably repeated in
succeeding generations, and the past determines the present.
Specifically, Darl understands how far the destructive and obsessive selfishness of Addie, revealed to the reader in her
single monologue, is responsible for the family's present
state. The decaying body which they are conveying with such
difficulty to its burial suggests the continuing and baneful
domination of the past.

Darl's determinist vision is related to his apparent
insanity through his attitude towards freedom of will. He does
not believe that human beings possess such freedom since in
a universe in which events are predetermined then the exercise
of choice must be an illusion. It is the fact that his convictions render people and their belief in the freedom and significance of their actions actually meaningless or absurd to
Darl that is the explanation of his madness, or, rather, of
his apparent madness. His laughter at the start of the journey
arises not precisely because he foresees the family's imminent
disasters but rather from his acute awareness of the dishonesty
of the motives of those involved, the probable hazards, and
the pointlessness of the whole undertaking. His desertion of
the wagon when it is struck by a log during the crossing of
the ford makes clear his feeling that the journey is absurd,
in contrast to the view of Cash and Jewel who risk their lives
to rescue the coffin. Cora's remark to her husband on Darl's
action raises the question of how far one can say that he is
insane: "'you're one of the folks that says Darl is the queer
one, the one that aint bright, and him the only one of them
that had sense enough to get off that wagon'" (*Tull*, p. 145).
Faulkner raises in this novel the question whether the real
insanity is not to believe that human beings have freedom of
choice and that their actions are invested with signficance
and value.

Whether Darl's insanity arises from or is the cause of
his determinism Faulkner does not choose to make clear, but
that the two are inseparably linked is made plain in the
nature of his harsh and inhuman vision of the meaningless
inexorability of cause and effect. The imagery of the novel
creates a pattern of circular movements which are repetitious,

pointless, and associated with death. Many of these images are focused on the journeying wagon as a symbol of the inexorability of events. The image of the spool, already referred to above, is paralleled by Darl's description of the buzzards, sinister reminders of death, circling overhead: "High against [the sky] they hang in narrowing circles, like the smoke, with an outward semblance of form and purpose, but with no inference of motion, progress or retrograde" (p. 216). The buzzards are impelled to pursue the rotting corpse by instinct rather than volition, and their movements are implicitly compared with the equally mechanical progress of the humans on the wagon below them. Darl's vision presents a detached, almost Godlike point of view as the wagon leaves the main road to head for the bridge which, as the Bundrens will learn, has been destroyed:

> It turns off at right angles, the wheel-marks
> of last Sunday healed away now: a smooth, red scoria-
> tion curving away into the pines; a white signboard
> with faded lettering: New Hope Church. 3 mi. It
> wheels up like a motionless hand lifted above the
> profound desolation of the ocean; beyond it the red
> road lies like a spoke of which Addie Bundren is the
> rim. It wheels past, empty, unscarred, the white
> signboard turns away its fading and tranquil asser-
> tion....The signboard passes; the unscarred road
> wheels on. Then Dewey Dell turns her head. The
> wagon creaks on. (p. 102)

The wagon and its occupants are reduced to a mere point on a geometrical figure as the Bundrens, in a fated, involuntary progress, trace out some huge pattern across the vast, dead landscape. The image of the spoke and rim presents the wagon as poised on the circumference of an enormous, slowly turning wheel of cause and effect which is impelling the family towards Jefferson in obedience to the will of the dead woman. The wheel image conveys Darl's view of the illusory nature of free will and of the power of the past, for the journey seems to be the consequence of Anse's promise to Addie to bury her with her own family (*Addie*, pp. 164-165). So, in Darl's vision, the Bundren family, trapped and compelled by the corpse representing the will of the dead mother which drives them forward, is involuntarily acting out its fate. However, Faulkner makes it clear that the origins of the journey are more complex than this, for each member of the family, with the exception of Darl and Jewel, has a secret and selfish motive for wanting to get to Jefferson: Anse wants new teeth and a new wife, Dewey Dell an abortion, Cash a gramophone, and even Vardaman covets a toy train. Thus the

novel leaves unresolved the question of whether it is Addie's
will and the promise she extorted from Anse that is responsible
for the funeral journey, or the dictates of Providence, or
the conjunction of trivial and selfish reasons of each member
of the family.

Darl's vision of his family and of their emotions and
motives during this critical period of their lives is conveyed
in terms as mechanistic as his view of the workings of destiny,
and here it is easier to see the link between his determinist
outlook and his insanity. For the qualities of insight and
detachment that make Darl so objective an observer are quite
divorced from emotional involvement. He feels neither sympathy
nor antipathy towards others, apart from his occasional concern for Cash's interests. His taunting of Jewel and Dewey
Dell is not inspired by a desire to hurt so much as a dispassionate curiosity, for Darl watches his family almost as
if they were of another species.

Frequently Darl's descriptions of human actions are so
abstract as to be mere schematizations: movement is frozen
into stasis, the organic becomes geometrical, and the willed
becomes mechanical. Typical of this vision is his description
of Dewey Dell getting into the wagon: "her leg coming long
from beneath her tightening dress: that lever which moves
the world; one of that caliper which measures the length and
breadth of life" (pp. 97-98). The geometrical image withholds
from the girl any recognition of her humanity or her individuality. Characteristically, Darl's vision analyzes the human
body into grotesquely isolated elements which are, moreover,
often portrayed as divorced from their emotional context, as
in Darl's description of Vardaman's reaction to his mother's
death:

> From behind pa's leg Vardaman peers, his mouth
> full open and all color draining from his face into
> his mouth, as though he has by some means fleshed
> his own teeth in himself, sucking. He begins to
> move slowly backward from the bed, his eyes round,
> his pale face fading into the dusk like a piece of
> paper pasted on a failing wall, and so out of the
> door. (p. 48)

There is no sympathy for the child's fear and bewilderment,
but only an almost scientific interest in the appearance of
the symptoms of these emotions. Exactly the same detachment
is employed to render Anse's reaction to his wife's death
when Darl sees the rain-drops that fall on his father's face
as mock tears parodying the grief that he knows his father
does not actually feel: "It is as though upon a face carved
by a savage caricaturist a monstrous burlesque of all bereave-

ment flowed" (pp. 73-74). And it is in similar terms that
Darl describes Tull emerging from the river after diving to
retrieve Cash's lost rule: "Vernon comes up, streaming, his
face sloped down into his pursed mouth. His mouth is bluish,
like a circle of weathered rubber" (p. 152). Another example
of the inhuman detachment of Darl's vision of his fellow
mortals even at moments of extreme distress is his description
of the attempt by Gillespie's son, Mack, to rescue a mule
from the barn which Darl himself has set on fire:

> He looks back at us, his eyes and mouth three round
> holes in his face on which the freckles look like
> English peas on a plate. His voice is thin, high,
> faraway.
> "I cant do nothing..." It is as though the sound
> had been swept from his lips and up and away, speak-
> ing back to us from an immense distance of exhaustion.
> (p. 210)

There is no acknowledgment of the fact that Mack is terrified;
instead, his appearance and voice are abstracted from their
emotional context and their superficial features are described
with dispassionate precision.

It is Darl's attempt to burn down the barn in which his
mother's body rests that leads to his family's decision to
commit him to an asylum. Their rejection of him precipitates
him into the complete insanity from which his final monologue
issues. Darl's act of arson brings together the main themes
of the book: the domination of the present by the past, the
inexorability of the decrees of fate, and the equivocal nature
of Darl's madness. Darl tries to destroy the corpse in order,
presumably, to halt the journey which he sees to be so dangerous and so costly to his family. The rotting body of the
wife and mother by whose will the family is undertaking the
journey and as a result of whose perverse selfishness Darl
and Jewel are emotionally and mentally maimed, represents
the power of the past to exercise a malign influence on the
present. Darl's initiative is a tragic act because he knows
that the past cannot be eluded and that destiny cannot be
thwarted. The attempt costs him everything, as he must have
known it would, for Dewey Dell and Jewel seize the opportunity
to gain their revenge by having him declared insane. Yet
Darl's conduct in firing the barn is no more insane than that
of his family in persevering with the journey at the price
of sacrificing Jewel's horse and crippling Cash for life.
Cash himself comes close to recognizing this when he reflects:
"Sometimes I aint so sho who's got ere a right to say when a
man is crazy and when he aint. Sometimes I think it aint none
of us pure crazy and aint none of us pure sane until the

balance of us talks him that-a-way" (p. 223). He feels that:
"when Darl seen that it looked like one of us would have to
do something, I can almost believe he done right in a way."
But Cash, for all his virtues, is too prosaic and unimaginative a man to be able to sustain this insight, and he decides
that the conventional judgment on Darl's conduct is the correct
one: "I dont reckon nothing excuses setting fire to a man's
barn and endangering his stock and destroying his property.
That's how I reckon a man is crazy. That's how he cant see
eye to eye with other folks."

Cash has the last word in the book, and delivers his moving
but inadequate judgment on Darl when he thinks of his fate
in the asylum and decides that: "it is better so for him. This
world is not his world; this life his life" (p. 250). In his
final monologue Cash describes the restoration, after the
burial of Addie and the arrest of Darl, of normality and continuity; but, in the context of the novel as a whole, they
are of an ironically equivocal kind. As the family prepares
for the return journey the ambivalent nature of that continuity
is made clear: Dewey Dell, forced to abandon her hopes of
an abortion, resigns herself to bearing the unwanted child,
while Anse, for whom the memory of Addie means so little,
appears with a new wife. The family has survived, but only
at a cost and by exorcizing and expelling the two most
interesting and tragically unconventional of its members.

NOTES

1. Even the intelligent and sensitive reading of the
novel by Olga Vickery, the essential starting-point for
critical discussion of the book, is unsatisfactory on this
issue; see Chapter 4 of *The Novels of William Faulkner:
A Critical Interpretation* (Baton Rouge: Louisiana State
University Press, 1964).

2. An important exception is the stimulating but not
wholly convincing article by Joseph Gold, which, although
focusing on many of the topics discussed in the present
article, arrives at very different conclusions: see "'Sin,
Salvation and Bananas': *As I Lay Dying*," *Mosaic*, 7 (Fall
1973), 55-73.

3. In allusions to the text, the page number is given at
the first reference, preceded by the name of the monologuist
only when this is not clear from the context; quotations
from *As I Lay Dying* are from the corrected edition (New
York: Random House, 1964).

VARDAMAN'S JOURNEY IN *AS I LAY DYING*

George Rooks

One of the most enigmatic characters of *As I Lay Dying*
has been Vardaman Bundren. Focusing their discussion on the
famous "My mother is a fish" statement, many early critics
erroneously termed Vardaman a Benjy-like idiot or a moronic
child. For the most part, however, recent critics have considered Vardaman a sensitive but normal child, and have sought
a mythic and psychoanalytic basis of his fish statement.[1]
Despite this more enlightened reading of Vardaman, I believe
that the continuing emphasis on the fish statement has ob-
scured key aspects of Vardaman's Addie-fish identification.
More important, Faulkner's development of the relationship
between Darl and Vardaman on the journey to Jefferson has
not been adequately explored, and Vardaman's subsequent rejection of the Addie-fish identification has been totally
overlooked. The purpose of this essay is to analyze Vardaman's
progression through the novel focusing on the traumatic
psychological disturbances which Vardaman experiences.

At the end of Anse's first section, we receive our first
hint of Addie's psychological importance to Vardaman. Out of
concern, Vardaman asks Anse about the condition of his
mother: "'Pa,' he says, 'is ma sick some more?'" (p. 37).[2]
Faulkner underscored this concern Vardaman has for his mother
when he commented that, in a sense, Vardaman's love for
Addie is the most sincere of all the Bundrens: "Well, it was
because of the child's dependence on his mother, and probably
to that child nobody else except the mother paid any attention
to him. She was something stable, and his love for her was
clinging to something that was stable in his world."[3] After
the doctor examines Addie, Vardaman sustains his first
psychological jolt while listening to the short conversation
between Anse and Peabody. With no regard for Vardaman's
presence, Anse callously seeks Peabody's confirmation that
Addie is going to die. Throughout the conversation, Peabody's
perception focuses on Vardaman: "He sits on the top step,
small, motionless in faded overalls. When I came out he looked

up at me, then at Anse. But now he has stopped looking at us. He just sits there" (p. 44). Anse's comments clearly stun Vardaman; through them he learns that the center and source of his stability is about to die.

Yet this information is not nearly as devastating to Vardaman as his experience at the death bed. Here, the details which Darl narrates are strikingly similar to Peabody's details of the previous bed scene, especially insomuch as they focus attention on Addie and Vardaman. Vardaman peers out from behind Anse's leg, but again Addie ignores Anse and concentrates her gaze on Vardaman: "She lies back and turns her head without so much as glancing at pa. She looks at Vardaman; her eyes, the life in them, rushing suddenly upon them; the two flames glare up for a steady instant. Then they go out as though someone had leaned down and blown upon them" (p. 47). Vardaman is the last person at whom Addie looks before she dies, and the effect of that final glance is not lost upon him: "From behind pa's leg Vardaman peers, his mouth full open and all color draining from his face into his mouth, as though he has by some means fleshed his own teeth in himself, sucking. He begins to move slowly backward from the bed, his eyes round, his pale face fading into the dusk like a piece of paper pasted on a failing wall, and so out of the door" (p. 48). We would expect the youngest and most impressionable person in the room to recoil in terror from such an experience; nonetheless, Darl's graphic image of Vardaman's face carries a foreboding of inevitable deterioration: "his pale face fading into the dusk like a piece of paper pasted on a failing wall."[4]

Faulkner brilliantly waits until after the scene at the death bed to give us Vardaman's first section (pp. 52–55), in which he struggles to understand what has happened to his mother. The change in Addie came with terrifying swiftness after the doctor's arrival and examination, and Vardaman reaches the conclusion that the doctor killed her. The ensuing episode with Peabody's team reinforces the idea that no one has taken the time to instruct Vardaman in conventional guidelines of childhood behavior. Earlier, when Anse orders Vardaman to clean the fish, Vardaman "cusses it like a grown man" (p. 30). Here he curses Peabody as "[t]he fat son of a bitch" prior to chasing the team away while screaming "You kilt my maw!" (p. 53). Faulkner underpins Vardaman's violent actions and words with an unmistakable intensity. As Bleikasten points out: "Vardaman's monologues trace the tenacious gropings of a child's intelligence towards a firmer hold on reality and towards self-assertion in the face of its disorder. His is a mind still steeped in emotion and imagination, but whose total energies strive feverishly toward order, toward the beginnings of

rationality." [5] However, as we shall see, Vardaman's encounters
with later obstacles suggest that he will be unable to complete
this journey to rationality and order.

In Vardaman's next section (pp. 62-64), he continues his
effort to comprehend his mother's change in form. Faced with
the body on the bed, he attempts to convince himself that
it was not Addie who was covered by the quilt. Probably echoing what one of the adults has told him, he asserts that his
mother "went away." He then asks someone: "'Did she go as far
as town?'"[6] and receives a reply which will later give him
hope as the journey to Jefferson begins: "'She went further
than town.'" Next, his mind logically turns to his own limited
experiences with death: "all those rabbits and possums"
killed by his family. He even considers briefly the possibility
that his mother is a rabbit, only to discard the idea because
of his experience in the corn crib. As in his previous monologue, Vardaman gropes with the chronological relationship
between the fish becoming not-fish, and whatever happened to
his mother. Between the time that he chopped the fish in the
dust and someone put it bleeding into the pan to be cooked,
his mother was not there anymore: "Then it wasn't and she
was, and now it is and she wasn't." When he thinks of the
horrible probability that the fish will be eaten, his desperate,
jolted psyche links together a confused series of causes and
effects: "And tomorrow it will be cooked and et and she will
be him and pa and Cash and Dewey Dell and there wont be anything in the box and so she can breathe" (pp. 63-64).[7] As
Vardaman leaps from one idea to another, it is obvious that
his chronological analogy between the fish's death and the
change in his mother has yet to take the form of an identification. Before an identification can be made he must account
for the body, and his corn crib experience has earlier helped
him to devise a crucial test: "... I couldn't breathe in the
crib and Cash is going to nail it up. And so if she lets him
it is not her" (p. 63).

Tenaciously armed with his analogy, and convinced that
his insensitive father will not respond to it, Vardaman in
desperation travels alone through a stormy Mississippi night
to get Vernon, the only other person who can corroborate
his analogy. Arriving at midnight, Vardaman futilely attempts
to explain to Vernon and Cora about the fish and his mother.
By the time they arrive back at the Bundrens' (who show no
concern for his absence or whereabouts), Vardaman's proof is
gone; the rain has washed away the traces of fish in the
dust. Turning his attention to the body, Vardaman feels
that as long as it remains unenclosed, it can receive the
air it needs to exist. Through the long night, he continually
slips into the bedroom and opens the window so that the wind

can blow in on the body. To keep Vardaman from opening the
window a third time, the Bundrens enclose Addie in the
coffin. Despite his fatigue and their efforts, the heroic
Vardaman gets air to the body one last time; the next morning
they find him "in his shirt tail, laying asleep on the floor
like a felled steer, and the top of the box bored clean full
of holes and Cash's new auger broke off in the last one. When
they taken the lid off they found that two of them had bored
on into her face" (pp. 69-70). Vardaman's intense strain is
noticed by Cora who describes his face as looking like "one
of these here Christmas masts that had done been buried a
while and then dug up" (p. 69).[8] Only after this grotesque
series of events, which end with the holes in the box being
plugged, is Vardaman forced to make his identification. Since
she let Cash enclose her, the body in the box cannot be his
mother; instead Vardaman declares "My mother is a fish" (p.
79). Unlike some critics have stated, Vardaman does not
identify his mother with the dead fish.[9] He does not conclude
that "my mother was a fish" or that "my mother is a not-fish,"
or even that "my mother is the fish"; instead he declares
that "my mother is a fish." Vardaman must believe that his
mother "is," so that his own existence will not be denied.

     Until this point the narrative has revealed no member
of the family who shows any concern over Vardaman's particular
vulnerability. In fact, Faulkner depicts the Bundrens as
expecting Vardaman to assimilate the facts surrounding Addie's
death alone. As Faulkner pointed out: "... nobody had paid
any attention to him. He saw things that baffled and puzzled
him, and nobody--none of the adults would stop long enough
to show him any tenderness, any affection.... when he brought
the fish home, something that happened from the outside
got the fish confused with the fact that he knew his mother's
body was in a room and that she was no longer his mother.
She couldn't talk or--anyway, suddenly her position in the
mosaic of the household was vacant."[10] Vardaman, concomitant
with his formation of the identification, returns to his previously stated idea: "It was not my mother. She went away
when the other one laid down in her bed and drew the quilt
up" (p. 63). Even after Vardaman has been forced to form the
Addie-fish identification to give his mother existence, he
remains cognizant of the body in the box. Vardaman still considers it his mother's body, even though it can no longer
be his mother.

     The events of the next morning in the Bundren kitchen
offer Vardaman's troubled mind no respite. Peabody reports
that Vardaman "come into the kitchen, hollering, swarming
and clawing at Cora when he found her cooking that fish"
(p. 81). In this attack Vardaman demonstrates a swelling

of emotions similar to that surge he experienced when he
attacked Peabody's team. Yet his actions seem less under
control here; instead of attacking a non-human entity,
he focuses his thrust on Cora. Though he has made the
Addie-fish identification, Vardaman views the cooking and
eating of the fish as the final steps in that terrible series
of events that took his mother away. If Cora cooks the fish,
he evidently feels that all immediate hope of his mother's
returning to her familiar form will vanish. We learn later
that Dewey Dell can quiet Vardaman only by telling him she
saw a fish in the slough. True to his persistent nature,
Vardaman next appears at the slough trying to catch the fish.
What he hopes to accomplish is unclear, though it would appear
that he merely wants to catch a fish to replace the one that
his family has eaten. At any rate, the knowledge that another
fish exists in the slough has a soothing effect upon Vardaman;
Tull describes him with "his eyes round and calm" (p. 87).

     In the first part of Vardaman's next section (pp. 94-96),
Anse tells Jewel to leave the horse behind: "'We'll all go
in the wagon with ma, like she wanted.'" Vardaman responds
to this comment in his thoughts: "But my mother is a fish.
Vernon seen it. He was there" (p. 94). Addie is his mother
and his mother is a fish, but Addie the fish-mother is not
in the box on the wagon. The box only holds the body which
Vardaman no longer considers his mother. At this point Faulkner
develops a new relationship for Vardaman which will dominate
the latter part of the novel. Darl initiates a surprisingly
sophisticated conversation with Vardaman in which he questions
his own existence in light of Addie's death. Darl first makes
the Vardaman-like statement that "'Jewel's mother is a horse.'"
When Vardaman presses him for more information, Darl becomes
the first and only character to respond to Vardaman's Addie-
fish identification.

> "Then mine can be a fish, cant it, Darl?" I said.
> Jewel is my brother.
> "Then mine will have to be a horse, too," I said.
> "Why?" Darl said. "If pa is your pa, why does
> your ma have to be a horse just because Jewel's is?"

Because he receives no statement to the contrary here, Vardaman
takes this ambiguous question to mean that Darl believes
Addie is a fish. This monologue reveals the first evidence
that Faulkner has given of a relationship between Darl and
Vardaman, and he marks this revelation by the first conversation that any character has had with Vardaman concerning
Addie's death.

     Shortly thereafter the wagon overturns at the flooded
river, and Darl describes the people on the opposite bank:

"Vernon and Vardaman are running along the bank, pa and Dewey
Dell stand watching us...." (p. 142). Once again Vardaman seems
to be reaching a crucial emotional juncture as evidenced by
his running away from Anse and Dewey Dell. Vardaman narrates
the passage in which the box falls into the water (pp. 143-
144). Under severe emotional strain, Vardaman fuses the Addie-
fish identification with the immediate reality of the coffin
in the water to produce a belief that Addie the fish was in
the box and has escaped through the holes he drilled. Faulkner
underscores Vardaman's desperate desire that Darl catch the
fish through a dynamic grammatical and punctuational change.
The first end stop punctuation occurs 360 words into the
section and is the longest such passage of *As I Lay Dying*.
Bleikasten says this about the stylistic elements of the
passage:

> ... here is a breakdown of language of which the
> most obvious signs are irregularities in spelling
> ("darl" for "Darl"), the absence of punctuation
> (except in the last five lines), and the disloca-
> tion of syntax.... [S]entences are started and lost,
> repeated and mixed up.... Reference to reality is cer-
> tainly still present; ... we still perceive the echo
> of words spoken, the reflection of things seen, but
> so jumbled and scattered that their sequential
> logic escapes us altogether.... [T]he discourse
> itself is reduced to frenzied verbal gesticula-
> tion.... Nothing is left but the dizzy anguish of
> a consciousness caught up in the event.[11]

Darl emerges without the fish, and Faulkner depicts the
effect of the excruciating moment of his rising on Vardaman
by changing to italics, the first time he has used this
device in any of Vardaman's sections. After the traumatic
experiences of discovering his mother is going to die,
watching her die, and then seeing the fish being cooked, it
seems to me that Faulkner uses the italic device to show
that this bizarre series of events has begun to take its
toll on Vardaman's psyche:

> ... Darl was strong and steady holding her under
> the water even if she did fight he would not let
> her go he was seeing me and he would hold her and
> it was all right now it was all right now it was
> all right
>   *Then he comes up out of the water. He comes a
> long way up slow before his hands do but he's got
> to have her got to so I can bear it. Then his
> hands come up and all of him above the water. I*

> *cant stop. I have not got time to try. I will try*
> *to when I can but his hands came empty out of the*
> *water emptying the water emptying away*
>   "Where is ma, Darl?" I said. "You never got
> her. You knew she is a fish but you let her get
> away. You never got her. Darl. Darl. Darl." (p. 144)

Despite Darl's culpability, Vardaman does not lash out at him
as he did at Peabody's team or at Cora. Instead he shows a
displaced bewilderment. No longer are his eyes round and calm;
Darl observes that "Vardaman backs along the rope, to the
tree, moving blindly, watching Vernon. When we come up he
looks at us once, his eyes round and a little dazed" (p. 150).
The identification, which originated as means of giving
Vardaman hope, now begins to render him less able to cope
with external events: *"he's got to have her got to so I can*
bear it."
     After the Bundrens retrieve the box, the journey proceeds
to Armstid's. Armstid hears "that boy yelling" and thinks he
must "have fell into the well or something" (p. 178). He finds
Vardaman chasing a buzzard around the barn and comments that
the hot day in the sun chasing buzzards has made Vardaman
"nigh as crazy as the rest of them" (p. 182). Vardaman's next
conversation with Darl (pp. 185-187) reinforces this new
interest in the buzzards, as well as his growing similarity
with Darl. Darl earlier described the buzzards as: "Motionless, the tall buzzards hang in soaring circles, the clouds
giving them an illusion of retrograde" (p. 89). Vardaman now
uses a starkly similar image as he describes the buzzards as
"little tall black circles of not-moving." In addition, Vardaman sheds further light on how grotesque the journey has
become. He boldly informs Darl that if the buzzard tries to
land on the wagon again he "wouldn't let him light on her."
As Lee Richmond comments: "That the buzzards scent carrion
would be part of Vardaman's rural learning, but that they
would feed on Addie's remains is a fact that jars him into
shocking recognition."[12] Through the use of "her" Vardaman
clearly reverts to his pre-river distinction between his
mother's body in the box which is not his mother, and his
mother the fish. Later in the section Vardaman repeats what
Darl has told him, and again his thoughts are in italics (as
are several passages in this section):

> *But Jewel's mother is a horse. My mother is a fish.*
> *Darl says that when we come to the water again I*
> *might see her and Dewey Dell said, She's in the*
> *box; how could she have got out? She got out through*
> *the holes I bored, into the water I said, and when*

> *we come to the water again I am going to see her.*
> *My mother is not in the box. My mother does not*
> *smell like that. My mother is a fish* (p. 187)

Only Darl understands what took place in Vardaman's mind at
the river, and rather than attempt to change Vardaman's belief
here, he resorts to another ambiguity which Vardaman takes
as fact. Darl seems to be waiting for the right moment to
discuss his conception of Addie's mortality with Vardaman.

Faulkner now allows the sections of Darl and Vardaman
to take temporary control of the novel. Vickery seems to be
one of the few critics to discuss this structure, and she
develops it in relation to Darl: "As Darl loses contact with
the external world and with objective reality, his resemblance
to Vardaman becomes more pronounced. When the wagon reaches
the Gillespies', their sections are juxtaposed five times.
The two of them have reached an understanding which is beyond
logic and reason.... Their shared delusion suggests that for
both of them the world of fantasy has become as real as the
concrete facts which we call reality."[13] I think this only
half states the case; just as Darl's resemblance to Vardaman
becomes more pronounced, we have seen how Faulkner has moved
Vardaman closer to Darl. This movement continues to be evidenced by the fact that Vardaman addresses virtually all of
his verbal communication to Darl. In his short seventh section (pp. 200-201) he questions his brother about the horrible
buzzards: "'Where do they stay at night, Darl?' I say. 'When
we stop at night in the barn, where do they stay?'" Vardaman
follows with a poetic observation that sounds like something
Darl would say: "The hill goes off into the sky. Then the
sun comes up from behind the hill and the mules and the wagon
and pa walk on the sun. You cannot watch them, walking slow on
the sun."

The next two sections, which primarily take place in
the moonlight at the apple tree, are the most crucial for our
understanding Vardaman's journey in *As I Lay Dying*. Darl
singles out Vardaman and takes him to Addie's casket: "The
breeze was setting up from the barn, so we put her under the
apple tree, where the moonlight can dapple the apple tree
upon the long slumbering flanks within which now and then she
talks in little trickling bursts of secret and murmurous
bubbling. I took Vardaman to listen. When we came up the cat
leaped down from it and flicked away with silver claw and
silver eye into the shadow" (p. 202). It seems cabalistic
the way Darl describes the "bursts of secret and murmurous
bubbling," and chant-like when he speaks of "silver claw and
silver eye." Indeed, as we have seen, Vardaman's experiences
in the novel seem to be ones of initiation into the problems

of existence and mortality. Vardaman continues the commentary
in his next section (pp. 204-207). Darl tells him to use his
senses:

> "Hear?" Darl says. "Put your ear close."
> I put my ear close and I can hear her. Only I
> cant tell what she is saying.

Darl tells Vardaman that she is "'talking to God'" because
"'[s]he wants Him to hide her away from the sight of man.'"
To Vardaman's question of why, Darl replies, "'So she can lay
down her life.'" Vardaman still does not fully understand
Darl's explanation, and he pursues that explanation with
another question: "'Why does she want to lay down her life,
Darl?'" In regard to Darl's intuition of Addie's dissatisfaction with Anse, Richmond remarks that "Vardaman cannot be expected to grasp Darl's superhuman vision."[14] Perhaps Darl perceives Vardaman's inability to completely understand this
facet of his conception for he chooses to direct the conversation in another direction:

> "Listen," Darl says. We hear her. We hear her
> turn over on her side. "Listen," Darl says.
> "She's turned over," I say. "She's looking at
> me through the wood."
> "Yes," Darl says.
> "How can she see through the wood, Darl?"
> "Come," Darl says. "We must let her be quiet.
> Come."
> "She cant see out there, because the holes are
> in the top," I say. "How can she see, Darl?" (p. 205)

At first Darl guided Vardaman to the box and instructed him
how to listen, but here Vardaman takes the initiative and does
not merely hear his mother's body; he *sees* her "looking at me
through the wood." Darl obviously has a highly unconventional
conception of his mother's mortality, but we should not be
surprised that Vardaman ultimately accepts it--even though
he doesn't completely understand the conception. Faulkner
said that a key part of the Addie-fish identification was that
"the other" could not talk. As soon as Vardaman hears words
from inside the box, his identification begins to dissolve.
After his experience of knowledge at the apple tree, Vardaman
is able to think of his mother's body and the box without
thinking about the fish. Nowhere in this section or at any
point in the remainder of the novel does Vardaman refer to
his mother being a fish, nor does he make any reference to
the Addie-fish identification. From the psychological perspective of Vardaman's ability to deal with the outside world,
the change in his belief has negative connotations. After all,

Darl's conception of Addie's mortality is indicative of the
same sort of madness which justifies carting him off to Jackson.
After he returns to his pallet, Vardaman does not take
Dewey Dell's advice and go to sleep. He goes to check where
the buzzards stay at night and sees "something that Dewey Dell
told me not to tell nobody" (p. 207). In his next section
(pp. 213-215), he describes how the "barn went swirling up
in little red pieces, against the sky and the stars so that
the stars moved backward." Whereas Darl's relative maturity
enabled him to perceive that the buzzards had "an illusion
of retrograde" (p. 89), Vardaman's limited experience causes
him to believe that "the stars moved backward." As the section
closes, Vardaman explains that Darl has returned to the casket
after his attempt at cremation has failed:

> "Where is Darl?" they said.
> He is out there under the apple tree with
> her, lying on her. He is there so the cat wont
> come back. I said, "Are you going to keep the
> cat away, Darl?"
> The moonlight dappled on him too. On her it
> was still, but on Darl it dappled up and down. (pp.
> 214-215)

By manipulating words and action, Faulkner has again moved
Vardaman and Darl closer together. Earlier Darl commented
that "the moonlight can dapple the apple tree," and here
Vardaman uses the same unusual verb to describe the moonlight.
Also, just as Vardaman told Darl that he wouldn't let the
buzzard "light on her," he perceives that Darl has lain down
on the casket to keep the cat off.
    As the family reaches Jefferson, Darl perceptively voices
his awareness that Vardaman's condition has deteriorated.
Earlier Darl described Vardaman's face "fading into the dusk
like a piece of paper pasted on a failing wall"; now he reports
that Vardaman "too has lost flesh; like ours, his face has an
expression strained, dreamy, and gaunt" (p. 216). Once in
Jefferson Vardaman becomes primarily concerned with the capture of his brother. He is anxious for everyone to know that
he did not betray Darl. Cash says that "Vardaman see him do
it, but he swore he never told nobody but Dewey Dell and that
she told him not to tell nobody" (p. 222). Significantly,
while Vardaman's last monologue (pp. 239-242) describes his
actions in the events surrounding Dewey Dell's attempted
abortion, eleven of twelve of his italicized thought patterns
center on Darl. Vardaman experiences the same initial difficulty in trying to understand Darl's craziness as he did in
trying to understand Addie's mortality. More than this, he
senses an acute loss as the train carries away his best friend:

"*He had to get on the train to go to Jackson. I have not been on the train, but Darl has been on the train. Darl. Darl is my brother. Darl. Darl*" (p. 242). These words recall Vardaman's dazed utterances at the river: "You never got her. Darl. Darl. Darl" (p. 144). Just as the Addie-fish identification stuns Vardaman by leaving Darl empty handed at the river, here Vardaman receives a similar shock when the train takes Darl away to Jackson. At the end of the journey, the materially deprived Vardaman[15] does not receive the red train that is behind the glass; we last glimpse him through Cash's eyes with his "mouth half open and half-et" banana in his hands (p. 249).

Richmond summarizes Vardaman's journey in the novel by asserting that he "develops the flexibilities which a human being needs to survive in the world of the living."[16] Vardaman does survive the journey, but he does so at a terrible cost to his psychological well-being. Addie's death and the subsequent trip to Jefferson provide Vardaman with continuous psychological shocks: (1) Anse's comment that Addie is going to die, (2) Addie's devastating death gaze, (3) Cash's enclosure of Addie in the coffin, (4) Cora's cooking of the fish, (5) the coffin falling in the water at the river, (6) the recurrent, horrible reality of the buzzards, (7) Darl's capture and removal to Jefferson. Indeed, Volpe perceives that by the end of the journey Vardaman "has probably suffered more psychological disturbance than anyone but Darl."[17] This may understate the case; Faulkner carefully draws Darl and Vardaman closer together, and gives the reader details which suggest Vardaman's psychological deterioration. Most important among these details is Vardaman's rejection of the Addie-fish identification in favor of Darl's conception of Addie's mortality. Though this rejection does indicate a certain flexibility on Vardaman's part, it has disturbing implications for Vardaman's future. With no source of stability, and nothing but indifference from his family, Vardaman concludes his journey with the seeds of a Darl-like madness implanted in his mind.

NOTES

1. For good brief summaries of the major trends in Vardaman criticism, see the only essays which deal exclusively with Vardaman: Floyd Watkins and William Dillingham, "The Mind of Vardaman Bundren," *Philological Quarterly*, 39 (April 1960), 247-51; and Lee J. Richmond, "The Education of Vardaman Bundren in Faulkner's *As I Lay Dying*," in *Renaissance and Modern:*

Essays in Honor of Edwin M. Moseley, ed. Murray J. Levith (Saratoga Springs, N.Y.: Skidmore College, 1976), pp. 133-142. Watkins and Dillingham conclude that Vardaman is not an idiot and that his "words and acts are those of a sensitive child suffering bereavement." Richmond argues that Vardaman's journey is not merely "to fulfill a dying mother's wish: it is a journey towards personal growth into a learning of loyalty, human suffering, and the acceptance of the difficulty of survival" (p. 142).

2. Page references cited in parentheses throughout the text refer to the Random House edition of *As I Lay Dying* (New York, 1964).

3. Frederick Gwynn and Joseph Blotner, eds., *Faulkner in the University* (New York: Vintage, 1965), p. 111.

4. When she later throws Vardaman out of the barn, Dewey Dell similarly describes Vardaman as "disappearing slowly into the hill" (p. 61).

5. André Bleikasten, *Faulkner's As I Lay Dying,* trans. by Roger Little (Bloomington: Indiana Univ. Press, 1973), p. 98.

6. A possible source of Vardaman's comments here is Anse's earlier question to Peabody: "'She's goin, is she?'" (p. 43) .

7. Robert Sanderlin explains the identification solely on the basis that the fish is symbolic of Christ (*Iesos Christos Theou Hyios Sofer-icthys*-fish, as used by early Christians). He perceptively sees Vardaman's hope in the fish as symbolic of the hope embodied in the crucifixion and resurrection. The problem with a consistent fish-Christ symbol is illustrated when Sanderlin cites this passage as suggestive of the Eucharist. If it is, how do we symbolically interpret Vardaman's brutal killing of the fish, or his attack on Cora in the kitchen? It is difficult to imagine that Vardaman is symbolically guilty of Christ-murder, or that he wants to thwart the taking of the Eucharist. See: Robert Sanderlin, *"As I Lay Dying*: Christian Symbols and Thematic Implications," *Southern Quarterly,* 7 (January 1969), 155-166.

8. To some degree, Faulkner undoubtedly means to undercut Vardaman's heroism through Cora's description. He remarked that by "Christmas masts" Cora meant "the comic faces that children buy in the stores for Halloween and Christmas time." *Faulkner in the University,* p. 127.

9. For instance see: J.L. Roberts, "The Individual and the Family: Faulkner's *As I Lay Dying*," *Arizona Quarterly,* 16 (Spring 1960), p. 28.

10. *Faulkner in the University*, p. 110.

11. Bleikasten, p. 63.

12. Richmond, p. 141.

13. Olga Vickery, *The Novels of William Faulkner* (Baton Rouge: Louisiana State Univ. Press, 1964), p. 59.

14. Richmond, p. 141.

15. The theme of Vardaman's relative deprivation is developed in Vardaman's second section (esp. p. 63).

16. Richmond, p. 142.

17. Edmond Volpe, *A Reader's Guide to William Faulkner* (New York: Noonday Press, 1964), p. 131.

THE HOUSE THAT TULL BUILT

Gail Moore Morrison

A number of commentators have remarked briefly on the importance and functions of the eight non-Bundren narrators of *As I Lay Dying*. Among them these characters share sixteen of the novel's fifty-nine monologues. Thus, nearly one quarter of the novel is presented through the eyes of such folk as the Bundrens' closest neighbors, Cora and Vernon Tull, and Samson and Armstid; their doctor and preacher, Peabody and Whitfield; and two townsmen from Mottson and Jefferson respectively, Moseley and MacGowan. As these characters exist at further and further geographic remove from the Bundren farm, so their sense of duty and obligation and their understanding and sympathy for the Bundrens' bizarre odyssey diminish while their outrage and sense of violated respectability increase. Taken collectively, these eight characters certainly function as "reverberators" for the actions of the Bundren family; their humorous and ironic remarks frequently provide comic relief to the grim--now tragic, now heroic, now pathetic--trek of the Bundrens.[1] In addition, their importance as choric commentators who provide a wider if not entirely objective frame of reference constructed around specific rural virtues and prejudices has been acknowledged.[2] But in general little concentrated attention has been provided them, either as foils to the Bundrens or as characters who considerably enrich the tonal and thematic complexity of the novel.

Of these characters Cora and Vernon Tull function as substantially important narrators. Their geographic proximity to the Bundrens qualifies them to provide more information about the central characters and their motivations than Samson or Armstid, for instance, whose monologues function largely to advance the action of the novel. More significant, however, is the fact that events in the Bundrens' lives serve as eliciting, precipitating factors in dramatizing underlying conflict in the Tulls' own. Their marriage, especially as it symbolizes a specific view of world and

self, stands in marked antithesis to that of Anse and Addie
Bundren. Through the Tulls' monologues emerges a considerably
more complex portrait of the stolid, commonsensical countryman Tull who never appears in the same kind of heroic light
that Jewel does, for example. Instead, he is revealed as a
man who humanely and uncomplainingly carries his own burdens
although he barely manages to articulate them and finds the
alternative of laying them down in defeat unacceptable.

Tull's introduction in the novel occurs through his wife
in her first two monologues, and on this subject, as on so
many, Cora demonstrates little perceptiveness. The single most
critical fact about Cora Tull is that she is a mistress of
misinformation. Effortlessly and unintentionally, she paints
a self-portrait of a petulant, hypocritical, envious, self-
professed "Christian" when she intends just the opposite.
Ironically immured safely behind empty religious rhetoric,
she judges and condemns the Bundrens even as her rhetoric
blinds her to the shallowness of her own actions. The dis-
crepancy between Cora's words and her actions is at first
merely implied but later is made increasingly explicit. Further,
as the novel progresses it functions as a rich source of comedy
that counterpoints the novel's opening sequence of action involving Addie's death. Appropriately, then, it is left to Addie
in her monologue casually to dismiss Cora and her empty words
of wisdom with the simple phrase: "Like Cora, who could never
even cook."[3] Thus Addie counters Cora's frequently reiterated
assessment about the cakes with which she is absorbed in her
opening monologue, that they "turned out right well" (p. 6),
to focus attention on the role Cora plays as foil to Addie
herself.[4]

This function aside, however, and even without recourse
to monologues by other characters who provide factual data
that frequently contradicts information provided by Cora,
close attention to Cora's three monologues more than suggests
the skepticism with which she must be viewed. In her own eyes,
her attentions to the Bundrens in their time of need has been
unstintingly generous and to the neglect of her "own family
and duties so that somebody would be with her [Addie] in her
last moments and she would not have to face the Great Unknown
without one familiar face to give her courage" (p. 21). However, as Addie's monologue and Cora's which precedes it reveal, very little sympathy actually exists between the two
women.

Of all Cora's claims, one of the most transparent is her
assertion that her attentions to the Bundrens have caused her
to neglect her own family and duties. For one thing, her two
children are grown, unlike Vardaman who would very much bene-
fit from some maternal attention from a kindly and sympathetic

neighbor; for another, the novel provides evidence that Cora is discomfitted by the Bundrens somewhat less than she acknowledges. In particular, the visit to the Bundrens chronicled in Cora's first monologue is an incidental stop made during the course of a longer and unrelated journey. The Tulls have detoured to the Bundrens' from a trip to town where the sale of Cora's cakes has been refused.

Further, although Cora has been visiting the Bundrens every day during Addie's illness, she seems to perform no useful function there. Jewel refers to the Tull women as "them others sitting there, like buzzards. Waiting, fanning themselves" (p. 14). Addie's imminent death has singularly little impact on Cora whose attention is engaged not by her neighbor's suffering but by her own worldly preoccupations. To assuage her boredom, Cora's thoughts and conversation, especially with her daughter Kate, revolve continually around her cakes and their disposition. Even Cora's fleeting attention to Addie is firmly placed within the context of her more immediate concern with the cakes: "'But not like the cakes Addie used to bake'" (p. 8). Cora is at pains to establish that the cakes cost nothing to make; her hens have laid so well that she has been able to fulfill all her orders for eggs, save the requisite number for baking, and sell an additional number to cover the cost of the flour, sugar, and firewood used for the cakes. Clearly Cora is apprehensive about Vernon Tull's perception of her wastefulness, for he is evidently a careful, meticulous guardian of his family's purse strings. As Dr. Peabody remarks about his summons to the Bundren home, "it was maybe Vernon Tull sending for me again, getting me there in the nick of time, as Vernon always does things, getting the most for Anse's money *like he does for his own*" (p. 40, my italics). In light of Tull's niggardliness, no doubt Cora *could* use the money from the sale of the cakes, but her explanation--"I can tell him that anybody is likely to make a miscue, but it's not all of them that can get out of it without loss, I can tell him" (p. 9)--will most likely appease her husband, or perhaps more accurately, her sense of obligation to him.

In light of her apprehension about Tull's reaction to her failure to market her cakes, Cora's comic defensiveness about them becomes slightly more sympathetic. Clearly, the lady doth protest too much: five times in the same short monologue she asserts that "[t]hey turned out real well" (p. 7). She may recognize grudgingly Addie's superior talents, but her tribute to them is patronizing, and the compliment, if it is one, is backhanded and seems thinly to disguise past resentments: "'First thing we know she'll be up and baking again, and then we wont have any sale for ours at all'" (p. 8).

Possibly Cora is attempting to capitalize on Addie's illness
by stealing her market; perhaps Miss Lawington rejects the
cakes on viewing them, using as pretext that the party they
were ordered for has been cancelled. But whatever the actual
circumstances, Cora's self-righteous rationalizing of the
rejection on the grounds that if it is the Lord's "will that
some folks has different ideas of honesty from other folks,
it is not my place to question His decree" (p. 8) rings hollow
indeed.

Cora's Christianity is merely a rhetorical façade, words
without substance unaccompanied by any substantiating action.
Later in the novel, Cora's counterparts Rachel Samson and Lula
Armstid prepare full meals for all of the Bundrens under much
more oppressive circumstances, despite their greater geographic
distance from and their correspondingly reduced sense of
friendship with the Bundrens and their heightened sense of
outrage. But Cora, who comes calling in the home in which her
closest neighbor lies on her deathbed, whose family will eat
only "[p]lain turnip greens" (p. 58) for supper on the night
of her death, does not so much as conceive of leaving behind
any of her cakes in a time-honored Southern tradition of
providing food for a bereaved or soon-to-be bereaved family.
Cora's own words condemn her: after all, the cakes have cost
her nothing; she probably won't be able to sell them at the
Saturday bazaar for her asking price of two dollars each, and
she apparently plans to take any unsold ones home for use by
her own family. "It's not everybody can eat their mistakes"
(p. 9), she excuses herself. Further, as the Tulls leave the
Bundrens a storm is brewing--"It's fixing to rain, sho" (p.
32), Tull affirms--so a possibility exists that even in their
box the cakes may be damaged by the rain and rendered less
palatable by the time the Tulls arrive home. In short, Cora
may observe the letter of Christian law in performing her
"duty," but she manifests precious little of its spirit of
compassion and generosity.

If the Tulls enjoy a material prosperity vouchsafed them
through their own hard work and thriftiness--perhaps even
their selfishness, as Cora's attitudes suggest--it sets them
in marked opposition to the poverty of the Bundrens. However,
Cora manifests a spiritual barrenness, a blind insensitivity,
to the world around her. While her preoccupation with money
blinds her, and conveniently so, to the Bundrens' abject
poverty and to the real as opposed to imagined services she
might render them, it also magnifies her comic simplicity
which contrasts so markedly not only to the incredibly rich
and complicated emotional lives of the Bundrens but also to
some understated but indisputably present complexity in the
dynamics of her own family. In her first monologue, for in-

stance, Cora's initial preoccupation with her daughter Eula's
necklace concerns its cost of only twenty-five cents and the
fact that it looks much nicer than that bargain sum would
indicate. Price and value are Cora's central concerns. Although
Cora narrates that "Eula watches...[Darl] as he goes on....
Her hand rises and touches her beads lightly, and then her
hair" (p. 9), whether she understands that Eula's motivation
in wearing the necklace runs something deeper is unclear. Eula,
in particular, seems to exhibit interest in the Bundren sons.
She speculates that after Addie's death "'Cash and Darl can
get married now'" (p. 32). Even Kate is temporarily side-
tracked from the absorption with her mother's cakes which allies
her so closely with Cora's emotional sterility. She inquires
about Jewel's marital availability and responds to Eula's
affirmative answer with something of Cora's vocal defensiveness: "'I reckon he will. I reckon so. I reckon there's more
gals than one around here that dont want to see Jewel tied
down. Well, they needn't to worry'" (p. 32).

Obviously, Eula's misplaced interest in Darl, fostered
perhaps by her mother's comic misperception of his character,[5]
is hardly tragic, but the implications of Eula's attraction
to him and Kate's dominant concern with money, both of which
reflect Cora's attitudes, suggest the likelihood of a permanent
physical barrenness in these two young women who seem ill-suited
to form appropriate attachments that will lead to homes and
families of their own. One, like her mother, is obsessed
with money, or the lack of it. The other searches for a mate
in a family where the eldest son grumbles only "'them durn
women'" (p. 85) and the second son is absorbed with his
mother's rejection of him and his sister's pregnancy.[6] Ironic
and humorous as it is, Cora similarly misperceives another of
the Bundrens. She dismisses the ripe and fertile Dewey Dell
merely as "a tom-boy girl" (p. 8).

However, the most telling illustration of Cora's emotional
sterility occurs in her empty cluckings about Vardaman: "'That
poor boy.... The poor little tyke'" (p. 32). She implies not
sympathy so much as censure, not concern at the distressed
child's condition so much as relief at being able to drive
away promptly at five o'clock. Ultimately, when the child
walks four miles in the mud and rain and dark to inform the
Tulls of Addie's death, Cora greets him with the depersonalized
"'He's a-ruining the rug'" (p. 67). She has a beautifully
paradoxical character: the materialistic Christian, the
righteous miser, using the words of God to justify the ways
of man.

Cora's predisposition towards Darl notwithstanding, the
extent to which her myopia distorts her perception of the
reactions of the various Bundren children to their mother's

death is determined by her obsessive concern with money. Because she affirms that Darl is the only Bundren child that
has "any natural affection" (p. 20), she is all too willing
to blame Anse and especially Jewel, "[a] Bundren through and
through, loving nobody, caring for nothing except how to get
something with the least amount of work" (p. 21), for their
eagerness for three extra dollars. She is blatantly incorrect
on all three charges about Jewel. Yet if Cora is not too wide
of the mark in sensing without understanding Darl's yearning
for some sign of maternal affection from Addie, her blinkered
vision is a rich source of comedy since it is Darl who drives
the favored and illegitimate non-Bundren son, Jewel, away
from his mother's side. Cora is all too willing to sell Jewel
short, evidently because of her outrage at Addie's favoritism
and ultimate sacrilege (in Cora's eyes) of setting "that selfish
mortal boy in His place" (p. 160). Jewel's monologue, which
precedes Cora's second monologue, reveals all too clearly the
depth of his attachment to Addie. Later, when Darl narrates
the moving story of Jewel's efforts to clear Quick's field
in exchange for his horse, Cora's assessment of Jewel as someone who gets something for the least amount of work assumes
an even greater irony. Cora dismisses Vardaman as "'almost
old enough now to be selfish and stone-hearted like the rest
of them'" (p. 22), and she disregards Addie's partiality for
Jewel to conclude that she had merely been "pretending" and
"it was between her and Darl that the understanding and the
true love was" (p. 23). Most absurd of all is Cora's projection
of her own economic concerns onto Addie when Cora attributes
Addie's interest in the coffin over which Cash labors so loving-
ly to the necessity of "having to watch him so he would not
skimp on it, like as not..." (p. 22). To Cora, it is a dog-
eat-dog world, and if God wills it that way, she can do nothing
except guard against being one of the eaten.

The question of why Cora is permitted to contribute to
the opening of the novel so much misinformation, some of it
immediately perceivable, much of it not, is an interesting
one. As the narrator of the longest monologues offered thus
far in the novel, the second and sixth, Cora's voice is clearly
self-interested, long-suffering, and above all disapproving.
While the first monologue establishes her attitudinal unreliability, her second establishes her factual unreliability, or,
to carry it one step further, her wilful distortion of facts
she knows to be true (Addie's preference for Jewel, for instance) when confronted with circumstances that she can't
otherwise explain because of the narrowness of her vision.
Through Cora, Faulkner suggests early in the novel what are
to become two of its central themes. Most obvious is that
noted by several commentators--"the theme of the separation

of words and acts"[7] which reaches its fullest and most complex
treatment in Addie's monologue. To be sure, Cora lacks Addie's
capacity for introspection, for emotional commitment, for
spiritual anguish, but her hypocrisy is thinly transparent.
Not only are her words about duty and obligation unaccompanied
by any supporting actions, they provide a convenient screen
which actually *protects* Cora from offering more than the
"doing" that might accompany them, or, in Addie's metaphor:

> ... when Cora Tull would tell me I was not a true
> mother, I would think how words go straight up in
> a thin line, quick and harmless, and how terribly
> doing goes along the earth, clinging to it, so
> that after a while the two lines are too far apart
> for the same person to straddle from one to the
> other.... [p. 165]

For Cora, the words of her Christian orthodoxy indeed come
"quick and harmless" for they never intersect the line of her
actions. A second theme announced by the intentionally fragmented structure of the novel as well as by Cora's trans-
mission of inaccurate information involves the exploration of
the knowability of truth and the apprehension of reality.
This theme is closely linked to the first by virtue of the
fact that man stores and transmits knowledge through language,
which as symbol is already at one remove from reality.

Because she is an outsider to the Bundren family, in
temperament, in values, and in sympathy, Cora may perhaps
be excused for the inaccurate portrait she offers of her
neighbors. But if she ill-prepares us for the many truths to
which she remains oblivious--to Vardaman's anguished confusion
at his mother's death, to Darl's determination to separate
Addie from the beloved Jewel at the moment of death, to
Jewel's capacity for back-breaking hard work and unquestioning
self-sacrifice--so she ill prepares us for the portrait of
her husband that emerges through the six monologues assigned
him and his appearances elsewhere in the novel. Only two
characters are permitted more monologues than Tull (Darl has
19 and Vardaman has 10), and this fact alone suggests that
he deserves more attention than he has been accorded thus
far. In addition, three of his monologues (sections 31, 33,
36) complement and supplement Darl's and Vardaman's accounts
of the climactic river crossing which marks the Bundrens'
passage into more hostile territory.

Despite Tull's cynicism about the Bundrens' motives in
taking Addie's body to Jefferson, Cleanth Brooks terms it
"a fine stroke to have Tull, the practical, earthy, and
common-sense countryman, tell part of it."[8] Evidence of these
qualities is provided at various times by other characters,

whose grudging admiration is thinly disguised, as, for instance, in this exchange between Cash and Darl:

> "... He [Tull] cut a sight of timber outen here
> then. Payed off that mortgage with it, I hear tell."
> "Yes. Yes, I reckon so. I reckon Vernon could
> have done that."
> "That's a fact. Most folks that logs in this
> here country, they need a durn good farm to support
> the sawmill. Or maybe a store. But I reckon Vernon
> could."
> "I reckon so. He's a sight."
> "Ay. Vernon is."   [pp. 135-136]

Even the aloof and impetuous Jewel who expresses annoyance
at Tull's interest in Bundren affairs accedes to Tull's good
sense when they attempt to retrieve Cash's tools from the
river:

> "Jewel," Vernon says, not loud, but his voice
> going full and clear along the water, peremptory
> yet tactful. "It'll be back here. Better come back."
>   [p. 152]

> "... It'd [the hammer] float three to one, al-
> most. Try the plane."
> Jewel looks at Vernon. Vernon is tall, too;
> long and lean, eye to eye they stand in their
> close wet clothes....
> "It wont float like a saw," Jewel says.
> "It'll float nigher to a saw than a hammer
> will," Vernon says.
> "Bet you," Jewel says.
> "I wont bet," Vernon says.
> They stand there, watching Jewel's still hands.
> "Hell," Jewel says. "Get the plane, then."
>   [p. 154]

Tull soon establishes himself as a more reliable as well
as a fundamentally more sympathetic narrator than Cora.
Furthermore and unexpectedly, he displays an inner complexity
of character that helps account for his fascination with the
Bundrens.

Although Tull's voice supplants Cora's as the outside,
distanced if not entirely objective or impartial narrator
who helps place the Bundrens' actions in the larger social
context of their community, Cora's obsessive preoccupation
with defending herself against what would be ridiculous
charges from her husband of wastefulness in baking the cakes
is contradicted by evidence of Tull's actual kindliness and

generosity, specific attributes lacking in his wife. Although
on the surface Tull's assumption of the position of outside
narrator seems designed to correct the increasingly evident
misinformation supplied by Cora, Cora herself calls into question his reliability as narrator. She asserts that she repeats
what is actually Tull's version of Anse and Jewel insisting
that Darl leave Addie to earn an extra three dollars and
affirms that Tull believes Addie "liked Jewel the least of
all" (p. 21). If these are Tull's errors, then his perceptions
of events are not informed by any more acute personal insight
than Cora's; however, they *are* informed by a far more genuine
sympathy for the Bundrens which causes the two lines of his
words and actions to intersect rather than to run forever
parallel as do Cora's.

This is not to say that Tull is *not* the practical, thrifty
farmer who gets the best value for his money and may have
intimidated his wife into fearing his censure when she does
not do the same. Despite his pity for Anse and his compelling
interest in the child Vardaman, Tull is after all a farmer
not blessed with four sons to assist him. This misfortune
notwithstanding, he is to all apparent purposes as successful
as Anse has been unsuccessful. Tull's opening monologue, section 8, narrates the events of the call the Tulls pay to the
Bundrens shortly before Addie's death and thus directly counterpoints Cora's opening monologue, section 2. It masterfully but
unobtrusively shows the balance of the values of self and other
achieved by Tull and therefore stands in pointed contrast to
Cora's monologue in which the first has blinded her to the
second.

During her sympathy call to the Bundrens, Cora's primary
concern is her cakes. By contrast, the Bundrens and their
tragedy have most of Tull's attention during the same visit.
He offers Anse his practical and sound albeit unsolicited
advice that the burial journey be started as soon as possible
while the roads are passable in light of the impending storm.
But when Anse remains obdurate, Tull retreats tactfully to
assure him that Darl and Jewel will "'get back in plenty of
time'" (p. 29). When Anse suggests that Addie has decided to
die because "'[h]er mind is set on it'" (p. 29), Tull thinks
that "[i]t's a hard life on women, for a fact" although he
feels compelled to qualify that generalization to the probable
exclusion of Cora: "Some women" (p. 29). Specifically, for
Tull these women include his mother and Addie Bundren. Vardaman with his large fish next absorbs Tull's attention, and
his meticulous description of the boy's activities contrasts
with Anse's relative indifference, which Tull marks three
times: "Anse calls him without looking around.... He dont
look around.... Anse dont look around" (p. 30). Yet, Tull's

pity for Anse's surprise and disbelief at Addie's dying as
well as his sympathy for Addie--she kept the inherently lazy
Anse "'at work for thirty-odd years. I reckon she is tired'"
(p. 32) Tull affirms--is clearly devoid of Cora's censure and
judgmental righteousness. While it is Cora who departs with
what are for her empty social amenities, "'If there's ere a
thing we can do'" (p. 31), it is Tull, father to two daughters,
who offers to help Anse, father to three grown sons, to harvest
his corn since "[l]ike most folks around here, I done holp
him so much already I cant quit now" (p. 32).

Tull's attention is real and his sympathy sincere if un-
complicated. Yet it is a nicely humorous touch that throughout
his visit he observantly watches Cash working on the coffin,
mentally noting it in the lulls of conversation: "We can hear
Cash a-hammering and sawing beyond the corner" (p. 29); "Cash
too, knocking and hammering at the boards" (p. 30); "Cash is
still trimming at the boards" (p. 31). Tull recognizes what
Cora fails to understand about Cash's labor: not his niggardliness but his craftsmanship. Thus Tull's secondary if real
interest in it surfaces at last when he can't help thinking
twice to himself, "If Cash just works that careful on my barn"
(pp. 31, 32).

Tull's next monologue, section 16, is largely a reverie
that becomes increasingly personal and contrasts markedly
with his usual public demeanor. It is prompted by Vardaman's
arrival in the middle of the night after Addie's death. Tull
is particularly affected by Vardaman's bedraggled appearance.
The boy's obvious confusion of the dead fish with his mother
both fascinates and horrifies the practical, stolid countryman.
As Tull so often does when he is particularly struck by something he has seen, he repeats an observation twice, in this
case that the child "looked just like a drownded puppy" (pp.
66, 67). Tull begins to ruminate, initially in general terms,
about "all the sorrow and afflictions in this world" (p. 67)
despite the fact that he believes that "the Lord aimed for
him to do and not to spend too much time thinking, because
his brain it's like a piece of machinery: it wont stand a whole
lot of racking" (p. 68). The reasons for this stance soon
become apparent. To think is to wander into trouble. Tull's
pondering the sorrow and affliction in the world promptly
leads him to consider briefly the nature of God which brings
him suddenly and perhaps unexpectedly square up against
matters closer to home: Cora's religious fervor. Although Tull
earlier revealed himself to be more than capable of standing
between Cora and her perceived "Christian duty"--in his refusal
to hitch the team up and rush Cora to the Bundrens--he lacks
the power of his convictions and eventually yields to her
insistence. However, an uncustomary criticism escapes him:

"sometimes," he reflects, "I think that Cora's a mite over-
cautious, like she was trying to crowd the other folks away
and get in closer than anybody else" (p. 67). The disloyalty
of this thought evidently takes him by surprise, however,
since he backtracks quickly to argue with his other, skeptical
self in an effort to persuade himself back into line: "I reckon
she is right" and "I reckon I am blessed in having a wife
that ever strives for sanctity and well-doing like she says
I am (p. 68).

But Tull's penance for his momentary lapse into independent
thought and judgment does not stop there. He concedes immediately (and comically, because the reader by this point is well
aware that Cora is wrong far more often than she is right)
that "Cora's right when she says all...[Darl] needs is a wife"
and that "Cora's right when she says the reason the Lord had
to create women is because man dont know his own good when he
sees it" (p. 68). He is willing, after all, to give Cora her
due; perhaps in the interests of domestic harmony he can do
no less, but the subsequent events of the night and early
morning cause that skeptical, faintly disapproving, vaguely
dissatisfied aspect of Tull's being to surface in mild rebellion
against the chains of Cora's orthodoxy and the emptiness of
her pat answers to Tull's questions about destiny, death, and
justice.

Ironically, it is not Addie's death that rubs a raw nerve,
for Tull clearly perceives that "'[w]herever she went, she
has her reward in being free of Anse Bundren'" (p. 86) whose
emotional if not physical sterility and passivity Tull cap-
tures in likening him both to a scarecrow and to a steer (p.
69). Rather, it is Cora's repeated statements about Vardaman's
disorientation being "'the hand of the Lord upon this boy
for Anse Bundren's judgment and warning'" (p. 68), paired
with the boy's pathetic efforts to raise the window in Addie's
bedroom and his boring holes in her coffin to enable her to
breathe that elicit Tull's more emphatic rebellion. If Cora's
God is an anthropomorphic projection of her own narrow vision,
Tull is not willing to dispute the possibility of her correct-
ness, but privately he clearly questions its justice: "If it's
a judgment, it aint right. Because the Lord's got more to do
than that. He's bound to have" (p. 70).

Tull's attraction to Vardaman, his sensitivity to Anse's
indifference to the child, and his own expressed skepticism
about Cora's God coalesce finally into a revelation of the
central underlying conflict of his own life:

> It aint right. I be durn if it is. Because
> He said Suffer little children to come unto Me
> dont make it right, neither. Cora said, "I have
> bore you what the Lord God sent me. I faced it

>   without fear nor terror because my faith was
>   strong in the Lord, a-bolstering and sustaining
>   me. If you have no son, it's because the Lord
>   has decreed otherwise in His wisdom....   [p. 70]

Unlike Cora, Tull has been profoundly touched by the circumstances surrounding Addie's death. The eliciting factor is,
of course, his concern for Vardaman, but Tull's unease is
deeper, and he persistently mulls over recent events and fragments of remembered dialogue in an effort to come to grips
with what has truly upset him. His rejection of Cora's willingness to see in Vardaman's confusion the punishing hand of
God ("It aint right") opens the way at last for what is poten-
tially a greater and more lasting repudiation of her. Tull's
troubling fascination not only with Vardaman and with Cash
but with the paradox of the lazy, ineffectual, passive Anse
who has managed to father four sons is finally accounted for
with his articulation of his own profound disappointment at
Cora's failure to conceive any sons.

Apparently Cora's empty Christian rhetoric functions partly as a mechanism for coping with her husband's discontent.
Cora may find refuge in rote Biblical justifications which
not only advance the notion of God's will supplanting that
of man, thereby absolving him of any responsibility for his
actions or those of others, but also justify those events
which man cannot control. Evidently Tull has been able to
make no such accommodation with his disappointment, but at
the same time it is a testimony to his humanity and tolerance
that he is unwilling to destroy Cora's. Thus, unlike Addie
who repudiates Anse when he disappoints her, Tull lapses
back into submission in his internal argument and closes the
monologue by reiterating, "I reckon she's right" (p. 70).
However, his repetition of the verb "reckon" four times in
the closing paragraph suggests concession rather than conviction. While Tull's fanciful vision of God turning over the
world to Cora to run grants her good intentions in making
certain changes, ultimately he is able to do little more
than wryly resume his habitual mask of acquiescence: "And
I reckon...[the changes] would be for man's good. Leastways,
we would have to like them" he says, and then more realistical-
ly retreats slightly: "Leastways, we might as well go on
and make like we did" (p. 70).

The depth of Tull's self-awareness in seeing in Vardaman
the son he never had and feeling skepticism about Cora's
devoutness is not profound. More accustomed to "doing" than
to "thinking," he is by nature neither introspective nor
reflexive. Yet the persistence of his overtures toward, or
on behalf of, Vardaman remains a poignant reminder of the

vacuum in Tull's life and ironically establishes him, rather
than Cora, as the novel's Good Samaritan. His charitable
acts counter the hollowness of Cora's words. At Addie's
funeral, narrated in Tull's third monologue in section 20,
for instance, Tull notes immediately Vardaman's absence. When
Dr. Peabody seems eager to implicate Vardaman in the business
of his runaway team, Tull is quick to protect the child by
offering to repair the buggy if it is damaged (p. 81). After
the funeral as he drives home to the tune of Cora's implacable
song, "I'm bounding toward my God and my reward" (p. 87),
Tull sees the boy fishing in the slough, that "hadn't had
a fish in it never" (p. 87). Juxtaposed to the self-centered
refrain and orientation of Cora's song is Tull's interest
in the child and his invitation for Vardaman to return home
with him to fish in the river. Cora steadfastly ignores the
child. So much for her "Christian duty."

Certainly other factors elicit Tull's attention to the
Bundrens. There is his perception of the hard life that Addie
has led married to Anse. There is also his kindly perception
of Anse's bereavement in the face of death. Contrast, for
instance, Tull's perception of Anse, "his face is different
too. He looks folks in the eye now, dignified, his face
tragic and composed" (p. 81), with Anse's own "'God's will
be done.... Now I can get them teeth'" (p. 51). Like Samson,
Tull is also undoubtedly aware of the fact that Addie's body
has not been embalmed and should be buried as quickly as
possible--hence the offer of the loan of his team to carry
Addie to Jefferson when Jewel and Darl are delayed in returning home by a broken wagon wheel. However, it is on the strength
of his attraction to Vardaman that the logical, practical
countryman does what he can't quite see himself doing. To be
sure, at the river crossing, he does not loan his mule to
the Bundrens, for he readily perceives that the risk is too
great. But Tull does assist Anse, Dewey Dell, and Vardaman
in crossing over the bridge that is now underwater. He
thinks,

> I...knew that I'd have to get back there someway,
> I knew it couldn't be, because I just couldn't
> think of anything that could make me cross that
> bridge ever even once. Yet here I was, and the
> fellow that could make himself cross it twice,
> couldn't be me, not even if Cora told him to.
> It was that boy.   [pp. 131-132]

The river crossing is disastrous for the Bundrens, but
it also precipitates a fuller articulation for Tull of his
recognition of what has been a vague and unfocussed sense
of dissatisfaction until the recent events of Addie's death

and funeral. It is clear to him that contrary to all his
best instincts he crosses the river for Vardaman's sake,
an action that otherwise the compliant and conciliatory Tull
would not perform, even were it put to the ultimate test of
Cora's command. Ironically, however, when Tull offers Vardaman
his hand, the physical contact between them reassures Tull as
much as it does the child: "I be durn if it wasn't like he
come back and got me; like he was saying They wont nothing
hurt you...and if I just stayed with him I'd be all right
too" (p. 132). The physical contact momentarily fulfills that
yearning loneliness that lingers just beneath Tull's surface
which the out-of-the-ordinary events have driven upwards into
consciousness. Simultaneously, it gives rise to a remarkable
yet fleeting assessment of his marriage which Tull couches in
the protective distance of a countryman's analogies. He glances
back across the river through the glimmering heat at his farm
and sees

> all the broad land and my house sweated outen it
> like it was the more the sweat, the broader the
> land; the more the sweat, the tighter the house
> because it would take a tight house for Cora, to
> hold Cora like a jar of milk in the spring: you've
> got to have a tight jar or you'll need a powerful
> spring, so if you have a big spring, why then you
> have the incentive to have tight, wellmade jars,
> because it is your milk, sour or not, because you
> would rather have milk that will sour than to have
> milk that wont, because you are a man.   [p. 132]

Tull's years of industriousness stand in marked contrast
to Anse's laziness, as does his sense of having structured
those labors around Cora and all that as wife and mother
she represents. In his analogy, the tight house Tull attempted
to build for Cora is likened to a spring holding jars of milk
and Cora herself is analogous to the milk. When the containers
are unsuitable, when the spring is not powerful enough to
cool the milk or when the jars are not tight enough to protect
it, the milk spoils but is still valuable "because it is your
milk, sour or not." What Tull suggests is that Cora's container,
the house he has built for her, the life they have led, has
not been "tight" enough. It has not been able to protect either
of them from life's inevitable disappointments, specifically,
their failure to produce a son and Cora's resulting disillusion
and protective isolation behind the barriers of her religion.
The spring has not been cold enough, the jar not tight enough,
and Cora may have "soured."

But Tull is a character of a different mold. As the passage
concludes, his thoughts follow the pattern employed in an

earlier monologue during his vision of God turning the world
over to Cora to run: "Leastways, we would have to like them
[the changes Cora would make in running things]. Leastways,
we might as well go on and make like we did" (p. 70). That
is, in the first sentence he affirms one position, and because
it is untenable, he retreats a step or two to qualify it
with another in the second sentence that more accurately depicts his true feelings which are being uncovered layer by
layer. In his spring-jar-milk analogy, his first position is
that "it is your milk, sour or not." Cora is his wife, for
better or for worse; sour or not, she still functions as an
incentive to labor, to build, to sweat, because she is his.
However, because that statement posits an alternative (unsour
milk) that seems more desirable than (and thus denigrates)
his actual state (sour milk), Tull reconsiders and affirms
his deep-rooted commitment to his wife at the very moment
when he is most vulnerable and most tempted to lament his
life as the act of clutching Vardaman's "hot and confident"
hand (p. 132) drives home to him the emotional void that the
absence of a son has generated: "because you would rather
have milk that will sour than to have milk that wont, because
you are a man" (p. 132). In short, the ultimate value of man's
endeavors rests not at all in their outcome, which dooms him
to unavoidable disappointment, i.e., Tull labored long and
hard to protect his milk from souring. Rather, the essence
of his manhood lies in the challenge of those labors which
inevitably carry with them the danger of failure. Tull's
acceptance of that danger, the possibility of defeat and
failure, is the measure of his manhood. Tull is able to
accept less than the ideal; he is man enough not to yearn
hopelessly after an unattainable perfection, or, in his
metaphor, for the placidity and dullness of a world where
milk never spoils. Thus, despite his own grievances, Tull's
life-affirming attitude toward his marriage contrasts markedly
with the life-denying posture assumed by Addie who is both
defeated and destroyed by her perception of the souring of
her own life, especially in relation to Anse.

His rationalizing notwithstanding, this is Tull at his
best: dignified, unsentimental, and devoid of the least iota
of self-pity. But Tull is not a paragon of unlimited patience
and tolerance. The rise to consciousness of his sense of
Cora's imperfection and his declaration of both his acceptance of it and his commitment to her are obviously precipi-
tated by his increased contact with Vardaman. What effect its
surfacing will have on Tull's subsequent relationship to Cora
is impossible to tell for certain because after his sixth
monologue, the Bundrens leave Tull's farm behind and he exits
from the novel as one of its narrators. Before he does so,

however, Tull's reconstruction of his conversation with Cora
about the river crossing suggests that his epiphany is in some
measure cathartic. Not only does it reaffirm his own confidence
in his capacity to cope with the disappointments of existence,
but it seems to hint of the emergence of a new Tull, one who
is less browbeaten, less cowed by what Cora says and does and
believes, and one who is correspondingly more certain of his
capacities to risk love, labor, and loss in an imperfect
world.

What happens during their brief exchange in section 36
occurs nowhere else in the novel: Tull contradicts Cora, with
good humor, but pointedly. He remarks a simple fact which has
long been apparent to the reader, and that is Cora's inconsistency. In this case, she lauds Anse for refusing to cross
the river on the wagon, an endeavor the "hand of God" (p. 145)
dooms to failure, but at the same time condemns Anse for
failing to take his proper place with his sons. Tull complains,
"'I dont know what you want, then.... One breath you say they
was daring the hand of God to try it, and the next breath you
jump on Anse because he wasn't with them'" (p. 146).

Because Cora has no answer for Tull's unspoken charge of
hypocrisy, she retreats behind the protective barrier of her
song, by now a familiar withdrawal from the realities around
her. Tull describes it as "that singing look in her face like
she had done give up folks and all their foolishness and had
done went on ahead of them, marching up the sky, singing"
(p. 146). The end of the Bundrens' marriage provokes a re-
assessment by Tull of his own out of which the suggestion is
offered in his final exchanges with Cora that he has emerged
as a stronger partner. No longer tormented by his own secretly
nursed grief for a son, but sensitive to its effect on Cora,
Tull can perhaps begin to deal with Cora's own defense
mechanisms by countering rather than accepting them in the
blind faith that Cora is "right." He can, in short, risk
disagreement, disharmony, and the conflict which he has so
meticulously avoided.

These do not threaten his commitment to Cora. Instead,
they affirm rather than deny his new perception of the ingredients of his manhood which lead him to reject Cora's
determinism and perceive at last the irony of her vanity in
believing in her own status as one of the chosen. In the face
of a reality which is inevitably less than ideal, one in
which there remains always the possibility that despite one's
best efforts, milk may still turn sour, Tull affirms not only
the value of striving for tight jars but the challenge of
failure. Thus, by extension, for Tull the Bundrens' losses
in crossing the river are not owing to the condemnatory hand
of God; rather the chance taken is the measure of their

humanity, their manhood. Appropriately, Vardaman, because he
is a child, Dewey Dell, a woman, and the ineffectual, in-
decisive Anse do not ride the wagon across the river. They
are not men and are therefore not to be tested. Tull is
understandably short with Cora who perceives the event as
another extension of God's will rather than as the action,
or the "doing" in Tull's diction, by which man establishes
his identity.

Tull's widely different reactions to the men who are tested
thus assume a logical order in light of the gradual clarifica-
tion of his own attitudes toward the tension between words
and actions. Darl's inactivity mystifies Tull, so he is
content to abandon diagnosis of Darl's dilemmas to Cora,
who, as always, is wide of the mark. Jewel remains at the
greatest distance for Tull although ultimately, despite
Jewel's initial hostility, he accedes to Tull's instructions
for retrieving Cash's tools and testifies to Tull's inherent
worth. On the other hand, Tull's obsession with Vardaman is
deeply emotional and threatens disloyalty. So strong is his
attraction to the child as surrogate son that Tull refuses
to call him by name, a perhaps too painful reminder that the
boy belongs to another family and bears a name given him by
another man. Tull's attraction to Cash is characterized by
a similarly frustrated paternalism; but with Cash his in-
articulate yearning toward the confused and disoriented child
gives way to his sympathy and admiration for the boy grown
into the man Tull's own son might have become: Cash, the careful craftsman who is worthy of respect and admiration and
dedicated to the values Tull understands best, those of
"doing" rather than "thinking." Nonetheless, Tull is not above
offering solace to the grown man as he does to the child
Vardaman. At Addie's funeral before Cash speaks of his disgust
with the women who have reversed Addie in her coffin, Tull
attempts to console him: "'You couldn't have holp it'" (p. 85).
Tull's overture is well-intentioned if not particularly
articulate. Later, during the river crossing he is more
comfortable demonstrating the depth of his sympathy for Cash
through the more familiar medium of his actions when he ven-
tures into the water to assist Jewel in recovering Cash's
tools.

While Tull expects to profit by utilizing Cash's skill
as a carpenter, his admiration for Cash's meticulousness
is unbounded: "I have seen him spend a hour trimming out a
wedge like it was glass he was working, when he could have
reached around and picked up a dozen sticks and drove them
into the joint and made it do" (p. 82). But Tull's concern
extends beyond the value of Cash's labor--extends deeply
enough to concern about the man himself to elicit the un-

characteristically frenetic behavior in the moment of crisis
at the river: Tull tries to "catch sight of Cash because he
couldn't swim, yelling at Jewel where Cash was like a durn
fool" (p. 147). He also shouts at Anse whom he has until now
been so unwilling to condemn: "'See what you done now? See
what you done now?'" (p. 147). The moment of crisis for Tull
is an intimate one, and his involvement is surely reflected
in the wonderfully rhythmic urgency of his account of the
accident. Tull, the man who has no sons, stands on the river
bank to bear testimony to Anse's passive but ruthless willingness to throw his own away.

Tull exhibits several admirable qualities throughout
the novel, including his capacity for hard work, his intelligence, his generosity, and his sensitivity toward
children and women. Nevertheless, Tull remains a pathetically
comic character in many respects. His refusal to call Vardaman
by name, his willingness to concede "right" to Cora when she
is so demonstrably "wrong," his fear of "thinking," his
compulsive thriftiness, and his inability to counter Cora's
automatic parroting of Scripture cause him to fall decidedly
short of heroic or tragic stature. He is unable to deal in the
abstractions which torment and destroy Addie and Darl, although
some of their concerns are his as well. His efforts to articulate his own inner conflicts are frequently hesitant and
guilt-ridden and fumbling. Yet he possesses a measure of quiet,
nearly stoic, dignity which counterpoints the more articulate
anguish of other characters who lament their burdens and
chronicle their rejections. Tull's disappointment and dissatis-
faction--his lack of a son, Cora's empty piety and all that
she has become--never reduce him to Anse's rationalizing self-
pity because the house that Tull has constructed is more
tightly built. In addition to compassion and tolerance, Tull's
labors affirm both risk and responsibility as necessary
ingredients of manhood in an imperfect world as well as his
ability to manifest them both, deny them howsoever the Bundrens
and others like them will.

NOTES

1. Olga W. Vickery, *The Novels of William Faulkner: A
Critical Interpretation* (Baton Rouge: Louisiana State University Press, 1964), p. 65.

2. André Bleikasten, *Faulkner's As I Lay Dying* (Bloomington: Indiana University Press, 1973), p. 59.

3. William Faulkner, *As I Lay Dying* (New York: Vintage,
1964), p. 166. Subsequent quotations are taken from this edition and are indicated parenthetically in the text.

4. Catherine Patten, "A Study of William Faulkner's *As I Lay Dying* Based on the Manuscript and Text," Diss. New York University, 1972, pp. 114-120. Patten discusses revisions made between manuscript and published text which show Faulkner using Cora increasingly as a foil to Addie.

5. Tull reports that "Cora's right when she says all... [Darl] needs is a wife to straighten him out" (p. 68).

6. Both Cash and Darl make a number of comments that suggest their revulsion from sexual experience and hence heightens their unsuitability as prospective husbands. For instance, Darl describes Dewey Dell: "Squatting, Dewey Dell's wet dress shapes for the dead eyes of three blind men those mammalian ludicrosities which are the horizons and the valleys of the earth" (p. 156).

7. Vickery, p. 65. Cleanth Brooks in his chapter on the novel in *William Faulkner: The Yoknapatawpha Country* (New Haven: Yale University Press, 1963), sees a variant of this theme, "the nature of the heroic deed," as central to the novel and relates it to the Bundren characters (pp. 142-143). See also Bleikasten, pp. 133-137.

8. Brooks, p. 155.

AS I LAY DYING: THE INSANE WORLD

William Rossky

   If we look in one direction, toward which William Faulkner
himself seems to point, we may see As I Lay Dying as a rather
simple affair. "I took this family," says the author, "and
subjected them to the two greatest catastrophes which man can
suffer--flood and fire, that's all."[1] By "subjected them,"
Faulkner seems here to suggest that the external plot, the
Bundrens' meeting and dealing with physical difficulties,
is chiefly a testing of human endurance. But the very
patterns of reflective internal monologue and of emotional
conflict assure us that the story is about more than an encounter with physical hardships. Of what more it consists
Faulkner also indicates when he tells us that Vardaman is
"trying to cope with this adult's world which to him was, and
to any sane person, completely mad."[2] As I Lay Dying is not
only a testing of man but, like the novelist's other most
highly regarded works, a testing of the texture of existence.
It is a probing which evokes a vision of existence as insane,
absurd; of man as little and comic yet capable of a significant,
if limited, Quixotic answer to the madness of life. And Darl's
terrible laughter,[3] which has much in common with Houston's
"sardonic humor" before "the prime maniacal Risibility,"[4]
becomes the keynote of the novel.
   Darl is the seer; his vision is beyond time--the largest
in the book. Faulkner himself remarks that Darl, though mad,
may "see more than the sane man,"[5] and repeatedly the novel
confirms this view of Darl. Although he is not present, he
can see Addie's death, and his vision is authenticated by
Peabody's account,[6] he knows Dewey Dell's secret and Jewel's
true parentage. As Tull says: "It's like he had got into the
inside of you, someway. Like somehow you was looking at yourself and your doings outen his eyes" (p. 119). Darl "sits
at the supper table with his eyes gone further than the food
and the lamp, full of the land dug out of his skull and the
holes filled with distance beyond the land" (pp. 25-26).
The land has been "dug out"; he is beyond earth and time,
sees "beyond the land." "It was like he was outside of it

179

too..." (pp. 226-227). If he can at times act externally,
even conventionally, within the world, he also stands in space
where he surveys the whirling globe.

And what he sees evokes the terrible laughter. Viewed
from Darl's vantage point, man is a "clotting" in the chaos
of "the myriad original motion" (p. 156). For Darl, seeking
"home," it is even a question whether man "is" (p. 76); the
unperceptive person, like Jewel, who does not recognize the
absurd world, can easily believe that "he is," (p. 76) but also
remains, Darl sees, "[l]ike a little boy in the dark" when
confronted by death (p. 18). Darl feels the grim incongruity
of procreation that leads to the grave: "It takes two people
to make you, and one people to die. That's how the world is
going to end" (p. 38). "How do our lives ravel out into the
no-wind, no-sound, the weary gestures wearily recapitulant:
echoes of old compulsions with no-hand on no-strings: in sunset we fall into furious attitudes, dead gestures of dolls.
Cash broke his leg and now the sawdust is running out" (pp.
196-197). In this existence, man is little--a stuffed doll
with "gestures"--without power or meaning to sustain him.

Darl's vision of man as a "clotting" in "the myriad
original motion" expresses particularly the ironic futility
of man's restless stir on earth. Seen within the immense
roiling complexity, man's own hectic motion becomes a little,
temporary stasis: His very "fury" is "quiet with stagnation"
(p. 156); his action, a "furious attitude," a "dead gesture."
As Darl watches Jewel and his horse, they stand in a tableau,
a "rigid terrific hiatus," "rigid, motionless, terrific"
(p. 12). In the timeless cosmic whirl, puny man's very
violence seems static--a motionless frenzy, a "furious"
stance. The whole novel conveys the feeling of human motion
slowed or stopped,[7] and even the title, perhaps, is meant to
convey some sense of this: in life, for all our "terrific"
activity, we lie dying.

But if, despite the evidence, which includes Faulkner's
statements about Darl, it be objected that we cannot accept
a madman's understanding, we have only to turn to the echoes
of Darl's vision in other characters to see Faulkner sustaining his refrain. Darl's view of the incongruous world which
provides no true "home" for man reverberates sympathetically
in Peabody's comment on man's pride as a "furious desire to
hide that abject nakedness which we bring here with us,"
and which we carry with us through life and into the grave
(p. 44). Of course it appears in Addie's belief, even though
that belief drives her to wish to live more completely, that
"living was terrible" (p. 163), that living is dismally a
preparation for dying (pp. 161, 164-165), and in her perception of the enormous incoherence between "words"--what man in

his simple acceptances, slogans, and catchwords believes,
or wishes to believe, true--and the complex, often painful
reality that "goes along the earth" (p. 165). But it also
appears in Vardaman, who, in trying to become a man,[8] attempts
pathetically, and for the most part ineffectually, to bring
the incongruities of experience together into a meaningful
pattern--especially those of life and death--and who dimly
sees irrationality in earthly justice: By what justice is
he deprived? Because he lives in the country? "I did not
said to God to made me in the country. If He can make
the train, why cant He make them all in the town because
flour and sugar and coffee" (p. 63).

Most frequently the characters tread cautiously around
the edge of Absurdity, sometimes peer over the rim of the
canyon, and then withdraw precipitously. In his pity for the
child Vardaman, Tull comes close to that edge: "If it's a
judgment, it aint right. Because the Lord's got more to do
than that. He's bound to have" (p. 70). "Because He said
Suffer little children to come unto Me dont make it right,
neither" (p. 70). But Tull sidles only once up to the abyss.
He gives it up and echoes Cora's "trust in my God and my
reward" (p. 70); despite his virtues, he generally prefers
to remain unconscious, insists that the best thing is not
to tax one's brains as Darl does--best to use it "no more
than needful" (p. 68). And earthbound as she may be, Dewey
Dell knows that woman's "coming unalone is terrible" (p. 59).
Even Moseley, the druggist, recognizes sympathetically and
ironically that life isn't what it might be, that "life
wasn't made to be easy on folks," that, as he suggests, its
very difficulty makes people good so that they may die and
get out of it (p. 192). Even Anse sits stunned like a poled
steer in dim reaction to the final absurdity, death. But of
all those who turn their backs upon the grim reality, Cash,
musing profoundly on who in this world are the sane or the
insane, comes closest to seeing it clearly--for a moment,
indeed, stands with the "fellow in every man that's done
a-past the sanity or the insanity, that watches the sane
and the insane doings of that man with the same horror and
the same astonishment" (p. 228). Cash has here more than a
glimmer, but he cannot live long in the consequent "horror
and ... astonishment." Cash, who can put property above
morality--"It was either send him to Jackson, or have
Gillespie sue us..." (p. 222), and who becomes, as Darl
makes clear, a Judas to Darl--"'I thought you would have
told me,' he [Darl] said"--(p. 227) is surely not, as some
have suggested, the mature point of view of this novel. If
at the end, after helping to dispose of Darl, Dewey Dell

placidly munches bananas, Cash, though somewhat less callous, also finds a rather easy retreat from complexity in the notion of a gramophone that trickily "shuts up like a hand-grip, with a handle" and somewhat practically contemplates the restful effect of a "little music" after a tiring day's work (p. 248). As Cash himself says of Darl, "This world is not his world; this life his life" (p. 250). It is the world of Dewey Dell and Cash and Tull who, if they glimpse the abyss, nevertheless veer away lest they see it too clearly.

The most prevalent critical view of *As I Lay Dying* is to regard it as a novel of kinship, with Addie acting as psychological center. And whether Addie be considered the center of the novel or not, she is surely a psychological force acting upon the rest of her family. To a degree, at least, the children do react to and complete themselves in terms of Addie's attitudes toward them. Clearly, as Darl indicates, he is motherless and therefore homeless. Through his horse, Jewel acts out not only his intense, near-incestuous love for Addie but also the rage and hostility which the son is apt to feel for the source of his painful conflict. For Jewel the horse is properly a "sweet son of a bitch" (p. 13). If Dewey Dell and Vardaman are incomplete persons, "vegetable" and "idiot," as has often been suggested, perhaps their deficiency may be ascribed to Addie's lack of love for them, although, since Dewey Dell does exhibit feeling, especially in her anguish over the "too soon" on earth which will not even permit her to mourn her mother (p. 114), and Vardaman is not idiotic but, according to Faulkner, simply a "puzzled" child,[9] how this may be done is perhaps a little obscure.

In any event the significance of the Addie-Jewel-Darl relationships extends beyond the psychological. Absurdity is revealed in another pattern. In her attempt to live her own life vitally, to seek fulfillment through her violence, love and sin, Addie creates for others, ironically, complexity and pain. The particular irony is frequent in Faulkner: Man raises his hands toward a dream; but we are all manacled wrist to wrist so that, as one of us raises his hands, perhaps very nobly, he jerks his neighbor's wrists painfully. Trying to express oneself in life, says Judith in *Absalom, Absalom!*, is "like trying to, having to, move your arms and legs with strings only the same strings are hitched to all the other arms and legs...."[10] In that book it is the assertions of their identity, not only in Sutpen but in Charles Bon and even in Wash, which, interacting, precipitate tragedy, just as the demands of the "I-Am" in Joe Christmas in *Light in August* or Mink Snopes in *The Hamlet* and *The Mansion* pull violently at the lives of others. That Addie in her search

for self-realization is admirable makes particularly pointed
the irony of this aspect of the human dilemma.

The total vision of life, of the universal and terrible
incongruities of existence, which is essentially Darl's vision
and to a degree Addie's, inspires, then, Darl's sardonic yet
poignantly anguished laughter: "'Why do you laugh?' I said.
'Is it because you hate the sound of laughing?'" (p. 243).
It is hateful laughter because it rises in a vision of a
cosmic absurdity in which the others live almost unaware,
the vision of a bitter and painful joke that evokes hysteria.
And "*Darl. Darl is my brother. Darl. Darl*" (p. 242); and
again, "Darl is our brother, our brother Darl." We are all
in it--brothers in this sense--yet tragically, bitterly, as
the end of the novel makes clear through the treatment of
Darl, we are *not* brothers in it. Hysterically, this is what
our existence is like. "Yes yes yes yes yes yes yes yes"
(p. 244).

And yet it is in this world that man appears comic. Despite
some scholarly tendency to treat the novel either as a strict-
ly serious work or as a comedy, it is neither but both--it
is serio-comic. And consideration of at least one source of
that tone deepens our understanding of the vision of experience
created by the novel: little man is Tull, Jewel, and Anse
at the flooded river, seeing, as Darl says, only with the
"dead eyes of three blind men" for whom Dewey Dell's "mammalian
ludicrosities ... are the horizons and the valleys of the
earth" (p. 156). Blind within the immense reality, his sight
limited to the landscape of earth, man falls into comically
small postures; in this vast context, little "clottings"
are seen *as* little and comic. It is as if within the huge
circle of myriad absurdity the pinpoint of man's furious motion
is made to seem not only static but also, because so blind
and so dwarfed, often ridiculous. By contrast, his stances
become Lilliputian "ludicrosities."

Almost all the figures, except Addie and Darl, thus somewhere assume comic postures; repeatedly the action or the
belief--the stance--is comically limited, narrow, often ego-
centered. Placed against the universe which Darl perceives,
Vernon Tull's judiciously considered pronouncement that "all
he [Darl] needs is a wife to straighten him out" (p. 68) is
bathetic--hilarious in view of the sort of "straightening"
of which Tull's wife, Cora, is capable. In this context, Cora
is particularly ludicrous. Even as she is handled technically,
Cora is more stream of mouth than stream-of-consciousness;
she seems always to be talking *to* someone and is perhaps the
most truly unreflective character in the book. She is almost
invariably wrong in her judgments and, if she is correct, it
is for the wrong reasons. Her stance which glibly ignores

difficulty in existence and in which she sees herself as
unquestionably the apple of the Lord's eye, receiving her
revelations directly from the Source and rising in a cloud
of clichés inevitably to what she repeatedly and somewhat
smugly calls her "reward" (pp. 21, 86, 87), is highly comic.
But most of all, of course, is this true of the attitude of
that "clotting," Anse. In the light of Darl's understanding,
Anse's extremely egocentric interpretation of the universe
becomes incongruously funny. Anse sees everything in ludi-
crously narrow, personal terms. From his toothlessness to
the building of the road, all his tribulations are somehow
the work of a personally inimical, vengeful something or someone. If it rains, he stands gazing "at the sky with that
expression of dumb and brooding outrage and yet of vindica-
tion, as though he had expected no less..." (p. 73). Or his
difficulty is somehow both Addie's fault and due: "I dont
begrudge her the wetting" (p. 74). So comically and limitedly
egocentric is Anse's interpretation of the universe that when
Cash breaks his leg, Anse says, "But *I* [italics mine] dont
begrudge her it" (p. 156). His little obsession in the
"original motion," of course, is his new set of false teeth.
Even the demonic Jewel, stalking through the novel with his
wooden-Indian glare, cracks the seriousness of the novel as,
in a ridiculous exaggeration of his code of honor, he helps
his horse to preserve its integrity: says Jewel, rudely refusing a well-meant offer of free feed, "He aint never been
beholden to no man" (p. 110). And as Darl properly understands,
man's psychic thrashings may come ultimately to the comic,
as well as serious, fact that Jewel's "mother was a horse"
(p. 202). In this framework, Dewey Dell, traipsing up the
cotton row and setting an arbitrary magic number of filled
sacks to rationalize her venture into the woods with Lafe or
trying, so to speak, a hair of the dog that bit her to bring
about the abortion, is a highly comic figure--unquestionably
here a "mammalian ludicrosity." So too Cash, practical Cash,
measures to the half inch everything in the insanely un-
measurable world--he fell, he says, "Twenty-eight foot, four
and a half inches, about" (p. 85)--and evades the frightening
gambit of thought, which he has himself proposed, by settling
for the new gramophone. In the light of the reality of Addie's
death, Vardaman's yearning for the red trains on the gleaming
track is the comic epitome of all the little desires and
postures. His somewhat satisfied insistence at the end on
the sanity of the family--"*Pa and Cash and Jewel and Dewey
Dell and me didn't go crazy. We never did go crazy*" (p. 241)--
is another comic attitude. Vardaman has joined "this world."
He will do; dedicated to red trains, he will make out. But
the comic stance is perhaps best captured in the tableau at

the end of the novel as Bundrens with mouths gaping and half-
eaten bananas in their hands are confronted by Anse, his new
false teeth, and his new pop-eyed wife. Repeatedly, in the
Absurdity of the universe, the stasis of little man becomes
comic.

Of course the humor stems also from other sources. Like
all the life in *As I Lay Dying*, the comedy is rich and varied;
comedy lies within comedy. We may see Anse, for example, as
the clown many find him--a feckless oaf at times, at whose
helplessness we may laugh--and also as a lazy rogue who, lacking Falstaff's zest, has yet a rather shrewd, almost Falstaff-
ian ability to slide humorously over or through life and thus
to triumph over others. As Armstid says, "I be durn if Anse
dont conjure a man, some way. I be durn if he aint a sight"
(p. 184). Anse has at least a little in common with the fat
knight who conjures Prince Hal. Or we may even see the Bundrens
as rather Molière-like figures of social excess and thus as
objects of humor.

More central to our understanding perhaps is the fact that
the blind comic stance has its often simultaneously serious
side--and that not merely because of the grim absurdity in
which it exists. For despite the smallness of the postures
of Bundren-man, despite, even because of, his narrow, egocentric view of the world, he is, in a limited way, heroic. Not
only his statement that he "subjected" the Bundrens to fire
and flood but other of his comments on the family suggest that
Faulkner regards them in this way. Asked about the critical
opinion that his "characters carry a sense of submission to
their fate," Faulkner offered the Bundrens as one of two
illustrations from his fiction of characters that "pretty well
coped with" their fate and, significantly, even included Anse
and Dewey Dell as specific examples.[11] If, except for Addie
and Darl, the Bundrens live blindly by the "word"--specifically
the "convention"[12] of fulfilling a burial wish--they suffer
by the "word" and achieve by it a blundering kind of success.
Enduring Faulkner's fire and flood, they come through. And
even if we adopt in part the now familiar critical gambit of
emphasizing that several members of the family also have
comparatively selfish motives for taking Addie's corpse to
Jefferson--that Anse wants new teeth, Dewey Dell an abortion,
and Vardaman red trains--we cannot ignore the repeated stress
on the desire to fulfill the "given promise" (p. 34) nor
even the small element of value and even of vigor and assertion that lies in these perhaps inadequate or trivial wishes.

Further, in *As I Lay Dying*, both "words" and the petty
desires are part of a world of "seems"--illusions by which men
live in the insane world. Most of us, as Addie points out, live
not by reality but by "words"--illusions. The world of "seems"

permeates the book. It rises from the structure, from the very
shifting kaleidoscope of changing points of view and the consequent shifting perspectives on the action and characters.
Peabody's objective vision sees even death not as a "phenomenon of the body" but as "merely a function of the mind--and
that of the minds of the ones who suffer the bereavement"
(p. 42); and, as we have seen, in his reverie on the theme of
reality and appearances Darl not only wonders whether he "is"
but declares that Jewel is not what he appears.

Oddly enough it is the practical, sane Bundrens who,
ignorant of the true nature of existence, live in a world of
illusion, even of dream. And this limited vision, although
it makes them comic, also makes them heroic: they are lesser
Quixotes, whose illusions, like Don Quixote's, not only
help them to endure trials, but, even like the knight on *his*
journey, to transform their world--to move the unwilling Tulls
and Armstids and the whole horrified, outraged, nose-holding
community to subserve their view and objectives.[13] As they
top the rise of a hill, moreover, and look over Jefferson, we
see them, again like Quixotes, looking "strained, dreamy, and
gaunt" (p. 216). We have here a perhaps significant echo of
the figure of Dilsey, described near the opening of the last
section of *The Sound and the Fury*, her "skeleton" rising
gauntly above "the somnolent and impervious guts," her very
body asserting the victory of spirit over flesh. In their way
the Bundrens are as unbelievable and mad as Cervantes' hero,
but, as with the knight, for the reader the question is Cash's
question: Who is crazy, after all? They live by "seems" and
succeed by "seems." "This world" demands a gramophone. To live,
to "cope" with this life, some need Vardaman's red train, or
Cash's belief in the sacredness of property, or Jewel's
devotion to a corpse and a wild horse, or respect for a
senseless "dying wish,"[14] or perhaps a new set of teeth. Blind
illusion helps man to live; if with Don Quixote--and Darl--
we finally recognize reality, we die.

But the victory of the Bundrens, of course, is comparatively a small one; for they lack vision. On the other hand,
Faulkner's questioning heroes of this period--Darl, Quentin,
and Horace Benbow--see the incongruities, see the insanity
of existence; but they drown in it. After *As I Lay Dying* we
await the hero who can recognize the absurdity and yet can
live in it, or else a hero who sees meaning in an ostensibly
chaotic world. Some inkling of such a figure, of course, we
have had in Dilsey in *The Sound and the Fury*. And a strong
hint of such a person appears, for example, in Byron Bunch
of *Light in August*: defeated, for the moment, Byron stands
looking up at a tree-covered hill, symbol of a vast indifference
to pygmy man, but concludes that he can "bear a hill, a man

can,"[15] quite in contrast to Hightower, who at one point sees
the "puny, unhorsed figure" of man defeated constantly in an
absurd world (p. 70). But it is really not until, in *The Hamlet*, we encounter Ratliff, the sensitive *and* the sane man,
who sees the "maniacal Risibility" but whose humanity and sympathy are created in and by the world and who faces it with
humor and integrity, that vision and ability to "cope" with
vision exist in the single character. Still later, seen in
"The Bear" through Ike McCaslin's eyes, pattern begins to
emerge from the ostensible chaos--the order of God's Wilderness which tests and creates the spirit of man, if he will
let it, molding him to self-discipline, courage, pity, and
love. Knowing the complexity of existence, Faulkner is never
completely sanguine; and, if his runner in *A Fable* is the
man who, somewhat like Ratliff, represents both "knowing and
caring,"[16] such a combination of virtues leaves him at the
end of the novel victoriously crying, "I'm not going to die.
Never"--but from a body so broken and scarred that, physically,
it is scarcely human. Developing out of the "sound and fury"
theme of the earlier novel, *As I Lay Dying* evokes a vision
of man's existence with which Faulkner has felt impelled to
deal recurrently, although with forever changing perspective,
through succeeding works.

NOTES

1. *Faulkner in the University*, ed. Frederick L. Gwynn and
Joseph L. Blotner (New York: Random House, 1965), p. 87.

2. *Ibid*, p. 111.

3. *As I Lay Dying* (New York: Random House, 1964), pp.
99, 100, 227, 243-244. All page references to *As I Lay Dying*
in the text of this essay are to this edition.

4. William Faulkner, *The Hamlet* (New York: Random House,
1940), pp. 215, 216.

5. *Faulkner in the University*, p. 113.

6. Noted by William J. Handy, "Faulkner's *As I Lay Dying*,"
in *Modern Fiction: A Formalist Approach* (Carbondale: Southern
Illinois University Press, 1971), p. 85.

7. Hyatt H. Waggoner, *William Faulkner: From Jefferson
to the World* (Lexington: University of Kentucky Press, 1959),
p. 76, notes this sense of "arrested motion"; interpreting
the novel through myth, Barbara M. Cross, "Apocalypse and
Comedy in *As I Lay Dying*," *Texas Studies in Literature and*

Language, 3 (Summer 1961), 252, finds that the Bundrens often appear in "the stylized immobility of totem or frieze."

8. Significantly, trying to imitate his elders, he "spits over his shoulder like a man" (p. 358).

9. *Faulkner in the University*, pp. 110-111. Richard Stonesifer, "In Defense of Dewey Dell," *The Educational Leader*, 22 (July 1958), 27-33, and Jack G. Goellner, "A Closer Look at 'As I Lay Dying,'" *Perspective*, 7 (Spring 1954), 51, were almost alone in the 1950's in seeing Dewey Dell as genuinely human. Goellner (p. 45) also anticipates Faulkner's remarks on Vardaman as a puzzled child.

10. Modern Library ed. (New York, 1951), p. 127.

11. *Lion in the Garden: Interviews with William Faulkner, 1926-1962*, James B. Meriwether and Michael Millgate, eds. (New York: Randon House, 1968), pp. 253-254.

12. "Convention" is Faulkner's word for it. (*Faulkner in the University*, p. 112).

13. Faulkner often spoke of *Don Quixote* as a particular favorite of his, one which he reread annually. See, e.g., *Faulkner in the University*, pp. 50, 150; *Lion in the Garden*, pp. 110, 251, 284.

14. *Faulkner in the University*, p. 112.

15. (New York: Modern Library, 1967), p. 401.

16. *Lion in the Garden*, p. 247.

AS I LAY DYING AND THE WASTE LAND: SOME RELATIONSHIPS

Mary Jane Dickerson

Surely one of As I Lay Dying's most distinctive features
is its revelation of William Faulkner's mythopoeic imagination
at work: "I took this family and subjected them to the two
greatest catastrophes which man can suffer--flood and fire,
that's all."[1] These elemental and primal forces, the resonances
of myth and ritual present in the journey motif and the landscape of the South itself create a visible world of relentless
motion that affects us with the power we generally attribute
to poetry. Indeed, André Bleikasten says, "The whole novel
tends toward being a poem."[2] Certain evidence indicates that
Faulkner, in writing As I Lay Dying, knew the vegetation myths
in Frazer's The Golden Bough.[3] And his source for his title
in the Eleventh Book of The Odyssey, the words of Agamemnon
to Odysseus, would bear out his familiarity with Greek myth:
"As I lay dying the woman with the dog's eyes would not close
my eyelids for me as I descended into Hades."[4] T.S. Eliot uses
Frazer in The Waste Land, which Faulkner probably read when
it appeared in The Dial in November, 1922, prior to its
publication in book form later the same year.[5] We know that
Faulkner, in at least one other instance, deliberately and
carefully used a paraphrase of a line in an Eliot poem as I
assume he was using The Waste Land in a more subtle way here.[6]

Perhaps the best general statement of the "waste" theme
is revealed by Darl's perceptive comment on the action of the
novel: "The river itself is not a hundred yards across, ...
as though we had reached the place where the motion of the
wasted world accelerates just before the final precipice."[7]
His apocalyptic image underscores the ultimate futility of
the burial journey and the sterility of the wasted lives of
the characters. The waste in both the novel and the poem reflects the depleted condition of life when men and women are
no longer alive to the needs of others.

This central meaning makes Addie Bundren's attitudes
toward spring--the season of the resurrection of life--more
ironical: it was the worst time of the year to her because
she did not want to be stirred to life. With the same ironic

189

rejection, the people of *The Waste Land* do not rejoice at
the return of spring; rather, they prefer to remain encased
in the death-like sleep of winter:

> April is the cruellest month, breeding
> Lilacs out of the dead land, mixing
> Memory and desire, stirring
> Dull roots with spring rain.
> Winter kept us warm, covering
> Earth in forgetful snow, feeding
> A little life with dried tubers.[8]

Addie remembers: "It would be quiet there then, with the
water bubbling up and away and the sun slanting quiet in the
trees and the quiet smelling of damp and rotting leaves and
new earth; especially in the early spring, for it was worst
then" (p. 161). She tried to reject life, which she felt
most painfully in the awakening of spring, and sought instead
a warm covering in death. Rather than seeking a regeneration
in life herself, she calls on her son Jewel to save her, in
words evocative of the New Testament—an ironic testament to
her spiritual loss: "He is my cross and he will be my salvation. He will save me from the water and from the fire. Even
though I have laid down my life, he will save me" (p. 160).
As well as showing how she has finally cut herself off from
all her children except Jewel, Addie's words reveal the
spiritual loss in the lives of this family whose livelihood
is tied to the cycles of the earth—they are unable to live
attuned to its life-giving sources just as the people in
Eliot's *The Waste Land* separate themselves from these elemental
sources of life.

Eliot's words "memory and desire" point to a significant
convergence at the center of both the poem and the novel:
the intertwined, inextricable relationship of the spiritual
and the sexual in our lives. Frazer connects spring with sexual
fertility, but sex for Addie held frustrations as well as the
wellsprings of her major connections with life. She saw her
life as empty as she believed Anse to be: "I would think
about his name until after a while I could see the word
as a shape, a vessel, ... a significant shape profoundly
without life like an empty door frame; and then I would
find that I had forgotten the name of the jar" (p. 165).
Another irony here is that Addie speaks of the central
frustrations of her life—sex and childbearing—through the
metaphor of Anse as a vessel, a jar. It is as if she rejects
her own sexuality, her own life source through such an object-
ifying of Anse as an emptied vessel. Eliot's Fisher King
echoes Addie's acknowledgment of a barren existence: "I sat
upon the shore/Fishing, with the arid plain behind me/Shall

I at least set my lands in order?" (11. 424-426). Addie
has set her house in order, accepting death as her only
possible answer: "And so I have cleaned my house" (p. 168).
But setting lands in order and leaving a clean house are
sterile substitutes for leaving without having communicated
and loved or without having worked out some meaning for life.
Dead people against a dead landscape.

Both works appear to use the vegetation myths, with
reference to the changing seasons, but invert the ancient
attitudes toward the life cycle, thereby reversing the central
significance of the myth. Eliot's notes to *The Waste Land*
point out that he was drawing upon Jessie Weston's book,
From Ritual to Romance, for his title, plan and much "incidental symbolism", and upon *The Golden Bough* for general
information.[9]

The fertility myth and its rites are immediately percep-
tible in the titles of three of the four sections in Eliot's
poem, and these titles alone would provide convincing evidence of the relationship of *As I Lay Dying* to *The Waste Land*.
"The Burial of the Dead" suggests the ceremonial atmosphere
of the funeral scene and the subsequent journey to bury
Addie Bundren according to her wishes. The men are stiff and
shy in their unaccustomed Sunday dress, the women are singing
mournful hymns, and the journey resembles a processional scene
with the wagon followed by Jewel on his prancing spotted horse.
The title in the poem is related to the pagan burial ritual,
which finds symbolic explanations in the concept of winter
as the time when living things die in contrast to spring as
the revival of life. "The Fire Sermon" supplies a parallel
to Darl's thwarted attempt to burn Addie's rapidly decaying
body. In both instances, the fire carries the double implications of purification and destruction. Eliot uses references
to Buddhist and Christian concepts of purification through
the cleansing effects of fire, and this section of the poem
also contains references to the consuming passion of lust.
Darl set fire to the barn housing Addie's body to purify and
cleanse; Jewel rescued his mother's coffin to save her from
the fire's destruction. "Death By Water" hints of Frazer's
dying god, who is annually resurrected in the spring. The
line (317) "He passed the stages of his age and youth" seems
to echo the resurrected god, and when Addie's coffin spills
from the wagon into the menacing river, her prophecy that
Jewel was to save her from the water is borne out. Jewel
saves her from the water, but the irony is that she is already dead. She and Phlebas are dead, and the ritual purification
by water cannot restore them. Both Faulkner and Eliot link the
physical loss to the decay of the spiritual.

The poem and the novel translate man's state through symbols suggestive of nature rituals and turn the myth into

meaningful paradox that suffuses both works with a strong
vein of irony. The planting of the corpse at the end of Section
I of *The Waste Land* recalls the resurrection of the Corn-God
Osiris; the burial of Addie at the end of the Bundren's
apocalyptic-ridden journey finds each Bundren attempting a
futile stab at the renewal of life: Anse gets himself a new
pair of teeth and a new wife, reminding us of Eliot's Lil
who is urged "To get yourself some teeth" (1. 144) so that
she can remain sexually attractive to her husband Albert;
Cash is looking forward to hearing the widow's gramophone--
which conveys to the reader the same sense of enervation as
does Eliot's reference to the typist's gramophone in *The Waste
Land* when "She smoothes her hair with automatic hand,/And
puts a record on the gramophone./'This music crept by me upon
the waters'" (11. 255-257).

Water is important to the ritualistic atmospheres of both
the poem and the novel: it is depicted as a negative, feared
element in ironical juxtaposition to the view of water as a
source of life in the pagan vegetation ritual. The people in
both works turn away from facing life completely and choose
instead the tragedy of a living death: "We who were living
are now dying" (1. 329). Darl sees the river as an uncontrollable and elemental force--a dangerous hindrance to Addie's
burial; "It looks peaceful, like machinery does after you have
watched it and listened to it for a long time. As though the
clotting which is you had dissolved into the myriad original
motion, and seeing and hearing in themselves blind and deaf;
fury in itself quiet with stagnation" (p. 156). In comparison
to *The Waste Land's* arid plain, it is the river which to Darl
is desolate: "Above the ceaseless surface they stand--trees,
cane, vines--rootless, severed from the earth, spectral above
a scene of immense yet circumscribed desolation filled with
the voice of the waste and mournful water" (p. 135). Darl
sees the land and the water alike as waste. Madame Sosostris
prophesies: "Fear death by water" (1. 55), and later in the
section "Death By Water," Phlebas the Phoenician, who has
met death by drowning,

> Forgot the cry of gulls, and the deep sea swell
> And the profit and loss.
> > A current under sea
> Picked his bones in whispers. As he rose and fell
> He passed the stages of his age and youth
> Entering the whirlpool.
> > > > (11. 313-318)

Tull describes Cash in the water: "He looked just like a old
bundle of clothes kind of washing up and down against the
bank ... laying there in the water on his face, rocking up

and down a little, looking at something on the bottom" (p.
148). The current caused Cash to break his leg when it
turned the wagon over and dumped Addie's body into the raging
river. The water operates as an inimical force in the novel,
not as a source of salvation.

The section "A Game of Chess" contains references that
have corresponding incidents as *As I Lay Dying*. Lil is told
to buy herself a new set of teeth--to improve her appearance.
Anse wants teeth to enjoy his food, but as soon as he has the
teeth, he acquires a new wife. Lil has taken pills to induce
abortion, "to bring it off" (1. 159); Dewey Dell tries to buy
pills to abort the child she already carries. "What you get married for if you don't want children?" (1. 164) asks a friend of
Lil's. Addie Bundren resented her children's births; the line
from the poem concentrates the irony of using the fertility
myths to portray modern man. Two more lines echo descriptions
of Anse and Jewel, and underline the lack of sensitivity
they feel for others:

> Those are pearls that were his eyes.
> "Are you alive, or not? Is there nothing in your head?"
>   (11. 125-126)

Tull notices that Anse's "eyes look like pieces of burnt-out
cinder fixed in his face, looking out over the land" (pp.
30-31). The phrase "looking out over the land" recurs several
times in *As I Lay Dying*, recalling the dominant and powerful
image of the Fisher King looking over his kingdom in *The
Waste Land*. Darl sees Jewel's face as empty and unfeeling:
"Still staring straight ahead, his pale eyes like wood set
into his wooden face, he crosses the floor in four strides
with the rigid gravity of a cigar store Indian dressed in
patched overalls and endued with life from the hips down..."
(p. 4). And Darl sees them all as wasted lives with no real
direction: "How do our lives ravel out into the no-wind,
no-sound, the weary gestures wearily recapitulant: echoes
of old compulsions with no-hand on no-strings: in sunset
we fall into furious attitudes, dead gestures of dolls"
(p. 196-197).

Faulkner uses Darl in much the same way that Eliot uses
Tiresias. Tiresias can be identified as the speaker of the
poem, but not the protagonist. Darl is the one in the novel
who seems closest to being Faulkner's voice. Tiresias is,
as one critic has put it, "the supreme metamorphosis that
brings together all the metaphoric transformations and thus
is qualified to summarize their experience,"[10] and Darl is
the one with the sensitivity to uncover the desires and
motives deeply imbedded in the "wooden-faced" features of
the characters in the novel.

Darl has been sent away with his family's belief that he
will bear some of the Bundrens' more immediate problems:
his knowledge of Dewey Dell's pregnancy, any act of recrimina-
tion that Gillespie might bring against them for the barn
burning, and his knowledge of Jewel's birth. Darl's family
refuses to try to understand his sensitivity; indeed, they
see it as a madness injurious to themselves. Darl knew all
their secrets. An examination of *The Golden Bough* suggests
that Darl may be identified with Frazer's study of the scape-
goat in primitive life. Frazer's discussion explains that men
were sent away as scapegoats to carry the disease or evil
afflicting the people with them.[11] The Bundrens watch the
train leave with no visible expression of grief. Rather, in
Darl's words which objectify his departure, "There is about
it [the wagon] that unmistakable air of definite and imminent
departure that trains have, perhaps due to the fact that
Dewey Dell and Vardaman on the seat and Cash on a pallet in
the wagon bed are eating bananas from a paper bag" (p. 244).

The novel and the poem employ the journey to define the
stages of man's mental, spiritual, and physical states. The
poem is about a visionary search for the water of life. We
see the Fisher King fishing at the poem's end, but without
regeneration his fate will be as hopeless and as predestined
as that of Phlebas the Phoenician sailor. The journey in the
novel is represented physically, but finally the characters'
lives are more selfishly directed than before: they have
known no true regeneration of the spirit or of the flesh.
They have not learned to give, to sympathize, or to control.
Addie's life and death and the ritualistic journey to bury
her should have made them more conscious of the individual
directions of their lives. Only Darl saw that "Life was
created in the valleys. It blew up onto the hills on the old
terrors, the old lusts, the old despairs. That's why you
must walk up the hills so you can ride down" (p. 217). Eliot
says in *The Waste Land*:

> There is not even solitude in the mountains
> But red sullen faces sneer and snarl
> From doors of mudcracked houses....
>   (11. 343-345)

Darl sees a similar image when they come up the hill into
the town: "We follow the wagon, the whispering wheels,
passing the cabins where faces come suddenly to the doors,
white-eyed" (p. 219).

Death is as much the main thread of meaning in *As I Lay
Dying* as it is in *The Waste Land*. A death in which there is
the hope of salvation is unknown. The will to believe in anything good and real is frustrated by the burdens of life,

and so the Bundrens return to their hill, passing through
the valley, where the old despairs, old fears, and old lusts
await them. The death suffered by the characters is worse
than physical death; they are dead to life while still alive.
Frazer, in *Folk-Lore in the Old Testament*, tells the story
of the distorted message that a hare delivered from the moon
to men: "As I dying live again, so you dying will die for
ever."[12] Eliot's lines strongly resemble Frazer's except
that they reverse the meaning: "He who was living is now
dead/We who were living are now dying" (11. 328-329). We also
recall Addie's words about the futility of existence: "I could
just remember how my father used to say that the reason for
living was to get ready to stay dead a long time" (p. 161).
The Fisher King was maimed, but his suffering was sacrificial,
offering hope for resurrection just as Christ's death symbolizes eternal hope.

Life will go on for the Bundrens. Dewey Dell's child will
be born; they have a new mother; Anse has a new set of teeth
and a new wife; Cash has a gramophone. It is important that
they survived and, in some measure, accomplished what they
journeyed to do. But, as Tull observes, "They would risk the
fire and the earth and the water and all just to eat a sack
of bananas" (p. 133). Finally, whatever *The Waste Land*'s
particular influence on the workings of Faulkner's mythopoeic
imagination in *As I Lay Dying*, his remarkable accomplishment
lies in the realm of a fiction transcending itself through
subtleties of language and symbol to become a poetry with its
own visionary power.

NOTES

1. Frederick L. Gwynn and Joseph L. Blotner, eds.,
Faulkner in the University (New York: Vintage, 1965), p. 87.

2. André Bleikasten, *Faulkner's As I Lay Dying*, trans.
Roger Little (Bloomington: Indiana University Press, 1973),
p. 43.

3. See especially Carvel Collins, "The Pairing of *The
Sound and the Fury* and *As I Lay Dying*," *Princeton University
Library Chronicle*, 18 (Spring 1957), 114-123. Also Barbara M.
Cross, "Apocalypse and Comedy in *As I Lay Dying*," *Texas
Studies in Literature and Language*, 3 (Summer 1961), 251-258;
Robert M. Slabey, "Myth and Ritual in *Light in August*,"
Texas Studies in Literature and Language, 2 (Autumn 1960),
328-349. Also see Walter Brylowski, *Faulkner's Olympian Laugh:
Myth in the Novels* (Detroit: Wayne State University Press,
1968), p. 84n.

4. Joseph Blotner, *Faulkner: A Biography*, I (New York: Random House, 1974), pp. 634-635.

5. Donald Gallup, in *T.S. Eliot: A Bibliography* (New York: Harcourt, Brace, 1953), gives the date that *The Waste Land* was first published in the United States in book form as December 15, 1922, by the American publishers Boni and Live-right, who were to publish the first two novels of William Faulkner in 1926 and 1927. *The Waste Land* also appeared in the same issue of *The Dial* (73, July to December, 1922) as an installment of *Many Marriages* by Anderson, a book that Faulkner discusses in his appraisal of Sherwood Anderson ("Sherwood Anderson," *Princeton University Library Chronicle*, 18 [Spring 1957], 89-94; first published April 26, 1925, in *The Dallas Morning News*). After attacking the book, he writes: "However, this story won the Dial prize in its year, so I am possibly wrong" (p. 91). Another comment about an Anderson novel, *A Story-Teller's Story*, seems to indicate that at this time Faulkner was reading *The Dial* with interest, and fairly closely: "... but taking the book as a whole I agree with Mr. Llewellyn Powys in the Dial: it is not his best contribution to American literature" (p. 93). If Faulkner read the particular issue of *The Dial* that featured *The Waste Land*, he might have read the review in the following issue by Edmund Wilson in which Wilson briefly discusses the sources of the poem and gives enough information about them to interest and inform a reader of the review (Edmund Wilson, Jr., "The Poetry of Drouth," *The Dial*, 73 [December 1922]).

6. James Meriwether, in *The Literary Career of William Faulkner* (Princeton: Princeton University Press, 1961), quotes Faulkner as writing his editor that in *Requiem For A Nun* he wanted "to paraphrase Eliot, 'In the beginning was the Word,'" in the title of the narrative prologue to Act II (p. 36). The poem he was consciously working with here was "Mr. Eliot's Sunday Morning Service."

7. *As I Lay Dying* (New York: Random House, 1964), p. 139. All subsequent page references will appear in the text immediately following the quotation.

8. T.S. Eliot, *The Complete Poems and Plays, 1909-1950* (New York: Harcourt, Brace & World, 1950), 11. 1-7. Cited hereafter in the text with the lines following.

9. Eliot, *Complete Poems and Plays*, p. 50. I do not believe that Faulkner knew Weston's book other than Eliot's reference to it. Any material he might have absorbed from the work, he probably received through *The Waste Land*.

10. George Williamson, *A Reader's Guide to T.S. Eliot* (New York: Noonday Press, 1957), p. 146.

11. Sir James G. Frazer, *The Golden Bough*, abridged ed. (New York: Macmillan, 1922), p. 628.

12. Sir James G. Frazer, *Folk-Lore in the Old Testament* (New York: Macmillan, 1927), p. 22. Though the quotation reminds us of the title of Faulkner's novel, Carvel Collins has shown that the title actually comes from the Eleventh Book of a specific translation of the *Odyssey* which Faulkner knew well enough to quote at length (see footnote 3). More recently, Joseph Blotner has made the line even more specific through Faulkner's own quoted speech (see footnote 4).

ANNOTATED CHECKLIST OF CRITICISM

Listed below are articles and books in which *As I Lay Dying* is given scholarly and critical treatment, along with a few dissertations and theses of special significance. The list is selective for those works published before 1974 and inclusive for those published from 1974 to 1982. None of the essays collected in this volume is listed in this checklist. In the annotations, a few references are made to works not listed here; these are keyed to Thomas L. McHaney, *A Reference Guide to William Faulkner* (G.K. Hall, 1976), where the items are listed and annotated. Those items I have not seen are marked with an asterisk.

Adamowski, T.H. "'Meet Mrs. Bundren': *As I Lay Dying*--Gentility, Tact, and Psychoanalysis." *University of Toronto Quarterly*, 49 (Spring 1980), 205-227.
   Discusses the novel in light of Freud's concepts of pre-Oedipal and Oedipal psychological patterns.

Alldredge, Betty. "Spatial Form in Faulkner's *As I Lay Dying*." *Southern Literary Journal*, 11 (Fall 1978), 3-19.
   Uses Joseph Frank's concept of "spatial form" as an entry to a discussion of Addie's monologue and her effects on her children. Covers old ground but makes some interesting comments on Cash's limitations.

Allen, William Rodney. "The Imagist and Symbolist Views of the Function of Language: Addie and Darl Bundren in *As I Lay Dying*." *Studies in American Fiction*, 10 (Autumn 1982), 185-196.
   Argues that the characterizations of Addie and Darl are meant to reflect the contrasting views of language held by the Imagist and Symbolist poets Faulkner read in his youth.

Annas, Pamela. "The Carpenter of *As I Lay Dying*." *Notes on Mississippi Writers*, 8 (Winter 1976), 84-99.
   Harking back to Olga Vickery's 1950 article, argues that Cash emerges as a creative and redemptive force. Examines his progress through his relation to Addie and Darl. Old ground.

Backman, Melvin. "Addie Bundren and William Faulkner."
    Faulkner: The Unappeased Imagination: A Collection of
    Critical Essays. Edited by Glenn O. Carey. Troy, N.Y.:
    Whitston Publishing Co., 1980. Pp. 7-23.
An unconvincing psychobiographical approach arguing that
the writing of *As I Lay Dying* was Faulkner's rejection of his
poetic temperament. Thus Darl and Jewel represent aspects of
the poet Faulkner, Addie the figure of strength he was seeking.
Includes some discussion of the horse-symbol in Jungian psychology.

Bakker, J. "Faulkner's World as the Extension of Reality:
    As I Lay Dying Reconsidered." *Costerus*, 26: *From Cooper*
    to Philip Roth: Essays on American Literature. J. Bakker
    and D.R.M. Wilkinson, eds. Amsterdam: Rodopi, 1980. Pp. 57-
    68.
Studies the irony deriving from the shifting of perspectives
among the novel's characters. Does not go much beyond Brooks
(1963).

Bassett, John Earl. "*As I Lay Dying*: Family Conflict and Verbal
    Fiction." *Journal of Narrative Technique*, 11 (Spring 1981),
    125-134.
A treatment of the inadequacy of Addie's attitudes towards
words and their effects on her children; antedated by Vickery
(1950 and 1959) and others. Includes a paragraph on the novel's
analogues to and reversals of the *Odyssey* and Joyce's *Ulysses*.

Beach, Joseph Warren. "Stream-of-Consciousness." *The Twentieth*
    Century Novel: Studies in Technique. New York: Appleton-
    Century-Crofts, 1932. Pp. 516, 520-522.

A brief and highly appreciative early notice of Faulkner as
a practitioner of the stream-of-consciousness method. In *AILD*
many of the monologues are actually soliloquys.

Bleikasten, André. *Faulkner's "As I Lay Dying."* Revised
    edition. Translated by Roger Little. Bloomington: Indiana
    University Press, 1973.
The only published book-length treatment of *AILD*. A comprehensive introduction to the major aspects of the novel.
Bleikasten synthesizes the best of what had already been done,
and often goes beyond it. There is some treatment of the
manuscript and typescript, and two facsimile pages are provided.
The place to begin a study of the novel.

Bradford, M.E. "Addie Bundren and the Design of *As I Lay Dying*."
    Southern Review, n.s. 6 (October 1970), 1093-1099.
Argues on the evidence of the title and the placement of
Addie's monologue that she does not die until the end of the
novel; that she is the auditor of all the other monologues; and

thus she is the center of the novel. A gimmick treatment that
is still occasionally taken seriously. Antedated by Julia
Randall (McHaney, 1951 B51).

Brady, Ruth H. "Faulkner's *As I Lay Dying.*" *Explicator*, 33
     (1975), item 60.
     Like Watkins and Dillingham (1960), argues that Vardaman is
neither crazy nor retarded, as some early readers thought.

Brooks, Cleanth. "Odyssey of the Bundrens (*As I Lay Dying*)."
     William Faulkner: The Yoknapatawpha Country. New Haven:
     Yale University Press, 1963. Pp. 141-166. Notes: "Darl's
     Self-Consciousness," "Vardaman as an Idiot," "Addie and the
     Experience of Community," "Faulkner's Debt to Hawthorne,"
     "Addie as Heroine," "Home-made Coffins." Pp. 398-401.
     A perceptive assessment of the novel, with emphasis on its
theme of heroism. Still the best treatment of the book's complexity of tone. Interesting comments on the effects of what is
narrated by whom. The notes address specific problems in the
novel, or misconceptions of previous critics.

Broughton, Panthea Reid. "Faulkner's Cubist Novels." In *"A
     Cosmos of My Own": Faulkner and Yoknapatawpha 1980*. Doreen
     Fowler and Ann J. Abadie, eds. Jackson: University Press
     of Mississippi, 1981. Pp. 59-94.
     Includes a brief treatment of *AILD*, placing it in Faulkner's
"modern" period, in which his work combined a concern for univer-
sals, a romantic intensity of feeling, realistic detail, and
cubist techniques; concludes that the reader is meant to respond
only to its aesthetic patterns and to remain emotionally distanced from the Bundrens.

————. *William Faulkner: The Abstract and the Actual*. Baton
     Rouge: Louisiana State University Press, 1974. Pp. 35-36;
     176-177.
     Brief discussion of two of Faulkner's revisions from manu-
script to typescript.

Brown, Calvin S. "Faulkner Glossary: A Supplement." *William
     Faulkner: Materials, Studies, and Criticism*, 3 (April 1981),
     30.
     Identifies a historical source for Faulkner's reference to
the "Birdsell" farm wagon.

*Brumm, Anne-Marie. "The World as Madhouse: Motifs of Absurdity
     in Virginia Woolf's *Mrs. Dalloway*, William Faulkner's *As I
     Lay Dying*, and Jean-Paul Sartre's *Le Mur*." *Neohelicon*,
     4 (1976), 295-330.

Capps, Jack L. *As I Lay Dying: A Concordance to the Novel*.
     Ann Arbor: University Microfilms International, for the

Faulkner Concordance Advisory Board, 1977.
Includes significant typescript variants in addition to the 1964 edition. A useful research tool.

Coindreau, Maurice Edgar. "Lettres Étrangerès: William Faulkner." *La Nouvelle Revue Française*, 236 (June 1931), 926-930. Translated by George Reeves. "William Faulkner." *The Time of William Faulkner*. Columbia: University of South Carolina Press, 1971. Pp. 25-30.
An appreciative early assessment by Faulkner's translator.

———. "William Faulkner in France." *Yale French Studies*, X (Fall 1952), 85-91. Rpt. *The Time of William Faulkner*. Edited by George Reeves. Columbia: University of South Carolina Press, 1971. Pp. 75-84.
An account of the early attention paid to Faulkner in France, including the publication of Coindreau's translation of *AILD*, with a preface by Valery Larbaud. Prints portions of letters from Larbaud to Coindreau concerning the book.

Collins, Carvel. "The Pairing of *The Sound and the Fury* and *As I Lay Dying*." *Princeton University Library Chronicle*, 18 (Spring 1957), 114-123.
Important article identifying the source of Faulkner's title. Treats use of myth patterns in *AILD* and *The Sound and the Fury*; suggests Greek parallels for *AILD*.

Cook, Sylvia Jenkins. "Faulkner's Celebration of the Poor White Paradox." *From Tobacco Road to Route 66*. Chapel Hill: University of North Carolina Press, 1976. Pp. 39-63. *AILD*: 41-46.
AILD is not a novel about class. The Bundrens are both heroic and fallible, and Faulkner's techniques work to humanize them. Accepts mistaken idea that Vardaman is an idiot.

Cox, Dianne L. "A Critical and Textual Study of William Faulkner's *As I Lay Dying*." Ph.D dissertation, University of South Carolina, 1980.
Together with Patten (1973) and Bleikasten (1973), one of the three most extensive studies of the novel. A detailed reading is provided, along with a textual apparatus based on a study of the MS and corrected TS.

Cox, Leland H., Jr. "*As I Lay Dying*." *William Faulkner: Biographical and Reference Guide*. Gale Author Handbook, Vol. 1. Detroit: Gale Research, 1982. Pp. 140-146.
A judicious introduction to the novel for the non-specialist.

Cross, Barbara M. "Apocalypse and Comedy in *As I Lay Dying*." *Texas Studies in Literature and Language*, 3 (Summer 1961), 251-258.
AILD manifests ironic interplay between its farcical action

and its apocalyptic language. Discusses the book's mythic structure and concludes it is an anti-epic in which each triumph is
a defeat.

Dabit, Eugène. "William Faulkner.--*Tandis que j'agonise*."
     Revue Europe, 18 (15 October 1934), 294-296.
     A novelist's appreciation of *As I Lay Dying*, touching briefly
on its realism; lyricism; the irony and harshness of the style;
the equal importance of characters, setting, natural elements,
and sensory imagery; and the interior monologue technique.

D'Avanzo, Mario L. "Reason in Madness: Darl's Farewell Scene in
     As I Lay Dying." *Notes on Contemporary Literature*, 9 (January
     1979), 9-10.
     Identifies the reference to Iago (*Othello*) in Darl's last
monologue, and discusses the nickel/spyglass/pig passage. Antedated by Ditsky (McHaney 1970 B22); Woodbery (McHaney 1971 B107);
and Rosenman, 1975.

Despain, LaRene. "The Shape and Echo of Their Word: Narration
     and Character in *As I Lay Dying*." *Massachusetts Studies in
     English*, 6 (1979), 49-59.
     Schematizes the narrators of *AILD* into three types: external
narrators; internal monologists, and talkers. Darl is in a class
by himself, using formal essayistic style.

————— and Roderick A. Jacobs. "Syntax and Characterization
     in Faulkner's *As I Lay Dying*." *Journal of English
     Linguistics*, 11 (March 1977), 1-8.
     Compares the syntax of Molly Bloom's monologue (*Ulysses*) to
those in *AILD*, focusing especially on Darl's monologues and their
differences from those of other narrators. Includes syntactical
analysis of a few sentences.

Dickerson, Mary Jane. "Some Sources of Faulkner's Myth in 'As
     I Lay Dying'." *Mississippi Quarterly*, 19 (Summer 1966),
     132-142.
     Builds on Collins (1957) to explore the novel's mythical
frame of reference. The plot combines compatible elements of the
traditional journey motif and vegetation myth.

Ditsky, John M. "'Dark, Darker Than Fire': Thematic Parallels
     in Lawrence and Faulkner." *Southern Humanities Review*, 8
     (Fall 1974), 497-505. *AILD*: 502-503.
     Brief exploration of parallels between the harvest scene in
The Rainbow and elements in Addie's monologue, as well as Dewey
Dell's account of her seduction by Lafe.

Douglas, Harold J., and Robert Daniel. "Faulkner and the Puri-
     tanism of the South." *Tennessee Studies in Literature*, 2
     (1957), 1-13. Reprinted as "Faulkner's Southern Puritanism."

Religious Perspectives in Faulkner's Fiction: Yoknapatawpha and Beyond. Edited by J. Robert Barth. Notre Dame: University of Notre Dame Press, 1972. Pp. 37-51. *AILD*: 43-46.

Argues that Hawthorne's *The Scarlet Letter* was a direct influence on *AILD*. Suggests that Tolstoy had an influence on Faulkner's double-plot structure.

Franklin, R.W. "Narrative Management in *As I Lay Dying*." *Modern Fiction Studies*, 13 (Spring 1967), 57-65.

Accuses Faulkner of inconsistencies in narrative management, anachronisms and implausible elements. Based on an inadequate understanding of the narrative technique of *AILD*. Has had an unfortunate amount of influence on other critics.

Franklin, Rosemary. "Animal Magnetism in *As I Lay Dying*." *American Quarterly*, 18 (Spring 1966), 24-34.

A useful explanation of the historical meaning of Cash's phrase, and an overstated application of this concept to Cash's "I made it on the bevel" monologue.

Friedman, Melvin J. "Le monologue intérieur dans *As I Lay Dying*." *La Revue des Lettres Modernes*, V: *Configuration Critique de William Faulkner*, II (Winter 1958-1959), 331-344.

Describes the narrative technique of the novel. Quotes representative passages to illustrate the differing quality of consciousness of Darl, Dewey Dell and Vardaman. Faulkner's voice intrudes.

————. "The Symbolist Novel: Huysman to Malraux." *Modernism: 1890-1930*. Edited by Malcolm Bradbury and James McFarlane. New York: Penguin Books, 1974. Pp. 453-466. Reprinted Atlantic Highlands, N.J.: Humanities Press, 1978.

Includes brief discussion of Faulkner's use in *As I Lay Dying* of "symbol and metaphorical suggestion to delineate character."

Garrett, George. "Some Revisions in *As I Lay Dying*." *Modern Language Notes*, 73 (June 1958), 414-417.

The first attempt to study the evidence of the manuscript. Limited to the two pages available for inspection at the time, but from this evidence Garrett refutes the misconception that the book underwent no revision.

Goellner, Jack Gordon. "A Closer Look at 'As I Lay Dying'." *Perspective: A Quarterly of Literature and the Arts*, 7 (Spring 1954), 42-54.

Points out and attempts to correct some of the earliest misconceptions about the novel. Crux of the novel is in the tangle of relationships within the Bundren family. Builds on Vickery (1950) and modifies her view that Cash has grown during the course of action.

Gold, Joseph. "'Sin, Salvation and Bananas': *As I Lay Dying*."
    Mosaic, 7 (Fall 1973), 55-73.
    Argues that the novel's central subject is religion and that
it constitutes Faulkner's contribution to the faith/works debate.
Isolated insights, among which are the points that Whitfield is
a parody of Rev. George Whitefield, and that Anse owes something
to the Biblical Job.

Goodman, Charlotte. "The Bundren Wagon: Narrative Strategy in
    Faulkner's *As I Lay Dying*." *Studies in American Fiction*,
    7 (Autumn 1979), 234-242.
    A study of the symbolic functions of the wagon. Many errors
of fact and interpretation.

Gray, Richard. "The Individual Talent: Faulkner." *The Literature
    of Memory: Modern Writers of the American South*. Baltimore:
    Johns Hopkins University Press, 1977. Pp. 197-256. *AILD*:
    222-229.
    A study of varying perspectives on the individual characters
provided within the novel, with special emphasis on Dewey Dell
as an example. Comments on the complexity of tone. Tends finally to reduce the novel to Addie's "message."

*Gresset, Michel. "Postface." *Tandis que j'agonise*. Paris:
    Gallimard, 1973. Pp. 247-254.

————. "Le Scandale." *Faulkner ou la fascination, I: Poétique
    du regard*. Paris: Klincksieck, 1982. Pp. 217-238. *AILD*:
    220-226.
    This brief section of Gresset's meditation on Faulkner's
poetics of vision contrasts Jewel, who is only eyes and ends
blind to his identity like Oedipus, with Darl, who is purely
vision and ends in madness as the object of his own regard; it
discusses the sense of scandal manifested in the extremes of
horror and astonishment, both of which derive from vision.

————, ed. "Valery Larbaud et les débuts de Faulkner en
    France." *Preuves*, 184 (1966), 26-28.
    Prints letters of Larbaud to Coindreau--and one of R.N.
Raimbault to Coindreau--of the 1931-1933 period. The letters
deal with Coindreau's translation of Faulkner and Larbaud's
preface to his translation of *As I Lay Dying*. Two of these
letters are also printed in Coindreau, 1953.

Hammond, Donald. "Faulkner's Levels of Awareness." *Florida
    Quarterly*, 1 (1967), 73-81.
    Exploration of the means by which Faulkner overcomes the
technical problems presented by the inarticulateness of his rural
characters. Brief treatments of Darl, Vardaman, Dewey Dell.
Shows that the transitions from one level of thought to another
are accomplished through Faulkner's use of italics and verbal

keys.

Hemenway, Robert. "Enigmas of Being in *As I Lay Dying*." *Modern
    Fiction Studies*, 16 (Summer 1970), 133-146.
    Treats the characters' attempts to come to terms with death
and being. Detailed examination of Darl's "emptying for sleep"
passage and Darl and Vardaman's is/are discussion.

Howe, Irving. *William Faulkner: A Critical Study*. New York:
    Random House, 1952. Pp. 42-44, 127-142. Revised edition,
    1962. Pp. 52-56, 175-191. Third edition, Chicago: Univer-
    sity of Chicago Press, 1975. Pp. 52-56, 175-191.
    Sets *AILD* within the historical and legendary setting of
Yoknapatawpha. Discusses the relationship of Addie to each of
her children. Finds *AILD* the warmest and kindliest of Faulkner's
novels, but is not very appreciative in its assessment of it.

*Idei, Yasuko. "A Quest for Identity and the Meaning of the
    Be-Verb in *As I Lay Dying*." *Kyusha American Literature*
    (Fukuoka, Japan), 19 (1978), 32-44.

Irwin, John T. *Doubling and Incest/Repetition and Revenge: A
    Speculative Reading of Faulkner*. Baltimore and London:
    Johns Hopkins University Press, 1975. Pp. 53-55.
    Claims that Darl's love for Addie is displaced in an inces-
tuous love for Dewey Dell. Argument is derived primarily from
plot similarities with *The Sound and the Fury*.

Kartiganer, Donald M. "*As I Lay Dying*." *The Fragile Thread:
    The Meaning of Form in Faulkner's Novels*. Amherst: Univer-
    sity of Massachusetts Press, 1979. Pp. 23-33.
    Attempts to demonstrate that *AILD* is a failure because, in
it, plot works counter to consciousness. Useful comments on
Vardaman and Cash.

Kawin, Bruce. "Faulkner, Beckett, and Jabès." *The Mind of the
    Novel: Reflexive Fiction and the Ineffable*. Princeton:
    Princeton University Press, 1982. Pp. 251-298. *AILD*:
    258-272.
    Raises some questions about the narrative voice of *AILD*
similar to those addressed in Ross (1979) and Bradford (1970),
but fails to answer them satisfactorily.

Kinney, Arthur F. "Style as Vision: Accomplishment." *Faulkner's
    Narrative Poetics: Style as Vision*. Amherst: University of
    Massachusetts Press, 1978. Pp. 121-244. *AILD*: 161-177.
    Studies the narrative consciousness of the novel, with
special attention to Darl and Addie. Darl is paired, first
with Jewel as his secret model, then with Addie. Her death
presages his own.

Kirk, Robert W. "Faulkner's Anse Bundren." *Georgia Review*,
19 (Winter 1965), 446-452.
Sees Anse as the central and comic figure. Points out his
desire to *seem* a part of things and to attain dignity.

Kloss, Robert J. "Faulkner's *As I Lay Dying*." *American Imago*,
38 (Winter 1981), 429-444.
An uneven, often far-fetched discussion of sexual behavior
and perversions in relation to Addie on the part of her sons.
Based more on an external application of Freudian meanings to
the book's images than on a close reading of the novel.

Komar, Kathleen. "A Structural Study of *As I Lay Dying*."
*Faulkner Studies: An Annual of Research, Criticism, and
Reviews*, I (1980), 48-57.
Argues that the novel exhibits two broad structural patterns
in tension with one another: a mythic pattern motivated by plot,
with Addie at center, and a pattern of consciousness with Anse,
ironically, at center. Provocative, but not completely satisfactory. Ignores the non-Bundren narrators.

Lanati, Barbara. "Il Primo Faulkner: *As I Lay Dying*." *Sigma*,
19 (September 1968), 83-119.
A general assessment of the novel, touching on the characters
and their language, structure and narrative technique. Provides
a day-by-day plot summary. Suggests Mrs. Morel of Lawrence's
Sons and Lovers and Hester Prynne of Hawthorne's *The Scarlet
Letter* as analogues for Addie. Suggests Bunyan's *Pilgrim's
Progress* as a model for some of the allegorical features.

Larbaud, Valéry. "Préface." *Tandis que j'agonise*. Translated
by Maurice Coindreau. Paris: Gallimard, 1934. Pp. 9-14.
Rpt. as "Un roman de William Faulkner. *'Tandis que j'agonise'*." *Ce vice impuni, la lecture. Domaine anglais*.
Paris: Gallimard, 1936. Pp. 218-222.
Praises the novel's presentation of an unfamiliar part of
the United States, the truth of its characterizations, its epic
and dramatic qualities, and comments on the interior monologue
technique.

*Leath, Helen Lang. "'Will the Circle Be Unbroken?' An Analysis
of Structure in *As I Lay Dying*." *Southwestern American
Literature*, 3 (1973), 61-68.

Le Breton, Maurice. "Le Thème de la Vie et de la Mort dans
As I Lay Dying." *La Revue des Lettres Modernes*, V:
Configuration Critique de William Faulkner, II (Winter
1958-1959), 292-308.
Studies the characters Addie, Darl, Dewey Dell and Vardaman
and how they deal with problems of isolation and being or self.
One of the few treatments of the characters' perceptions of the
concrete world.

208 An Annotated Checklist of Criticism

Levins, Lynn Gartrell. *Faulkner's Heroic Design: The Yoknapataw-pha Novels*. Athens: University of Georgia Press, 1976. Pp. 94-114.

AILD evokes the epic journey and the Christian pilgrimage. Analogues are the Apocalypse, *Divine Comedy*, *Piers Plowman*, *Pilgrim's Progress*, Exodus, the *Odyssey*, the *Aeneid*. Also treats the theme of heroism.

Lilly, Paul R., Jr. "Caddy and Addie: Speakers of Faulkner's Impeccable Language." *Journal of Narrative Technique*, 3 (September 1973), 170-182.

Relates Faulkner's concept of poetry, which implies a transcendence of language, to the narrative form of *AILD*. Argues that Addie's images are all variations on the container enclosing an explosive force. Provocative.

Little, Matthew. "*As I Lay Dying* and 'Dementia Praecox' Humor." *Studies in American Humor*, 2 (April 1975), 61-70.

Treats the conjunction of rustic characters and subtle psychological characterization in *AILD* as two strains of American humor: native and dementia praecox. Overly schematic.

Lyday, Lance. "Jewel Bundren: Faulkner's Achilles." *Notes on Contemporary Literature*, 10 (March 1980), 2.

Notes, without interpretative comment, some similarities between Jewel and Homer's Achilles, the most significant being that both retire from their endeavors when horse and mistress, respectively, are taken from them, but later return to participate.

McCarthy, Paul. "Several Words, Shapes, and Attitudes in *As I Lay Dying*." *Notes on Mississippi Writers*, 14 (Spring 1981), 27-37.

A study of the characters' use of the words "straight," "circles," and "angles" that breaks little new ground.

Mellard, James M. "Faulkner's Philosophical Novel: Ontological Themes in *As I Lay Dying*." *The Personalist*, 48 (October 1967), 509-523.

Examines the relevance of various philosophical stances--idealism, nominalism and realism--to the novel's characters without claiming that *AILD* belongs to any particular philosophical school.

*Mickevic, Boris. "Kogda nastal moj cas." *Neman*, 27 (1978), 70-75.

An introduction to the Russian translation of *AILD* by Galina Usovaja.

Middleton, David. "Faulkner's Folklore in *As I Lay Dying*: An Old Motif in a New Manner." *Studies in the Novel*, 9 (Spring

1977), 46-53.

Ostensibly a treatment of *AILD* as an inversion of the folk motif of the grieving husband who carries his wife's corpse with him because he can't bear to part with her. Actually devoted to defending the thesis that Anse is aware of Addie's revenge and he deliberately tries to turn the tables on her.

Millgate, Michael. "*As I Lay Dying.*" *The Achievement of William Faulkner.* New York: Random House, 1966. Pp. 104-122.

Places *AILD* in the context of Faulkner's other works; examines function of multiple viewpoints; describes the MS and TS evidence for the time it took Faulkner to write the novel; suggests some sources and analogues. Still an excellent general introduction to the novel.

Morell, Giliane. "'Pourquoi ris-tu', Darl?—ou le temps d'un regard." *Sud*, 14/15 (Summer 1975), 128-148.

A wide-ranging discussion of the images of vision in *AILD*. Fruitful comparison of the river-crossing scene with "Nympholepsy." Argues that Darl is denied vision (access to Addie) until the end, when—mad—he "sees" his parents in the spyglass.

Orfali, Ingrid. "Silences de *Tandis que j'agonise.*" *Delta*, 3 (November 1976), 19-21.

Explicates Addie's comments about words briefly; then takes this theme as an analogy for the whole novel. What is not said is as important as what is. Darl contradicts himself about what he is doing in the night with his shirt up, but the reader concludes for himself because Faulkner has provided a "silent" text parallel to (or between the lines of) the discourse presented in the monologues.

*Palumbo, Donald. "The Concept of God in Faulkner's *Light in August*, *The Sound and the Fury*, *As I Lay Dying*, and *Absalom, Absalom!*." *South Central Bulletin*, 34 (Winter 1979), 142-146.

Parsons, Thornton H. "Doing the Best They Can." *Georgia Review*, 23 (Fall 1969), 292-306.

A revaluation of Jewel, Cash and Anse, focussing on the themes of sacrifice and endurance. Points out that none of the characters undergoes change or development, but rather the reader re-adjusts his judgments about them as more evidence is provided. Recognizes the complexity of characterization, but perhaps over-emphasizes the "sacredness" of the promise made to Addie.

Patten, Catherine M., R.S.H.M. "A Study of William Faulkner's *As I Lay Dying* Based on the Manuscript and Text." Ph.D. dissertation, New York University, 1973.

Usefully brings MS evidence to bear on several topics: narrative management, characterization, the triptych and imagery, humor and irony (Cash and Anse), and myth. The most thorough

examination of Faulkner's revisions (slightly marred by its lack
of attention to the TS), and the most detailed compilation of
information and quotes from the MS, the dissertation also provides
fruitful discussions of many critical issues in the novel.

Pierce, Constance. "Being, Knowing, and Saying in the 'Addie'
    Section of Faulkner's *As I Lay Dying*." *Twentieth Century
    Literature*, 26 (Fall 1980), 294-305.
    Discusses Addie's attempt to escape self-consciousness in
terms of Heidegger's *Identity and Difference*. Thesis-ridden;
offers little that is new.

Pilkington, John. "The Way of Naturalism: *As I Lay Dying*."
    The Heart of Yoknapatawpha. Jackson: University Press of
    Mississippi, 1981. Pp. 87-110.
    An overview of the novel's composition and plot, with random
comments about problems of technique, certain characters, and
the theme of heroism. Adds nothing to Millgate (1966) or
Bleikasten (1973).

Pitavy, François L. "Through Darl's Eyes Darkly: The Vision of
    the Poet in *As I Lay Dying*." *William Faulkner: Materials,
    Studies, and Criticism*, 4 (July 1982), 37-62.
    A fruitful study of Darl's imagery and modes of perception
comparable in approach to Rossi (1973).

Powers, Lyall H. "*As I Lay Dying*." *Faulkner's Yoknapatawpha
    Comedy*. Ann Arbor: University of Michigan Press, 1980.
    Pp. 50-72.
    The overriding thesis of this book leads Powers to view the
Bundrens as exemplars of the "naked human goodness" of the simple
folk and Darl as having the clearest sense of self-identity.

Reed, Joseph W., Jr. "*As I Lay Dying*." *Faulkner's Narrative*.
    New Haven: Yale University Press, 1973. Pp. 84-111, 283.
    Examines imagery patterns, thematic patterns and narrative
patterns.

Reed, Richard. "The Role of Chronology in Faulkner's Yoknapataw-
    pha Fiction." *Southern Literary Journal*, 7 (Fall 1974), 24-
    48.
    Claims Faulkner was inconsistent about the time of conception
of Dewey Dell's baby. Easily refuted.

Richmond, Lee J. "The Education of Vardaman Bundren in Faulkner's
    As I Lay Dying." *Renaissance and Modern: Essays in Honor of
    Edwin M. Moseley*. Edited by Murray J. Levith. Saratoga
    Springs: Skidmore College, 1976. Pp. 133-142.
    Traces Vardaman's progress through the action of the novel,
concluding that he acquires the emotional equipment he needs to
survive. Misreads. Superseded by Rooks, in this volume.

Robinson, Fred Miller. "Faulkner: *As I Lay Dying*." *The Comedy of Language: Studies in Modern Comic Literature*. Amherst: University of Massachusetts Press, 1980. Pp. 51–88.
     Offers a fruitful discussion of Bergsonian comedy in the novel's characters, of the theme of form versus reality as a source of comedy, and of the complexity of the novel's vision.

Rosenman, John B. "Another *Othello* Echo in *As I Lay Dying*." *Notes on Mississippi Writers*, 8 (Spring 1975), 19–21.
     Antedated by Ditsky (McHaney 1970 B22) and Woodbery (McHaney 1971 B107). Rosenman's interpretation distorts the novel to fit the symbolism imported from Shakespeare.

————. "A Note on William Faulkner's *As I Lay Dying*." *Studies in American Fiction*, 1 (Spring 1973), 104–105.
     Finds a verbal parallel for Dewey Dell's "I wish I had time to let her die" in *Macbeth* V.v. 17–18. Overstates similarities in characters.

————. "Physical-Spatial Symbolism in *As I Lay Dying*." *College Literature*, 4 (Spring 1977), 176–177.
     Examines the first monologue, focusing on how the scene may be used to introduce students to the central relationship between Darl and Jewel and the contrast between the man of action and the man of reflection. Slight.

Ross, Stephen M. "'Voice' in Narrative Texts: The Example of *As I Lay Dying*." *PMLA*, 94 (March 1979), 300–310.
     Primarily theoretical in approach, using *AILD* as an example of the problems encountered in defining voice in narrative fiction. A far less satisfactory refutation to the charges made by Franklin (1967) than is Ross's earlier article, though it tries to do so on other grounds, denying that Faulkner used interior monologues in the novel. Does not deal satisfactorily with the function of Faulkner's italics.

Rossi, Beatrice. "Faulkner's Poetical Universe in *As I Lay Dying*." Maîtrise, University of Paris, Danton-Sorbonne, 1973.
     Studies the imagery of the novel for what it reveals about the patterns of the characters' emotional concerns. Rossi is the first to apply this very fruitful approach to the novel in any sustained fashion. The first half of the thesis is the best treatment of Darl's imagination in existence. The second half––on Addie––is less satisfactory, but often worthwhile.

Sawyer, Kenneth B. "Hero in *As I Lay Dying*." *Faulkner Studies*, 3 (1954), 30–33.
     Refutes Warren (1946). Despite the occasional heroic acts in *AILD*, the Bundrens' quest cannot be conceived as heroic. Only Jewel achieves tragic proportions.

Seib, Kenneth. "Midrashic Legend in Faulkner's *As I Lay Dying*."
   Notes on Modern American Literature, 2 (Winter 1977), item 5.
   Argues unconvincingly that the "skeletal plot of *As I Lay
Dying* is taken from the Hebrew scripture known as the Midrash."

Seltzer, Leon F. "Narrative Function Vs. Psychopathology:
   The Problem of Darl in *As I Lay Dying*." *Literature and
   Psychology*, 25 (1975), 49–64.
   Claims that Darl embodies the characteristics of both the
schizoid and the hysterical personality, and thus lacks psychological plausibility. Attempts to explain the "incongruities
in Darl's character" and the novel's "major aesthetic imperfec-
tions" by examining the validity and consistency of the psychological concepts Faulkner employed in characterizing him, and
thus to correct critics' tendency to accept Darl on Faulkner's
terms.

———— and Jan Viscomi. "Natural Rhythms and Rebellion: Anse's
   Role in *As I Lay Dying*." *Modern Fiction Studies*, 24
   (Winter 1978-79), 556-564.
   Argues that Anse prevails by bringing all of his family in
line with his values of passivity, and that he undertook the
journey in order to stabilize his family and immobilize his
rebellious children. Errs in conflating Faulkner's concepts
of enduring and prevailing and in setting up a false dichotomy
between natural, resilient characters and unnatural, self-
destructive ones. Does not recognize Anse's limitations.

Shoemaker, Alice. "A Wheel Within a Wheel: Fusion of Form and
   Content in Faulkner's *As I Lay Dying*." *Arizona Quarterly*,
   35 (Summer 1979), 101-113.
   A discussion of each of the Bundrens and some other characters, held together by the observation that there are two con-
flicting perspectives in *AILD*: the Bundrens', which sees the
journey as heroic necessity, and the outsiders', which sees it
as absurd. Takes up Bradford's (1970) argument that Addie is
the auditor of all the monologues, and belabors the evidence
for Addie's continuance as a ghost.

Simon, John K. "The Scene and the Imagery of Metamorphosis in
   'As I Lay Dying'." *Criticism*, 7 (Winter 1965), 1-22.
   A study of the scenic imagery, which establishes an
apocalyptic vision independent of any mythic or literary
framework. Works through the subjective presentations of scene
by various narrators to arrive at a common, composite scene
underlying them. Stimulating, but open to question. Does
nothing with the last third of the novel.

————. "What Are You Laughing At, Darl?: Madness and Humor in
   As I Lay Dying." *College English*, 25 (November 1963), 104-
   110.

Addresses the consistency of Darl as a literary creation and the relevance of his madness to the conclusion of *AILD*. Points out that in Darl's last monologue the first person is used with verbs of speech and knowledge; the third with action verbs. All the images presented by Darl as sources of laughter are of dehumanized humanity. A solid, helpful reading.

Sitter, Deborah Ayer. "Self and Object Representations in *As I Lay Dying*." *Hartford Studies in Literature*, 12 (1980), 143-155.
An attempt to demonstrate a psychoanalytical method that functions "independently of knowledge regarding Faulkner's life." Focuses on Darl as the "central ego."

Solery, Marc. "Addie Bundren: du corps au groupe." *Sud*, 14/15 (Summer 1975), 117-127.
The dead Addie is metaphorically the "author" of *AILD*. She reappears as a collective being in her children. She is, then, both corpse and "author"--and her children reflect this split. Too schematic, underdeveloped.

Stich, K.P. "A Note on Ironic Word Formation in *As I Lay Dying*." *Notes on Mississippi Writers*, 8 (Winter 1976), 100-103.
Indulges in word and number games to trick out a case for the novel as an allegory of Mississippi and the South; ignores the historical basis for the characters' dialects. Difficult to take seriously; perhaps this is a spoof of "close lexical and semantic analysis."

Stonum, Gary Lee. "Dilemma in *As I Lay Dying*." *Renascence*, 28 (Winter 1976), 71-81.
AILD is structured around various dilemmas, and presents a formal dilemma to the reader in its ambiguity. Includes a perceptive discussion of the function of verb tense and italics.

————. "The Referential Phase." *Faulkner's Career: An Internal Literary History*. Ithaca: Cornell University Press, 1979. Pp. 94-122.
Incorporates some of Stonum (1976). Examines *AILD* as exemplary of Faulkner's impersonal fiction of the 1930's, with its commitment to the primacy of worldly experience. *AILD* is the most extreme representation of the world as motion.

Strandberg, Victor. "Transition: From Freud to Marx." *A Faulkner Overview: Six Perspectives*. Port Washington, N.Y.: Kennikat Press, 1981. Pp. 56-88. *AILD*: 70-71.
Includes brief treatment of Darl in light of Freudian principles.

Turner, Dixie. *A Jungian Psychological Interpretation of William Faulkner's As I Lay Dying*. Washington, D.C.: University

Press of America, 1981.
A published thesis for a master's degree in education, offering superficial treatments of each Bundren as a Jungian archetype. Takes no account of Bleikasten (1973) or Williams (1977),
and is predominantly plot summary and quotations.

[Vickery], Olga Westland. *"As I Lay Dying." Perspective,* 3
    (Autumn, 1950), 179-191. Revised version: "The Dimensions
    of Consciousness: *As I Lay Dying." The Novels of William
    Faulkner: A Critical Interpretation.* Baton Rouge: Louisiana
    State University Press, 1959. Pp. 50-65.
Perhaps the most influential early study of the novel. Argues
that the central problem is not the fulfillment of a promise,
but Addie herself and her effects on her children. The action of
AILD moves toward a resolution of the tensions created by Addie
and perpetuated through Darl. The source of the popular interpretations that Cash grows through his suffering and that Peabody
offers a reliable interpretation of the action--though the latter
opinion is modified in the revised version.

Waggoner, Hyatt. "Vision: *As I Lay Dying." William Faulkner:
    From Jefferson to the World.* Lexington: University of
    Kentucky Press, 1959. Pp. 62-87.
A highly appreciative early assessment, focusing primarily
on imagery and characterization in terms of Christian themes.

Wagner, Linda W. *"As I Lay Dying*: Faulkner's All in the Family."
    College Literature, 1 (Spring 1974), 73-82.
Treats the love/hate relationships among the Bundrens. Sees
Addie as the moral center--even spokesman--of the novel and
defines the attitudes the reader is to take towards each of the
others on the basis of how each relates to Addie or where he
stands on the words/deeds issue.

Warren, Robert Penn. "Cowley's Faulkner." *New Republic,*
    12 August 1946, 176-180; 26 August 1946, 234-237. Rpt.
    "William Faulkner." *William Faulkner: Two Decades of
    Criticism.* Edited by Frederick J. Hoffman and Olga Vickery.
    East Lansing: Michigan State College Press, 1951. Pp. 82-
    101. *AILD*: 94-95.
Stresses the "sympathy and poetry" of *AILD* and the heroism
of the Bundrens. The novel demonstrates that not all poor
whites are Snopeses.

Wasiolek, Edward. *"As I Lay Dying*: Distortion in the Slow Eddy
    of Current Opinion." *Critique: Studies in Modern Fiction,*
    3 (1959), 15-23.
Deplores the lack of critical interest in what Faulkner
thought his "best" work and the prevalent view of the novel as
a heroic struggle to define kinship despite obstacles. A plea
for recognition of the novel's ironies. Finds Cash's last state-

ments "sententious," but identifies Addie's and Darl's points of view with Faulkner's.

Watkins, Floyd C. "*As I Lay Dying*: The Dignity of Earth." *In Time and Place: Some Origins of American Fiction.* Athens: University of Georgia Press, 1977. Pp. 175-189.
A study of how local history, culture and geography inform the novel. Includes photos of the Yocona River and a dog-trot cabin.

————. "The Word and the Deed in Faulkner's First Great Novels." *The Flesh and the Word: Eliot, Hemingway, Faulkner.* Nashville: Vanderbilt University Press, 1971. Pp. 181-202.
Takes Addie's rejection of abstractions as a critical standard for *TSAF*, *AILD* and *Sanc*. Points to similarities of plot and theme among the three novels. Provides an analysis of Darl's spoken language.

———— and William B. Dillingham. "The Mind of Vardaman Bundren." *Philological Quarterly*, 39 (April 1960), 247-251.
Corrects several critics of the 1950's who interpreted Vardaman as an idiot.

Watson, James G. "Faulkner: The House of Fiction." *Fifty Years of Yoknapatawpha*. Edited by Doreen Fowler and Ann J. Abadie. Jackson: University Press of Mississippi, 1980. Pp. 134-158.
Provides brief treatment of Darl's descriptions of the Bundren house and their relation to his psychology.

Weisgerber, Jean. "Evil and Fate: Raskolnikov (1929-1934)." *Faulkner and Dostoevsky: Influence and Confluence.* Translated by Dean McWilliams. Athens: Ohio University Press, 1974. Pp. 174-225. *AILD*: 192-195.
Claims that Addie's ideas often parody or invert those of Dostoevsky. Concludes that there is no case to be made for the influence of the Russian writer on this novel.

Werner, Craig. "Beyond Realism and Romanticism: Joyce, Faulkner, and the Tradition of the American Novel." *Centennial Review*, 23 (Summer 1979), 242-262. Revised version: "The Dangers of Domination: Joyce, Faulkner, Wright." *Paradoxical Resolutions: American Fiction Since James Joyce.* Urbana: University of Illinois Press, 1982. Pp. 9-32. *AILD*: 14-18.
Sees a progression from a direct and imitative Joycean influence in *Mosquitoes* to a more independent use of Joycean techniques to contribute to Faulknerian themes in *AILD*; and from a general mythic parallel in *AILD* to more specific use of the social myths of the Negro and the wilderness in *Go Down, Moses*. Isolated insights.

White, Michael. "Inverse Mimesis in Faulkner's *As I Lay Dying*."

Arizona Quarterly, 32 (Spring 1976), 35–44.
A confused treatment of narrative technique that stresses
the novel's similarities to classical Greek drama.

Whitely, Deborah. "Phenomenological Psychology and the Interior
    Monologue: Interpreting Whitfield's Passage." *CEA Critic*,
    44 (January 1982), 33–36.
Applies a Rogersian explanation for self-blinded behavior
to Whitfield's monologue and sees it as an attempt to preserve
his self-image. Mostly an exercise in semantics, this note only
partially deals with the evidence about Whitfield's motivations.

Williams, David. "As the Mother of Death Lay Dying: *As I Lay
    Dying*." *Faulkner's Women: The Myth and the Muse*. Montreal:
    McGill-Queen's University Press, 1977. Pp. 97–126.
Views Addie as an emblem of death, one aspect of the archetypal feminine, but she is also an archetypal madonna and thus
is "mythically ambivalent." So is Dewey Dell. Darl's resistance
to the mother archetype leads to psychic death.

Wittenberg, Judith Bryant. "Work as Redemption: *As I Lay Dying*
    and *Light in August*." *Faulkner: The Transfiguration of
    Biography*. Lincoln: University of Nebraska Press, 1979.
    Pp. 103–129. *AILD*: 103–117.
Conjectures that Cash's betrayal of Darl is Faulkner's
symbolic banishment of the disconnected intellectual in himself
as writer. Cash henceforth assimilates Darl's role and becomes
an actor-thinker, the artist who is fully engaged.

DATE DUE	BORROWER'S NAME	ROOM NUMBER
OCT 07 '96		